Instructor's and Counselor's Guide for Career Choices

An Interdisciplinary Curriculum for High Schools and Colleges

by Mindy Bingham, Sandy Stryker,
Rochelle Friedman, Ed.D.,
Laura Light, M.Ed.

Contributions by
Kenneth B. Hoyt, Ph.D.

Academic Innovations, Santa Barbara

Published by Academic Innovations
3463 State Street, Suite 267A
Santa Barbara, California 93105
(805) 967-8015   FAX (805) 967-4357

Manufactured in the United States of America

10 9

Foreword

Quick! What do you want to do with your life? You have 15 minutes to decide. Not enough time, you say? Of course you are right. Yet that's about how much time a typical American student spends with his or her high school career counselor.

The resulting lack of direction exhibited by so many young people is hardly surprising. It can lead to such serious problems as substance abuse, teen pregnancy, and dropping out of school. The economic consequences for society can also be seen in stagnating productivity and declining real wages. To reverse this trend schools and families need to get involved in the career-planning process early, making sure that all young people recognize their own ability to become valued and productive members of society.

According to a 1988 study in Eugene, Oregon, students stop coming to school because it doesn't interest them. It's boring. On the other hand, kids who see the relevance of getting an education don't drop out. Likewise, teens who get pregnant are likely to leave school. Children's Defense Fund President Marion Wright Edelman points out that young women who see options for their future are less likely to get pregnant.

The United States lags far behind other industrialized nations in helping its youth plan and train for careers. A recent study by the Commission on Skills of the American Work Force states that broad changes are called for in the way non-college graduates, in particular, are prepared for work. The report, "America's Choice; High Skills or Low Wages," warns that present practices will lead to a continuing decline in the American standard of living and the country's ability to compete in international markets.

Both the General Accounting Office and Educational Testing Service have reported that American high schools provide almost no assistance in choosing and preparing for careers for the majority of their students.

Concerned parents may be quick to blame school counselors for this oversight. However it must be pointed out that, on average, there is one counselor for every 500 students in American high schools. Most of their time is spent on students with special problems or special needs, or with those who seek out assistance. The "average" student, therefore, may see the counselor only once during his or her academic career—for that 15 minute session in ninth grade—when the balance of the student's high school schedule is determined.

The teens will be asked whether or not they plan to go to college but, generally, things don't get much more specific than that. Those who *do* expect to attend college will see some relevance in their high school education. Many of the other students, however, are left with no vision for a satisfying future. For them, school can become meaningless. And that's when they get into trouble.

"Future planning" is the key to dealing successfully with a wide range of problems affecting today's youth. Young people tend to live day-to-day. They don't stop and think about how their present actions will alter their future choices. They may be thoughtless, but they're not stupid. Once someone takes the time to point out that there *are* unpleasant consequences for dropping out, or convincingly good reasons to stay in school, they respond positively.

We know this approach works. For example, at San Marcos High School in San Diego County, California, 150 of 692 female students became pregnant during the 1983-84 school year. The community was understandably alarmed, but actually these figures aren't abnormally high. The school already had a sex education class, so they decided to add one of the *"Choices* Series" on career and life planning. The next year there were only seven reported pregnancies. Dozens of similar instances demonstrate that you can't simply tell kids to 'just say no' to drugs or dropping out or being sexually active. You have to give them a *reason*.

Career Choices takes a non-traditional approach to career planning, devoting most of its pages to helping readers determine who they are and what they want from life. Too many career planning classes, when schools *do* offer them, become little more than projects on how to use the library. Students are told to pick two or three possible careers—seemingly out of thin air—and write papers about them. Young people need to concentrate more on their own identities, their own passions and abilities, than they do on the average annual salary for a sales rep in Seattle.

Since career planning takes time, schools should be willing to give this topic the time and attention it deserves within the curriculum. We hope we have provided you with an interdisciplinary resource that can easily fit into such traditional classes as English, math, social studies or family life. All students need this information...and the sooner the better.

At this stage in their lives, young people need to establish their own identity and feel that they have an important role to fill. You can help teens discover the qualities that make them unique and the activities that make them feel good. By building their self-confidence you will help them learn to make decisions, set goals, and take responsibility for their actions. Urge them to take calculated risks and overcome any fears that may unnecessarily limit their achievement. Then stand back and watch them soar.

Contents

"To choose what you want to do, you first have to know who you are."

Introduction

Career Choices is designed to help young people deal with the two major tasks of adolescence: establishing and consolidating their identity and deciding what they want to do with their lives. It goes without saying that these are huge undertakings for individuals of any age. We believe, therefore, that teens can use all the help they can get.

Many people struggle with these issues well into adulthood. For some, they are never resolved. Since the chances are good that Mom and Dad are involved in their own mid-life identity crisis, adolescents can't always depend on getting support at home.

While most schools offer some kind of career planning class or seminar, the majority focus almost exclusively on career research or finding a job. Most of the time, when it comes to deciding who they are or what they want, students are left to their own devices.

We believe that schools can do a great deal more to insure the future success and satisfaction of their graduates. In *Career Choices*, we've brought together the things we have learned over years of working with adolescents, college students, teachers, and parents.

In 1983, Sandy Stryker and Mindy Bingham along with Judy Edmondson wrote a book entitled *Choices: A Teen Woman's Journal for Self-awareness and Personal Planning*. It was followed a year later by *Challenges*, a companion book for young men. These texts on pre-career awareness have now been used by more than a half million students in thousands of schools, and two national programs are based on the materials. They have proved to be extremely effective in raising the consciousness of young people regarding the importance of self-sufficiency and future planning, regardless of gender-linked prejudice.

3. As an old proverb says, "Tell me and I forget. Show me and I remember. But involve me and I understand." Repeating the successful format of its predecessors, *Career Choices* emphasizes discussions, interactive learning, exercises, and projects which involve the learner as a participant in his or her education.

4. Adolescents are motivated to learn when they see the relevance of a subject to their own lives. The skills they pick up in this way, however, can easily be transferred to other topics. Interestingly, these topics become relevant, too. This course allows students to develop and practice language arts skills and math skills in a very personal way. Once they have done this, they become more willing and able to apply composition and reading comprehension skills with more traditional language arts materials and to gain the computation skills necessary to be a productive adult in our increasingly complex society.

5. It's difficult for adolescents to make wise decisions about the future until they give some serious thought to their own values, passions, abilities, and goals. Traditional career education materials have omitted or neglected this essential part of the process. *Career Choices* is based on the theory that figuring out who you are and what you want is more important and more difficult than learning to fill out a job application or choose a college. Therefore, the major portion of this book deals with questions of identity, the key task of adolescence according to most developmental psychologists.

6. Few schools can afford enough guidance counselors, and few guidance counselors have sufficient time to provide the individual attention every adolescent needs in order to consolidate identity and make quality decisions about education and potential careers. By making these processes an integral part of the core curriculum, *Career Choices* assures that each student will get the comprehensive guidance that is so necessary during this crucial period of development and, at the same time, demonstrates the importance of learning to speak, write, and compute as well as he or she possibly can. When we started this project, we intentionally set out to do something different. This is not a typical career education course. Career and life planning are so essential to the educational experience of every young person that they should be integrated into the core curriculum of all secondary schools. What you are about to embark upon is a competency-based, interdisciplinary course that could be the most valuable learning experience of a student's high school career.

Goals and Objectives

While each state has specific education guidelines, all share one goal: **Today's graduates must be prepared for the workforce of the future.** *Career Choices* is uniquely adaptable for this purpose because it concentrates on outcome-driven goals:

PERSONAL SATISFACTION: Students will recognize the significance of high school and further education for their success and happiness. As self-directed individuals able to adapt to change, they will be equipped to become successful lifelong learners.

EMOTIONAL STABILITY: Students will develop a positive self-image and self-esteem, and the ability to cope with anxiety and stress.

COGNITIVE ACHIEVEMENT: In addition to basic skills, students will develop critical and creative thinking, problem-solving and collaborative skills, and the ability to adapt to change.

SOCIAL RESPONSIBILITY: Students will develop concern for others and a positive work attitude.

MOTIVATION: Upon completing this course, students will be self-motivated to prepare for employment or further education.

Broad-based, these outcomes are essential for ALL students. Because of the flexibility of *Career Choices*, YOU can tailor the program to suit the needs of YOUR students.

Evaluative Criteria

Students will:

1. Think about and project themselves into the future.

2. Understand the importance of planning for the future.

3. Become aware of the fact that everyone's life involves some difficulties, but that obstacles can and must be overcome.

4. Begin thinking about the income level they will need to maintain in order to live a satisfying life.

5. Learn to determine their own values and how these may relate to appropriate career paths.

6. Develop a step-by-step plan for achieving future goals.

7. Learn effective problem-solving and decision-making skills.

8. Learn an effective career research process.

9. Develop a ten-year action plan for achieving their career and life goals.

10. Gain an enhanced understanding of who they are, what they want, and how to achieve their goals.

11. Expand their educational goals or establish more realistic ones.

12. Learn to recognize and overcome societal expectations or self-doubts that could limit their career and life goals.

13. Be encouraged to base career plans on informed decisions rather than on the expectations of society, family, or other external influence.

14. Develop employment skills appropriate for success in the 21st century.

15. Learn to better cope with change.

16. Understand the value and benefits of good reading, writing, and computation skills.

Where to Use this Curriculum

The flexibility of the curriculum design makes *Career Choices* suitable for...

Mainstream 8th, 9th or 10th Grade Language Arts and/or Math Classes. Combining the *Career Choices* text and its theme of personal success with the supplements *Lifestyle Math* and/or *Possibilities*, the language arts anthology, allows ample opportunity for reading, writing, and computation assignments that students will complete with enthusiasm because of the subject's relevance to their own lives. Class discussions, too, will take on new energy and meaning as students address such topics as character, motivation, commitment, and compromise.

Launching Students into Tech Prep or School-to-Work Programs. As we ask adolescents to make sophisticated career and life decisions, it is essential to provide them with a comprehensive guidance experience if we want them to choose wisely. *Career Choices* integrates academics and guidance themes in a way that not only gives them greater understanding of themselves, but demonstrates the inextricable connection between success at school, success at work, and satisfaction in life.

Gifted Students Programs. Gifted student programs most often emphasize intellectual achievement at the expense of the practical and emotional needs of individual class members. *Career Choices* can be used alone or in a language arts or math program to help focus, challenge, and motivate gifted students as they develop the support systems they need.

Employment Seminars. *Career Choices* is a motivational tool, emphasizing identity search as an important supplement to basic career research and building skills. It is also very effective in demonstrating how academic classes are relevant to future employment and in instilling an attitude toward work that employers applaud.

A Guidance Curriculum and Counseling Program. As new state and federal regulations mandate more personal and career guidance for all students, *Career Choices* allows already overworked counselors to provide the kind of high quality information and advice that's needed for every individual in their school. The curriculum meets all mandated requirements and can be used effectively in individual and group counseling programs, as well as in the classroom. (When counselors *do* use *Career Choices* in the classroom, they become an important part of the teaching team.)

Equity Programs. *Career Choices* not only illustrates the need for all students to take responsibility for planning for their own future, but it also demonstrates how young women, in particular, can enhance their potential to be good parents and partners by seriously preparing for paid employment outside the home.

Family Life Courses. With components on problem solving, decision making, balancing lifestyles, budgeting, and planning for the future, this is an ideal Family Life course textbook.

At-risk Students. The text effectively demonstrates future benefits of completing high school and possibly post-secondary education. *Career Choices* also helps at-risk students understand that, in spite of individual challenges, they have the ability, resources, and responsibility to determine their own life patterns.

JTPA Summer Youth Employment Programs. *Career Choices* encourages young people who may already be disengaged from their lives as students to stay in school by demonstrating the relevance of education to future success. It clearly meets the federal requirements for "Academic Enrichment" and "Workplace Readiness."

Teen Parenting Programs. Students overwhelmed by the chores and responsibilities of parenthood are less likely to drop out of school when they receive the kind of support and encouragement that is infused throughout the *Career Choices* text.

How to Use this Guide

The *Career Choices* curriculum is a flexible program that can be used in many ways. Although this guide presents a number of possibilities, we encourage you to use your creativity to make the curriculum relevant and stimulating for your own classes.

Courses based on this text may run anywhere from six weeks to an entire school year. Most often, however, it is used over a nine-week quarter or an 18-week semester. Since text materials build on skills learned in previous chapters, we urge you to follow the sequence of the books.

The *way* you use the materials, however, can vary greatly. Many schools are currently restructuring, working with interdisciplinary education, teaching teams, Tech Prep and School-to-Work programs, and more. You will find that this curriculum can easily be adapted to meet your particular needs. For instance, you may choose to use only the *Career Choices* text with the *Workbook and Portfolio for Career Choices*, or you may choose to include the *Possibilities* and/or *Lifestyle Math* texts. You may choose to use all the texts within one course or team teach the materials over a number of disciplines.

The core of this *Instructor's Guide* includes chapter-by-chapter, exercise-by-exercise learning objectives, presentation suggestions and, where appropriate, exercises and activities. There's also room for you to add your own notes, comments, and ideas. Because more and more schools are incorporating interdisciplinary teaching teams into their restructuring plans, this curriculum can be used in a variety of configurations in traditional academic classrooms.

On pages 25 to 29, you'll find an overview of how to incorporate the anthology *Possibilities* for those of you who plan to use this optional literature component. Then, throughout Section Four, beginning on page 128, you'll find suggestions about where each literature selection could be assigned to reinforce both the understanding of the activity and the meaning of the literary work.

Information regarding *Lifestyle Math* is also included. The majority of the problems in *Lifestyle Math* augment the activities in Chapter Four of *Career Choices*. This text can be used by either math instructors in an interdisciplinary model, or by instructors from other disciplines who enjoy math, financial planning and economics. See page 314 for one example of an interdisciplinary approach.

Technology has made this personalized and relevant "math problem" possible. In the past, in order to make the correction process for busy instructors feasible, students completed irrelevant problems with only one answer. Today, for *Lifestyle Math*, a "correction key" is available for IBM-compatible computers. Since the nature of each student's portfolio depends on his or her personal goals and plans, there is rarely a "right" answer. This computer program will enable you—or your students—to correct computations easily and effectively.

Obviously, a language arts instructor will use the books differently than a math or career education teacher or a guidance counselor. Likewise, you will use the materials differently when working with gifted, mainstream, at-risk, Tech Prep, or School-to-Work students. We have, therefore, incorporated hints that may be helpful under a variety of different circumstances. Throughout the *Guide*, you'll find numerous resources that will be valuable as you begin planning your strategy for bringing *Career Choices* into your classroom. Throughout Section Four, beginning on page 128, we've dropped in classroom ideas and comments from teachers who use one or all of the *Career Choices* textbooks. In Section Five, you'll find a variety of supportive materials you may find useful as you build your program.

In addition, since the books present excellent exercises for hands-on learning and group discussion, we have included sections on group dynamics and classroom techniques.

We know you are capable, but we also know you are very busy! Therefore, we have included charts and worksheets that can be helpful. While the materials in *Career Choices*, the *Workbook and Portfolio for Career Choices*, *Possibilities*, and *Lifestyle Math* are copyrighted materials and may not be photocopied or reproduced in any fashion without the written permission of the publisher, you are granted permission to photocopy pages 67, 68, 92, 93, 107, 154, 163, 222, 223, 224, 225 and 231 from this *Instructor's and Counselor's Guide for Career Choices* for your own classroom use.

We are committed to your success. Therefore, we have on-staff curriculum specialists who are available to provide technical support as you incorporate this program into your school. Do not hesitate to pick up the phone and call us at (800) 967-8016 between 9:00am and 3:00pm PST. We stand ready to help in any way we can.

Connect Online with Academic Innovations

http://www.academicinnovations.com

Would you like to be able to access successful teaching strategies from your colleagues at any time? Are you interested in participating in a user's group with other teachers from across the country who use the *Career Choices* curriculum? Would you like to ask Mindy Bingham, the coauthor of *Career Choices*, questions about the curriculum?

Now you can with Academic Innovations' home page on the Internet. You can log on to find resources and ideas for using the curriculum, copies of our past newsletters, dates and locations of upcoming workshops, funding suggestions, specialty lesson plans and much more.

 When you see this logo throughout the remainder of this *Guide*, you'll know you can find a variety of additional resources at the URL (Internet address) noted. You'll want to log on and visit that site for additional information.

Question	Go to URL:	You'll find:	Helpful hints & tips
How would I approach a business in our community for help with funding our Career Choices program?	http://www. academicinnovations.com/ corpfun.html	A detailed explanation of how to approach the business community for funding	*Print out this page plus the text from all the hyperlinks in this section. Form a committee to strategize a plan using this information.*

You'll also find charts similar to this sprinkled throughout the *Guide*. Not only do these provide you with the URLs that address the question, but the chart also gives you helpful hints on how best to use the material found on these Internet pages.

Let Us Hear from You!

Would you care to share your observations and suggestions in future editions of this guide as well as in our training sessions? What has worked well for you? What innovations have you made? What other information would you find helpful? Let us know what you think!

Send you ideas to:

Academic Innovations
3463 State Street, Suite 267
Santa Barbara, CA 93105
(800) 967-8016, Fax (805) 967-4357
E-mail: academic@academicinnovations.com

We'd like to thank the numerous dedicated and innovative educators who have given us feedback and shared with us their exceptional teaching strategies. You'll find some of their comments and recommendations throughout the text.

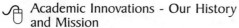 Academic Innovations - Our History and Mission

http://www.academicinnovations.com/company.html#profile

Meet our staff and consultants

http://www.academicinnovations.com/staff.html

Do you want to be included on our mailing list?

http://www.academicinnovations.com/news.html

Here's What We're Hearing...

It Works

The counselors reported a real difference when my students went to register for next year's classes: they knew what they wanted.

Elizabeth Farris
English teacher
San Gabriel High School
San Gabriel, CA

After utilizing Career Choices as a counseling instrument and a career cluster selection, less than 5% of our students are changing programs. This evidence supports our belief that the program is a key to career decision-making.

Jim Campbell, Ph.D.
Executive Director of
Delaware Tech Prep
Recipient of Dale Parnell Outstanding
Tech Prep Program Award

It's Easy to Use

Career Choices is great for the classroom teacher who doesn't know that much about career guidance.

Ernie Gomes, Science Chair
Casa Roble Fundamental
High School
Orangevale, CA

It has been easy to fit in other projects and lessons with Career Choices. They are the best career education materials I've used in 18 years. Thank you!

Bonnie Morris
Business and careers instructor
Anacortes High School
Anacortes, WA

It Motivates Students

[As a result of this text] many students recognized the need to buckle down more to reach their goals. Others made decisions regarding a career possibility or interest they had.

Linda Wolverton
9th grade English
Milford High School
Milford, OH

I wanted to thank you for the enlightening course, Career Choices....I know now that school really does pay off and that the longer I stay in school, the more likely I am to have a high paying job.

Thank you letter to the authors
from California student

It's Ethnic and Gender Fair

My students are 80% non-white minority students. The selections in [Career Choices and Possibilities] make them feel OK about themselves.

Julie Vetica
8th grade Language arts
Hargitt Middle School
Norwalk, CA

The first year, my biggest success was when students of different races found common ground and learned a language to talk to each other.

Susan Henneberg
9th grade English
Milford High School
Milford, OH

18

The results of this project were extraordinary. Participants were exposed to the writings of poets, visionaries, and other great authors. They learned the practical applications of math. For the first time, these students began to understand the correlation between knowledge, employment, and education. The success of the program amazed even the teachers, many of whom had dual master's degrees...By the fourth week, many parents had called to thank me for the changes they'd seen in their children. In previous years our dropout rate averaged 40%, this year it was only 3%.

Joe Werner, JTPA Administrator
Monterey County, CA

Before this class I thought everything would just fall into place. Now I realize that I have to make my future happen, it won't just work out good by itself. So how I do now will not only affect me for the rest of my life, it will also affect my children.

Student in Dee Fay's class
Ukiah High School
Ukiah, CA

Our Web Site

What educators are saying about the *Career Choices* curriculum

http://www.academicinnovations.com/
whatsay.html

[Young] women who never dreamed of higher education saw possibilities and opportunities. Many...were excited about going to college and spoke of the decision with bright eyes.

C. Sue Waldfogel Huff
Administrative Assistant
Silverado High School
Mission Viejo, CA

Career Choices *is definitely "politically correct" in terms of race, gender, etc.*

Linda Wulff
Chairperson, Communications Dept.
Waupun High School
Waupun, WI

Using *Career Choices* in English/Language Arts Curriculums

"Everybody is talented, original and has something important to say," according to Brenda Ueland, author of *If You Want to Write*. Many English teachers may doubt this statement. Students, too, may be prematurely downgrading their abilities and shortchanging their futures. But *Career Choices*, used effectively by English teachers, can confirm Ueland's statement, making teaching more rewarding, as teachers help students discover their talents and their dreams.

Using *Career Choices* to combine English and career education may, at first, seem unlikely to succeed on either level. After seven years of study and work with curriculum developers across the country, however, we are convinced that the English classroom is the ideal place to nurture and stimulate young imaginations and help students learn to articulate their needs and desires.

Adolescents, after all, have at least one thing in common: an avid interest in themselves and their futures. When class assignments help them find answers for their most urgent questions (Who am I? What do I want?), communication and critical thinking skills become suddenly relevant. As fictional characters are perceived as struggling with these same questions, literature, too, takes on new meaning.

According to poet Cecil Lewis, "We do not write in order to be understood; we write in order to understand." This is the theory behind the growing and important trend in American education called "writing across the curriculum." In *Writing to Learn*, William Zinsser declares, "We write to find out what we know and what we want to say. . . . how often as a writer I [have] made clear to myself some subject I had previously known nothing about by just putting one sentence after another. . . . Writing and thinking and learning were the same process. . . . I saw that 'writing across the curriculum' wasn't just a method of getting students to write who were afraid of writing. It was also a method of getting students to learn who were afraid of learning."

Students today need to learn two important things at the outset:

1. Who they are and what they want to do with their lives and;

2. How their education relates to achieving those future goals.

Since the traditional curriculum rarely takes these factors into account, it is not surprising that so many capable students don't make an effort to learn. They have not made the connection between their education and their future lives. The blurring of boundaries between one course and another that is now taking place in the interdisciplinary classrooms should help alleviate this problem. Once students understand that writing skills are called for in nearly all career fields, and that Miss Rosie or Walter Mitty might have interesting things to say about *their* lives, they are likely to pay more attention.

We highly recommend bringing a school counselor into this innovative learning process. He or she is likely to have a great deal of relevant information and may also be able to spot and help any students with special needs or problems. In addition, since there is an average of one counselor for every 500 students in most American high schools, the class provides an opportunity for the counselor to spend more time with more students. The final chapter in *Career Choices* asks students to write a 10-year tentative plan for their future, an assignment that can make it easier for counselors to guide teens as they plan the remainder of their high school education.

English classes, of course, are meant to pass on more than the ability to write a complete sentence. Most English teachers entered the profession because of their love for literature and their desire to share its riches with the next generation. In *The Call of Stories*, author, teacher, and psychiatrist Robert Coles proposes that literature is a meaningful and useful tool for determining who we are and how we should live our lives. This is evident to adult readers, but adolescents often do not have enough life experience to see the relevance. Once they begin exploring their own psyches and establishing their own identities, as this course allows them to do, they are more open to the messages found in books. As Coles says, "during those stretches of inward looking, novelists may be summoned in daydreams and reveries, or consulted directly, through recourse to a particular page, chapter, section of a particular story. We all remember in our own lives times when a book has become for us a signpost, a continuing presence in our lives. Novels lend themselves to such purposes because their plots offer a psychological or moral journey, with impasses and breakthroughs, with decisions made and destinations achieved."

At Harvard University, Coles has used literature as a basis for teaching social and political issues as well as graduate seminars in law, medicine, education, theology, and architecture. He goes on to say, "Students are forever trying to find a direction for their lives and forever discovering that there are currents and cross-currents to negotiate. Eliot's novels, and those of Dickens, Hardy, Tolstoy, remind them that as in life, so in great art. . . . Again, and again, instructed by novelists, students remind themselves of life's contingencies; and in so doing, they take matters of choice and commitment more seriously than they might otherwise have done."

The type of class we propose will help students develop the life skills, communication skills, and love of literature that will propel them into a satisfying future. We hope that you will join us in this pioneering educational experience.

Our Web Site

Great ideas from great educators   http://www.academicinnovations.com/ideas.html

How *Career Choices* Meets Common Learning Objectives for Language Arts, English, and Reading

1. ATTAINING PROFICIENCY IN GROUP PROBLEM SOLVING
As they plan what they will do with their lives and how they will achieve their goals, students work together to define, limit, and analyze the problem, gather information, cooperatively select and implement solutions.

2. MAKING INFERENCES FROM PRINTED INFORMATION
Activities which develop skills in using ideas and relationships to infer additional ideas follow reading of the texts. These skills can then be applied to literature interpretation.

3. IDENTIFYING THE AUTHOR'S POINT OF VIEW
After examining how their personal perspective affects their writing and reasoning, students should be able to identify the author's point of view.

4. READING AND UNDERSTANDING CONSUMER INFORMATION
The text contains numerous charts, forms, job applications, and similar materials essential to daily life experience.

5. WRITING BRIEF NARRATION, DESCRIPTION, AND EXPOSITION
The texts offer numerous options which reinforce writing proficiency. Suggested projects occur throughout the workbook and the anthology.

6. IDENTIFYING THEMES OF LITERARY WORKS
Once students identify their own passions, values, personality strengths, and life mission, their ability to identify (and identify with) the central theme of a literary work increases.

7. USING RESEARCH SKILLS TO COLLECT, EVALUATE, AND APPLY INFORMATION
As they research potential careers and life plans, students learn information retrieval, interview, problem-solving and decision-making skills.

Possibilities: A Supplemental Anthology for Career Choices

Career advice from John Updike and Robert Frost? Pep talks from Emily Dickinson and Albert Camus? Unusual perhaps, but no more so than the idea of using a language arts class to teach problem solving, risk taking, and the work ethic. That's the approach taken when you combine *Career Choices* and *Possibilities*. After spending a little time with the materials, you are likely to begin wondering why no one ever thought of doing this before.

Possibilities, the accompanying anthology, supports the major themes and lessons of *Career Choices*. It is the first text in our new *Authors as Mentors* series. The curriculum is flexible enough to be used in a variety of situations and with students of varying abilities.

Use *Career Choices* and *Possibilities* together as:

- a semester or year-long class in the English department.

- a team teaching opportunity for the English department and the school counselor, career technician, or family and consumer science instructor.

- a team teaching opportunity for the English department and the math and/or social studies department.

- two supporting integrated classes (for example, a freshman orientation class coupled with 9th grade English).

Most of the literature contained in *Possibilities* was selected because it is on recommended reading lists in many states. There are 50 essays, short stories, poems, speeches, and plays included in *Possibilities*.

Since "My Name is Margaret" is such an outstanding example of autobiographical incident writing, we use this selection to prepare for the CLAS Text Writing Sample.

– Julie Vetica
8th grade language arts teacher
Hargitt Middle School
Norwalk, California

A Literature-Based Curriculum

Possibilities was written to reflect the literature-based approach to teaching English/language arts. The lessons in this text employ a variety of strategies to appeal to the various learning styles found in any group of students.

The "into, through, and beyond" format helps students relate the themes found in the literature to their lives. We wanted to provide assignments that are relevant to the students' real world. We have taken an approach that builds upon what students already know and what they are working on in their own life planning process.

The "into" activity (journal entries) helps them get started and prepares them for the material they are about to read. After they have read "through" the material, the "beyond" questions and activities help students discover the meaning of the work and apply that data, theme, advice or information to their lives.

This curriculum works because adolescents have at least one thing in common: an avid interest in themselves and their futures. When classroom assignments help students find answers for their most urgent questions (Who am I? What do I want?), communication and critical thinking skills become more relevant. When fictional characters seem to be struggling with these same questions, literature, too, takes on new meaning.

By using this self-discovery theme, teachers quickly notice an improvement in students' general attitude toward writing, reading and math assignments. The motivation to practice these basic skills is elevated. It makes teaching more rewarding and helps students realize their talents and dreams.

Finally, the *Career Choices* curriculum achieves the goals of integrating academics with vocational/career education, one of the major objectives of the restructuring movement. The themes woven through the curriculum help students understand the need to prepare for a satisfying and fulfilling life. The literature selections in *Possibilities* underscore these themes, giving students the motivation to see their education as the important component for reaching their dreams and ambitions.

More specifically, *Career Choices* with *Possibilities* is an ideal launching course for Tech Prep and School-to-Work programs. This integrated curriculum helps adolescents enthusiastically assess and select a path or course of study that meets their various interests and aptitudes, while, at the same time, they develop an appreciation for the literature of our culture. This is truly the integration of academics and vocational/career education.

Career Choices/Possibilities Cross Reference

The following is a suggested cross reference guide. It is designed to assist you in deciding when to incorporate the stories, poems, essays, plays or speeches found in *Possibilities* with the corresponding activities and exercises in *Career Choices*.

Career Choices is a sequential curriculum. This outline assumes you are working through the *Career Choices* textbook from beginning to end in the order presented.

Chapter 1
Envisioning Your Future

The Secret Life of Walter Mitty (page 11)
> Read after reading pages 10-13 in *Career Choices*

Psalm of Life (page 19)
Dreams (page 24)
I Have a Dream . . . speech by **Martin Luther King, Jr.** (page 27)
> Read after completing page 14 in *Career Choices*

Work, an excerpt from *The Prophet* (page 33)
> Read after completing pages 15-17 in *Career Choices*

Richard Cory (page 37)
> Read after completing pages 18-21 in *Career Choices*

Question	Go to URL:	You'll find:	Helpful hints & tips
I'm an English/language arts teacher. Is the Career Choices and Possibilities curriculum appropriate for my classes?	http://www. academicinnovations.com/ indepth.html	A variety of stories about educators' experiences in a variety of disciplines.	*Choose the hyperlinks to Phyllis Stewart of IN, Doug Campbell of CA, Mary Ellen Fowler of FL, Roberta Freed of MN, Priscilla Gregory of TN and Scott Hess of WA.*
AND...	http://www. academicinnovations.com/ ela.html	A variety of comments by English/language arts teachers using *Career Choices*	*Print out for later reading.*

Chapter 2
Your Personal Profile

Sonnets From the Portuguese (page 40)
> Read after completing pages 28-29 in *Career Choices*

Alice in Wonderland (page 43)
> Read after completing pages 28-45 in *Career Choices*

I Know Why the Caged Bird Sings (page 47)
Sympathy (page 57)
> Read after completing page 28-49 in *Career Choices*

Life (page 61)
> Read after completing page 52 in *Career Choices*

Self-Reliance (page 64)
> Read after completing page 53 in *Career Choices*

Chapter 3
Lifestyles of the Satisfied and Happy

Growing Older (page 69)
> Read as an introduction to the "Looking into the Future" exercise on page 169 in the *Instructor's and Counselor's Guide*

I Shall Not Pass This Way Again (page 72)
> Read after completing pages 60-61 in *Career Choices*

Red Geraniums (page 74)
> Read after completing 66-69 in *Career Choices*

I feel the usage of these materials helped my students to see the relevance of English to their lives and helped them formulate a more mature career plan. These materials, I think, have also caused them to be more conscious of the quality of their assignments and the importance of doing well in school.

–Amy S. Heaton
Applied Communications/
Creative Writing Teacher
Horn Lake High School
Horn Lake, Mississippi

The writing was revealing and showed positive growth. They showed me how much they really know and that they are further ahead than we usually give them credit for.

—Jose E. "Tito" Chavez
English Department Chair
West Las Vegas High School
Las Vegas, Nevada

Chapter 7
Decision Making

The Monkey's Paw (page 127)
    Read after completing pages 168-174 in *Career Choices*

The Road Not Taken (page 139)
    Read after completing page 177 in *Career Choices*

To Build a Fire (page 142)
    Read after reading page 179 in *Career Choices*

Chapter 8
Goal Setting

Uphill (page 164)
    Read before beginning Chapter 8

The Myth of Sisyphus (page 166)
    Read after completing pages 182-185 in *Career Choices*

Prince of Tides (page 178)
    Read after completing pages 182-191 in *Career Choices*

Chapter 9
Avoiding Detours and Roadblocks

Hope (page 172)
Expect Nothing (page 175)
    Read together after completing pages 194-199 in *Career Choices*

A Dream Deferred (page 212)
    Read after completing pages 214-215 in *Career Choices*

Mother to Son (page 214)
    Read before completing pages 196-197 in *Career Choices*

A Noiseless Patient Spider (page 216)
All I Really Need to Know I Learned in Kindergarten (page 216)
    Read after completing pages 216-217 in *Career Choices*

Over the Hill to the Poor-House (page 221)
    Read before completing pages 208-209 in *Career Choices*

George Gray (page 225)
    Read after completing pages 216-221 in *Career Choices*

Chapter 10
Attitude is Everything

Chapter 11
Getting Experience

Chapter 12
Where Do You Go from Here?

I found all the selections to be very helpful. This book provided creative involvement which revealed a key ingredient in understanding the emotional component of career choices and well being. Students were challenged to develop their own personal values, goals and individual philosophy which will give meaning and value to their lives.

– Doris R. A-Martinez
Community and Student Services
Los Angeles Trade-Tech College
Los Angeles, California

Lifestyle Math

In far too many schools, students who demonstrate an interest in math are considered even more aberrant than those who like to read. "Only nerds like math." What's more, there is a strong belief among students that math is hard—too hard for them. And, besides, they believe it's totally irrelevant. In the movie *Peggy Sue Got Married*, Kathleen Turner, as the title character, spoke for generations of teens (especially female) when she told her math teacher she didn't have to do her homework because "I know for a fact that I am never going to use any of this."

Lifestyle Math effectively and dramatically demonstrates the fallacy of all these arguments. It makes math interesting, shows students they can do it if they try and, most important, it shows them math's relevance in their lives, today and into the future.

That, we think, is the greatest strength of the program for students at all levels: It motivates them to learn by making math relevant on a purely personal basis. A cornerstone of the module, for example, is an extension of the budget exercise found in Chapter Four of *Career Choices*. As young people begin to think about and plan for the kind of life they want to have by age 29, each step of the process accomplishes more than building math skills—step by step, the exercise builds motivation and commitment to prepare for the future by doing well in school today.

The innovative *Computerized Correction Key and Portfolio* for *Lifestyle Math* and the *Making It Real* Internet-based curriculum enhancement strengthen its effectiveness. (You'll find more information about these on the pages that follow.)

Lifestyle Math holds student interest by having them plan a party, buy the car of their dreams, plan a vacation, and much more. And they'll find that math is relevant, not at all nerdy, and—wonder of wonders—they can do it!

The Key to Success

Studies suggest that in order for students to be successful at math:

1. **They must see themselves as successful in math.**

   Lifestyle Math addresses student attitudes and math anxiety, and offers ongoing support and encouragement. With some initial help from you in these same areas, your class will soon view itself as quite capable of doing the work.

2. **They must have support and high expectations from family, teachers, and peers.**

   Again, the program is designed so that you and your students can support and encourage each other.

3. **They must understand what's in it for them, why math is important to their future success and satisfaction in life.**

   Lifestyle Math makes this abundantly clear. You'll never have a more engaged class, and you may play a rewarding part in helping some students chart entirely new courses for their lives.

Career Choices **instructors from all disciplines enjoy teaching this unit. They include:**
- Career educators
- Teachers of freshman orientation courses
- English/language arts instructors
- Business and economics teachers
- Family and Consumer Science professionals
- Special population instructors and program directors

A Supplemental Text for Students at All Levels of Math Proficiency

Lifestyle Math...is an excellent supplementary resource for math classes at all levels, including algebra, pre-algebra and basic skills.
– American Vocational Association catalog

Lifestyle Math is designed to be used in conjunction with the *Career Choices* curriculum and is an ideal supplemental activity for math classes at all levels. *Lifestyle Math* clearly demonstrates the link between education and life satisfaction, thus making math a relevant and essential subject that must be mastered.

Algebra and more advanced level math students should be able to complete the portfolio in 15 to 20 hours. The text provides an excellent review of basic skills, teaches important economic and financial formulas, and demonstrates how pursuing math in college will pay dividends in job and career satisfaction.

There are several possible ways to use the materials with these students. Perhaps some of them, at least, can work through the text on their own or together in small groups. You might offer extra credit for these students. *Lifestyle Math* can be used effectively as an energizer for the class, or you might allow weekly time for students to work on their portfolios after they complete a quiz or test. You'll find they look forward to working on this project and will view this as a reward. Or, perhaps you'll prefer to spend a week or two on *Lifestyle Math* at the beginning of the term as a review of basic skills and to start students thinking about the value of math in many different areas in their lives.

Pre-algebra students may need up to a quarter to complete the module. They, too, will be reviewing basic skills and applying them to real-life decisions. Students will have an opportunity to practice sophisticated problem-solving techniques relating to their own future expectations of success.

Young people still struggling with basic skills may need a full semester or even a full school year to complete the program. For them, you will want to supplement *Lifestyle Math* with more traditional lessons and drills. The good news here is that they will *want* to complete it and that they will finally come to realize how math relates to all other aspects of their life, present and future. This should prove motivational and may even be the key to their success.

The Key Principles of *Lifestyle Math*

1. It helps students take responsibility for their own learning by demonstrating the value of applying themselves to their math education.

2. It emphasizes the need for mastering basic skills by showing how they are used in everything from determining take home salary to planning an entertainment and vacation budget to saving for a comfortable retirement.

3. It exposes students to important mathematical formulas they will use throughout their lives (figuring mortgage payments, buying a car, preparing budgets for food, child care, health care, vacations, and so on).

4. It demonstrates the value of teamwork in problem-solving when used with small groups of students and encourages critical thinking and problem-solving skills for all individuals.

5. It suggests possible reasons why students might have been resistant to math in the past and helps them understand the payoff for time and energy invested in their math work.

6. It helps keep students in upper division math classes by providing them with reasons to apply themselves and struggle with difficult concepts. Otherwise they might drop out of math.

7. When used with optional technology supplements (see following pages), it helps students become comfortable using computers in their daily lives.

8. When used with the *Computerized Financial Planning Portfolio Disk*, it allows young people to quickly check the financial consequences as they change career and educational plans.

9. When used with *Making It Real*, it shows students how to gather information from the Internet and use the facts discovered there to make informed decisions in all areas of their lives.

TECHNICAL SUPPORT
For the *Career Choices* curriculum
(800) 967-8016, ext. 677

The *Computerized Correction Key* and Portfolio for *Lifestyle Math*

The optional *Computerized Correction Key and Portfolio* for *Lifestyle Math* consists of 47 mathematical problems and activities from the *Lifestyle Math* workbook.

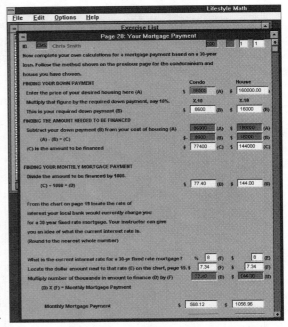

Until now, math problems have needed to be uniformly designed with one answer for each problem so teachers could check student work against a written answer key. This computer program allows students to quickly and accurately correct their own personalized math computations from their *Lifestyle Math* workbook.

All that's needed is at least one computer in the classroom or access to a computer lab along with our computer software program. Students work in their *Lifestyle Math* textbook, doing hand-written computations, then check their work with their own password-driven disk on the computer. At the end of the course, when students complete their workbook, their own computer disk can be upgraded by the Instructor to a Financial Planning Portfolio disk that can be used throughout their high school career to reassess their lifestyle expectations. This is an invaluable tool that motivates young people to increase their academic efforts accordingly.

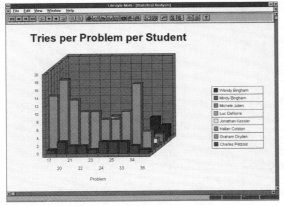

Teacher Assessment Tools Included

The software program also keeps track of valuable assessment information on individual students and on the class as a whole. For instance, it tracks how many times each student has attempted a task or how many times the class has attempted to solve a particular problem. On easy-to-read graphs, teachers can analyze the data and decide what mathematical skills need further work and tailor instruction accordingly.

Order your 60-Day Review Set of this New Software Today!*

Each review set comes with:

✓ A complete copy of the software program on disks to be reviewed for 60 days

✓ A comprehensive manual with step-by-step directions for loading and testing this software along with instructions for program set-up and class strategies

✓ A copy of the *Lifestyle Math* workbook

Hardware and Software Requirements

The program will run on any IBM/PC compatible machine running Windows 3.X, Windows 95 or Windows NT with at least 50 MB free space on the hard drive, and a minimum or 4 MB of RAM for Windows 3.X and NT, 8 MB of RAM for Windows 95.

---

* Call us at (800) 967-8016 for information and pricing.

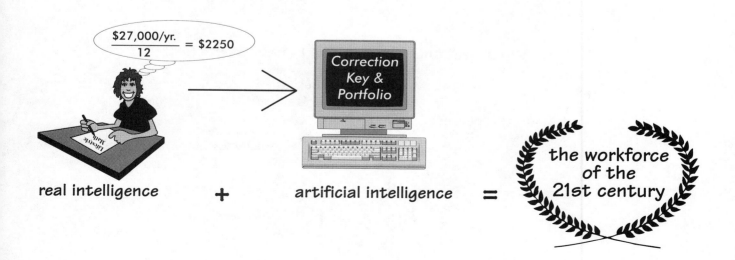

Internet Enhancement: *Making It Real*

In today's world, the truth of the statement "information is power" is commonly accepted. Therefore those who can use the Internet—an unlimited source of information—have more control than those who can't (at least when it comes to making good decisions for their own lives).

In the classroom, the Internet can bring excitement and relevance to just about any topic. And, like *Career Choices*, it motivates students to take the rest of their education more seriously. (For instance, if they are going to be corresponding with authorities on a given topic, they had better know what they are talking about, and they had better write a good letter. If they want to build relationships with people in other countries, it might be a good idea to learn new languages. To surf the Net effectively, it's helpful to know as much as possible about emerging technology.)

When you add the *Making It Real* component to your *Career Choices* program, you gain all these benefits while also allowing your students to more realistically apply the concepts they've learned in class. For example, you'll find an activity on page 226 that tells you how to help them research various careers using the databases of the classified advertisement sections of major newspapers. Class members will read about real jobs offered by real employers, with descriptions of the skills and aptitudes required, the salary range, and more. They can see how many jobs seem to be available, compare salaries in different parts of the country, even gain an understanding of the people who are likely to be competing with them for a particular position.

Salaries seem higher in San Diego than in Des Moines? We'll show you how to help students compare the culture, weather, and cost of living. (See page 264.) As plans become more detailed and personalized, they begin to seem more real. Students take them more seriously and are motivated to take the first steps necessary to achieve their goals. As they experience success, they become more motivated and seek out new areas for achievement.

When students see personal benefit in the task...

⇩

Motivation increases...then

Comprehension increases...then

Skill level increases...then

Self-esteem increases...then

Students experiences success...then

Internet Examples Throughout this *Guide*

Beginning on page 181 and throughout Section Four you'll find ideas for lesson enhancements using the World Wide Web as a resource (see pages 181, 226-227, 264, 285). These will be noted by this logo.

Please note that only a few possibilities are included in the *Instructor's Guide*. Because the web is a dynamic and constantly changing medium, we will update our *Making It Real* manual on a quarterly basis. You can be assured that only the most up-to-date and accurate web addresses are included. The Internet enhancement activities will be available to download from our Academic Innovations web site.

How to Get your Free Copy of *Making It Real*

The complete guide is available to schools who have adopted the *Career Choices* curriculum and registered for free technical support. Educators from qualified and registered schools will be given a special web address and annual password so they can retrieve periodic updates. They can then download the material to their hard drive and print out copies for their peers and students. Call our Technical Support Department to find out if your school qualifies and how to register.

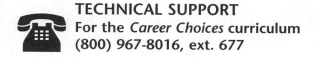

TECHNICAL SUPPORT
For the *Career Choices* curriculum
(800) 967-8016, ext. 677

Career Choices Meets the **NOICC** and **SCANS** Guidelines

"A new effective and integrated approach to career and life planning, Career Choices and the anthology, Possibilities, give schools a head start in addressing the recommended SCANS competencies and foundations skills."

– Gloria J. Conn
Member of the **SCANS** Commission

In response to concerns about the future of education and employment in America, the federal government established two committees to investigate the problems and make recommendations for solving them. The National Occupational Information Coordinating Committee (NOICC) attends to the occupational information needs of vocational education and employment and training program managers, and policy makers and the career development needs of youth and adults.

The purpose of the Secretary's Commission on Achieving Necessary Skills (SCANS), set up by the Department of Labor, is to help teachers understand how curriculum and instruction must change to enable students to develop skills needed to succeed in the high performance workplace.

Both groups have now released reports and issued guidelines that will greatly influence the direction of career education in the United States.

The NOICC guidelines, comprehensive and competency-based, aim to encourage quality career guidance and counseling programs and to recommend learning outcomes organized around self-knowledge, educational and occupational exploration, and career planning. NOICC officials say that using the National Career Development Guidelines will, among other benefits, provide students with a better understanding of the relationship of education to work and improve career decision-making skills.

On pages 300-303 of this *Instructor's Guide*, you will find a chart demonstrating how, chapter by chapter, the *Career Choices* curriculum meets these important guidelines. You will notice that the NOICC initiative calls for a curriculum nearly identical to that of *Career Choices*. For more information on the NOICC national guidelines, contact NOICC, 2100 M Street NW, Suite 156-a, Washington, DC 20037, or call the Curriculum and Instructional Materials Center at (800) 654-4502.

On pages 304-305, you'll find information on how *Career Choices* addresses the SCANS competencies. You can order the *What Work Requires of Schools* from the National Technical Information Service (NTIS), Operations Division, Springfield, VA 22151, or call (703) 487-4650. (Cost is $19.50).

Skills for the Future

Technology Enhancements for the *Career Choices* Curriculum

It is better to teach skills in context than in isolated situations.
This is as true for computer skills as it is for academic skills.

Most employers today require that new employees have at least minimal computer skills, whether they are coming in at entry level or beyond. If all your graduates leave you school with a working knowledge of the following programs, students going directly into the workforce from high school will have the skills necessary to compete for jobs with a career path and a future. Those young people going on to college or advanced training will not only be able to earn more than minimum wage as they work their way through school but will also have tools to help them excel in the classroom.

Checklist of skills required for the workforce of the 21st century:

☑ Keyboarding (at least 50 words per minute)

☑ Word processing*

☑ Using spreadsheets*

☑ Using presentation software*

☑ Using simple graphics/design software*

The *Career Choices* curriculum presents a variety of opportunities to practice these very important skills.

For example, note the suggestions in this *Guide*:

Tumwater High School's Integrated English and Technology Course, pages 54-55

San Gabriel High School's Presentation Project, page 276

You'll find an assortment of technology enhanced lesson plans that reinforce the development of the above skills on our *Making It Real* web site. They'll be noted by the logo at the top of this page. Be sure to register for technical support so you'll have access to these innovative ideas.

* Software programs available in most Office Suite packages such as Microsoft Office or Lotus SmartSuite.

Additional *Making It Real* activities are available through the Academic Innovations home page on the World Wide Web. For more information on how you can access these Internet enhancement activities, see pages 36 and 37 of this *Instructor's Guide*.

SECTION TWO

Teaching Strategies

Career Choices is ideal for the teacher who truly believes that any student can succeed in a supportive environment. This course is based on the premise that every person has strengths and that each person must be given the opportunity to use them and succeed. While the student is the worker, the teacher facilitates learning success!

Because of the flexible nature of the course, the instructor's creativity can come into play. Although a wide variety of stories illustrate the major themes of the text, teachers may supplement these with selections from other sources to make the topics even more relevant. Student volunteers may be willing to share personal dilemmas with the class, providing practice in decision making and problem solving.

Structured for small group input and hands-on learning, these course materials can create warm relationships with the class. A "we're all in this together" approach encourages group support and cooperative learning. Although the materials are markedly different from those traditionally used, they offer a creative way to facilitate authentic learning. For example, as a language arts course, *Career Choices* invites students to look at fiction from a new perspective as they begin to identify with the characters. Optional components of the program help young people become comfortable using computers and turning to the Internet for information they'll use in their daily lives.

We urge instructors to have students keep a personal journal through the course. This is a excellent strategy not only for the development of writing skills, but also for encouraging reflection and self-expression.

Career Choices affords a channel for school and community linkage. As the kind of program most communities and employers have sought in their schools, this innovative approach readily gains recognition and public support. Here is an ideal opportunity for teachers to showcase creative solutions to tough educational problems. See pages 90-94, 95, 123-127and 220-224 for more ideas.

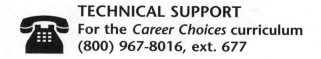

TECHNICAL SUPPORT
For the *Career Choices* curriculum
(800) 967-8016, ext. 677

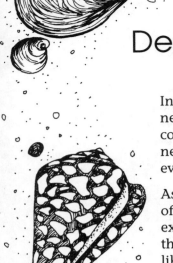

Designed for All Students

In recent years, schools have largely reinvented themselves to meet the needs of all their students, not just the minority who will be going on to college. Programs like Tech Prep and School-to-Work are particularly needed, and have been rightly applauded by parents, teachers, students— even the government.

As we look closely at these innovations, however, we see that some types of information must be assimilated by **all** students. Those in Tech Prep, for example, need as much career guidance as those in college prep classes; they'll make the same kinds of decisions, only at an earlier age. It seems like all kinds of young people are making potentially life-altering decisions at earlier ages, in fact, so all the more reason to teach them about making *good* decisions, setting goals, solving problems, taking initiative and calculated risks, overcoming anxieties and peer pressure, and so on.

Career Choices should be part of every young person's education, but it is up to each school to determine the most appropriate way to deliver its wisdom. For instance, many schools adopt it as the required 9th grade English/language arts course for at least one semester or trimester. Whether the text is used in language arts or family life courses, or in employment seminars, this *Instructor's Guide* offers enough suggestions so that teachers can work with it creatively and comfortably, knowing that they are meeting the needs of their students.

I found these materials adaptable to both my gifted and talented students and to my non-motivated students.

– Kathryn T. Harcum
English chairperson
North Caroline High School
Ridgely, Maryland

Our Web Site

Question	Go to URL:	You'll find:	Helpful hints & tips
My state framework calls for competency in goal setting, decision making, critical thinking and problem solving. Where and how does the Career Choices curriculum address these skills?	http://www. academicinnovations.com/ workport.html	A list of hyperlinks about how *Career Choices* meets a variety of learning objectives	*Surf through the hyperlinks with a copy of Career Choices beside you so you can review each noted exercise.*

Urban Students Get 36 Weeks of Career Guidance

At San Gabriel High School on the border of inner city Los Angeles, students in speech and communications classes are also receiving a full year of career guidance. The program, called Directions, draws on the activities in *Career Choices* for speech assignments, class discussion topics, group projects and more.

Doug Campbell, Chair of the Communications Department, recommended that all teachers go through the complete *Career Choices* textbook in sequence. This not only helped keep a uniform focus for all the classes, but also allowed students to build their awareness of the central issues: who am I, what do I want, and where am I going, in a natural progression, much like peeling the layers of an onion. At the center students discovered their true identity and were thus able to make better choices for their lives and their futures.

"Guidance counselors reported that students who had taken the Directions class seemed to have a plan when they came in at scheduling time," according to Doug. "They were clearly more involved in choosing their classes, rather than simply accepting the schedule given to them by the counselor. Students were actually seeing that there is a purpose for being in school."

The class also helped students get ready for success in the workplace by teaching such skills as working cooperatively, setting goals and making decisions. Class members teamed up to do mock interviews and practiced expository speaking by presenting reports they researched on careers. "This built up students' self-image and gave them more confidence to eventually enter the workplace," Doug said.

Most importantly, perhaps, he adds that "The one thing everyone learns in my class is that they always have a choice in life, and that they are always responsible for the choices they make. This year all of our freshmen (600 students) will take the course."

Student quotes from our evaluations:
"Life really is one choice after another."
"I learned I was smarter than I thought."
"I discovered skills I didn't know I had."
"I learned life (growing up) isn't so easy. I'm not so anxious."
"Now I know how hard it is for my parents.

–Elizabeth Farris
English Department Chair
San Gabriel High School
San Gabriel, California

Opportunities for a Team Teaching/ Interdisciplinary Approach

This curriculum is flexible enough to respect individual teaching styles as well as individual learning styles. The instructor who wants to implement his or her own creative plans alone can do so. For those who prefer a team teaching/interdisciplinary approach, however, the program offers outstanding potential, both for structured schools and less traditional settings.

A language arts instructor and guidance counselor could make an extremely effective team, with the counselor coming in once a week or so to lecture, facilitate discussion, or provide small group counseling or support. School counselors usually have a wealth of experience in dealing with people, yet their more customary duties do not permit them to fully utilize their talents. Many would enjoy taking part in this project. If they say they'd love to but just don't have the time, you might point out that they can accomplish many of their counseling and class scheduling goals using this curriculum in your classroom.

Many successful programs bring together language arts and technology teachers. Students learn about computers by using them to complete their language arts assignments. More ambitious programs have involved setting up mock businesses, videotaping student job interviews, and so on.

You may want to bring in the math teacher to talk about those exercises involving numbers and calculations. This is a good way to both integrate learning and illustrate what we can do in the real world. An optional component, *Lifestyle Math*, is designed to be used in the math classroom as a supplemental text for all math levels, or by the consumer education, business or economics instructor.

The career education teacher, family life instructor, and social studies teacher are other possible candidates to participate in a teaching team.

Our Web Site

Question	Go to URL:	You'll find:	Helpful hints & tips
Our interdisciplinary team is studying ways to structure our classes using the Career Choices curriculum. I need some ideas.	http://www. academicinnovations.com/ indepth.html	Hyperlinks to a variety of stories about 20 educators along with a summary of their creative approaches	*Choose the hyperlinks to Phyllis Stewart of IN, Robert Freed of MN, Scott Hess of WA, Barbara Larson and Peg Slusarski of NE. Print and share their stories with your teammates.*
AND...	http://www. academicinnovations.com/ interdis.html	A variety of interdisciplinary academic combinations for *Career Choices*	*Print, share and discuss these various possibilities with your teammates.*

Career Choices offers you options:

Independent

Career Choices / **Workbook and Portfolio**

Integrated

Career Choices / **Workbook and Portfolio** + **Possibilities** *A Supplemental Anthology for Career Choices*

Interdisciplinary

Career Choices / **Workbook and Portfolio** + **Possibilities** *A Supplemental Anthology for Career Choices* + **Lifestyle Math** *Your Financial Planning Portfolio*

+ Instructor's Guide

Instructor's and Counselor's Guide for Career Choices

Some Sample Combinations

ENGLISH/LANGUAGE ARTS OR COMMUNICATIONS
In many of the schools currently using the *Career Choices* curriculum, it is the English teachers who teach the course. Some instructors use only the *Career Choices* text with the *Workbook and Portfolio*, and some use the *Career Choices* text and *Possibilities*.

ENGLISH/LANGUAGE ARTS AND GUIDANCE DEPARTMENT
Many English/language arts teachers have teamed with the Guidance department to enrich the curriculum by having a guidance counselor come in at specific points to lead the lesson for the day. We have noted some particular activities in Section Four of this *Guide*. At the end of the course, students schedule planning sessions with their guidance counselor and use their *Workbook and Portfolio* as an integral part of their planning process.

FAMILY AND CONSUMER SCIENCE AND ENGLISH/LANGUAGE ARTS
Because of the guidance and career and family living expertise of the instructors in the Family and Consumer Science department, some schools have used this model. The family and consumer science teachers use the *Career Choices* text, while the English teachers use *Possibilities*. This is usually accomplished in a block format.

ENGLISH/LANGUAGE ARTS, MATH AND SOCIAL STUDIES
Schools using this format are usually divided into "houses" or clusters and work with block scheduling. The material in the *Career Choices* text is presented by the social studies instructor, *Possibilities* by the English teacher, and *Lifestyle Math* by the math teacher. Usually this course is a quarter or semester in duration, at the 8th, 9th or 10th grade level.

TECH PREP/SCHOOL-TO-WORK
Tech Prep and School-to-Work programs are using the *Career Choices* texts as one of their cluster options in the beginning of the program. The course is designed to help students choose a career path. A variety of instructors from different disciplines have chosen to teach this cluster.

CAREER EDUCATION
A career education instructor can effectively present the materials from *Career Choices* with the *Workbook and Portfolio* or use all the texts of the series.

CAREER EDUCATION AND ENGLISH/LANGUAGE ARTS
This combination of disciplines works especially well. The career educator presents the *Career Choices* text along with the *Workbook and Portfolio*, and the English/language arts instructor teaches from *Possibilities*.

BUSINESS EDUCATION AND ENGLISH/LANGUAGE ARTS
Many business education instructors are right at home with the material in *Career Choices* and *Lifestyle Math*. Teaming with the English/Language Arts department, using *Possibilities*, makes for an effective interdisciplinary approach to learning.

TECHNOLOGY EDUCATION AND ENGLISH/LANGUAGE ARTS
Because communication and computer skills are indispensable in the workplace and in post-high school education, these instructors can combine to form a powerful program for all students.

FRESHMAN ORIENTATION CLASS
This can be accomplished in a single class at the beginning of the 9th grade year, using the main text, or as a block-scheduled course, using all the texts within an interdisciplinary team.

A GUIDANCE CLASS: COUNSELOR IN THE CLASSROOM
In some schools, the counseling staff finds that one of the most efficient and effective ways to provide comprehensive guidance to students is in the classroom. Quarter and semester courses are designed and taught by the counselor using a combination of texts.

A SCHOOL-WIDE CLASS: ALL STUDENTS TAKE THE COURSE
At one school, in San Juan, California, the whole school took the *Career Choices* course over a one-year period. Class periods were adjusted so that once per week, at the same time, every instructor in the school taught from the *Career Choices* text along with the *Workbook and Portfolio*. Because the workbook is consumable, the students bought their own books.

*Our guidance counselors met with our freshmen classes once a month to present various ideas and units presented in **Career Choices**.*

– Linda Wulff
Chairperson, Communication Department
Waupun High School
Waupun, Wisconsin

Whole School Takes Career Choices

At Casa Roble Fundamental High School in Orangevale, California, every one of the 1,800 students enrolled took *Career Choices* during the '92-93 school year. With enthusiastic leadership and creative ideas from Ernie Gomes, Science Chair, and Linda Page, science teacher, the project flourished.

Every teacher in the school taught the course, which was held during a special period added at the end of the day. This presented a challenge. But as Ernie Gomes reports, *"Career Choices* is great for the classroom teacher who doesn't know that much about career guidance."

All students completed their own copy of the consumable *Career Choices* workbook. (Because they were allowed to keep their books, the students were required to pay for them.)

Besides the *Career Choices* activities, students were exposed to a wide variety of speakers at special breakout sessions and a day-long careers fair.

As a recipient of one of the state's five-year restructuring grants, the school has identified comprehensive career education as critical to its success. Next year, all freshmen will be divided into houses, and each house will complete a one-quarter course on careers. "The information found in *Career Choices* is something every student needs," Gomes concludes.

Reproduced from quarterly Focus on the Future *newsletter. To be added to our mailing list for this free publication, call (800) 967-8016.*

Cluster Concept Works

During the 1991-92 school year, Mission Bay High School of San Diego was one of the thirty California Investment High Schools. Chosen because of their innovative approaches and their dedication, the faculty set out to test various alternatives for improving the educational climate at their campus. Piloting the school-within-a-school concept—also known as houses or clusters—they assigned 100 students to a "house" which was team taught. This pilot not only enabled teachers to give more attention to each individual, but also to develop a feeling of community and commitment among the students.

Evaluating the results, school Counselor and Magnet Coordinator Steve Stangland reported, "During our year as an Investment High School, our pilot group of 100 students had better attendance, higher grades, reduced drop outs and fewer suspensions." Therefore, at the end of the year's experiment, all staff made a commitment to restructure with or without additional funds. As a consequence, the entire 9th grade is now divided into four houses and teams. Because the *Career Choices* program contributed significantly to success of the pilot project, that curriculum has been adopted for use throughout the 9th grade.

Joan Yost, English teacher and 9th grade team member, reported that her English, math and social studies team has decided to use *Career Choices* in an interdisciplinary way. Asked what she thought of the new curriculum, Yost enthusiastically responded, "I've shared information about *Career Choices* with friends at other schools because I think it is so terrific! And as I told the parents at our open house, I wish I had this when I was growing up."

Putting the Counselor In the Classroom

"As a guidance counselor—certified in both elementary and secondary schools—I commend you on dealing with the 'whole child,'" Wendy Hanslovan wrote us recently from St. Marys, a public high school in St. Marys, Pennsylvania, where she teaches a mandatory *Career Choices* class for freshmen. "Your multidimensional approach, I am sure, is the reason for the universal appeal of this curriculum."

Hanslovan and her colleagues in the counseling department are the exclusive instructors for the St. Marys High School class, which includes four or five sections each semester. Although some teachers from other departments would like to teach the material, the counselors are determined to remain in the classroom, believing fervently that this is vital information for their students and a quality guidance opportunity.

"Students are typically unassertive about choosing a career direction," says Hanslovan, noting that in the past, counselors often couldn't take the time to help each young person plan wisely for the future. And she knows how important the process is. "I knew I was going to college, but beyond that I had no clue. My counselor was no help and that is precisely why, eventually, I ended up in this career. I think it's important to our country, our society, and it's important to individuals, as well."

At St. Marys, the primary focus is on helping students choose an appropriate course from among six different career clusters and eventually find a satisfying career. *Career Choices* is extremely helpful in this process, Hanslovan says, because it helps young people clarify their thoughts about who they are and what they want before they begin making career decisions. "The students are relating to it," she states. "I cannot say enough good things about [*Career Choices*]."

TECHNICAL SUPPORT
For the *Career Choices* curriculum
(800) 967-8016, ext. 677

In-Depth Interviews with Innovative Educators

Over the last few years we have conducted in-depth interviews with educators across the country to learn how they used and adapted the *Career Choices* curriculum for each of their special populations. Their approaches are insightful and creative. If you are currently conducting a *Career Choices* program, are seriously considering its adoption or involved with educational restructuring at your school, you'll want to take the time to log on to our web site and read these innovators' stories. If you're not yet online, call our Tech Support Department for hardcopies of these interviews.

In-Depth Interviews with Innovative Educators

http://www.academicinnovations.com/indepth.html

Phyllis Stewart - Vincennes, Indiana

http://www.academicinnovations.com/int11.html

Learn how Phyllis Stewart, Tech Prep site coordinator and 30-year veteran teacher, integrated her *Career Choices* program with the English and computer keyboarding instructors. She shares her observations on why an integrated approach works.

Doug Campbell - San Gabriel, California

http://www.academicinnovations.com/int12.html

Learn how Doug Campbell and his staff created and implemented a year-long interdisciplinary class in communications for 9th graders using the *Career Choices* curriculum. Due to the success of this program it is now a required class for all 9th graders. Good ideas for anyone restructuring or starting Tech Prep or School-to-Work programs.

Mary Ellen Fowler - Broward County, Florida

http://www.academicinnovations.com/int13.html

Learn how English teacher Mary Ellen Fowler structures her class, Career Decision-Making and Critical Thinking Skills, in her school's Tech-Prep/School-to-Work program. She shares her innovative ideas, such as her exemplary speakers program and her parent orientation.

Roberta Freed - Little Falls, Minnesota

http://www.academicinnovations.com/int14.html

Learn how English teacher Roberta Freed and On-the-Job teacher Ron Hanenkamp created their integrated "Transitions" class for special education students. Roberta goes into detail that is sure to help any teacher with any population.

Priscilla Gregory - Vonore, Tennessee

http://www.academicinnovations.com/int15.html

Learn how and why English teacher Priscilla Gregory has a guidance theme for her college-bound students as well as her non-college prep students. Her unique community outreach program is worthy of replication.

Scott Hess - Tumwater, Washington

http://www.academicinnovations.com/int16.html

Learn from English teacher Scott Hess how his interdisciplinary team of six instructors put together their program, winner of the 1994 Washington Educators Association's "Leaders in Restructuring Award" for innovative programs. Scott also shares their ideas for "Keys to Successful Teamwork."

Dr. Jim Campbell - Delaware State Tech Prep Consortium

http://www.academicinnovations.com/int17.html

Learn from Dr. Campbell, 1993 winner of the Parnell Award for exemplary Tech Prep programs nationwide, the secrets for developing a successful Tech Prep program. He shares relevant statistics and discusses the need for comprehensive guidance.

Barbara Larson and Peg Slusarski - Columbus, Nebraska

http://www.academicinnovations.com/int18.html

Learn from business teacher Barbara Larson and English teacher Peg Slusarski how they designed their class BECI (Business and English Curriculum Integration program). They discuss in detail a planning process that has fostered cooperation among teachers and support from administrators while providing an excellent educational experience for students.

Teri Redl - Medina County, Ohio

http://www.academicinnovations.com/int19.html

Learn how School-to-Work Site Coordinator Teri Redl developed her class for potential drop-outs and the details of how she organized her lesson plans. Her strategies clearly demonstrate the strength of combining academic skills improvement with individual support and guidance.

Lorraine Rippey and Wendy Hanslovan - St. Marys, Pennsylvania

http://www.academicinnovations.com/int20.html

Learn how and why guidance counselors Lorraine Rippey and Wendy Hanslovan developed a classroom-based program where students get "ten months, instead of ten minutes of comprehensive guidance." Their team of three guidance counselors teaches four periods a day in this Tech Prep program.

Pat Marabella - Havre, Montana

http://www.academicinnovations.com/int01.html

Learn how Pat Marabella instilled a love of learning in his multi-cultural, at-risk group of students. Thirty percent of his students were Native American so his ideas for this population are worth looking at. Pre- and post-tests found significant increases in math and reading abilities.

Nancy Carter - Denver, Colorado

http://www.academicinnovations.com/int02.html

Learn how Nancy Carter structured her Summer Youth Program and about the students' significant gains in learning, based on an outside evaluation. One significant factor was that each student who successfully completed the program (100% attendance among other markers) received a unit of credit toward graduation.

Zora Tammer - Berkeley, California

http://www.academicinnovations.com/int03.html

Learn how Zora Tammer structured the six-hour day (over eight weeks) so that reluctant learners became motivated students.

Ron Eydenberg - Boston, Massachusetts

http://www.academicinnovations.com/int04.html

Learn how Ron Eydenberg brought academics into the worksite for his 500 Summer JTPA participants and the benefits of this approach.

Eric Stephens - Los Angeles, California

http://www.academicinnovations.com/int05.html

Learn how Eric Stephens adjusted his curriculum to the different learning styles of his at-risk population.

Deb Mumford - Denver, Colorado

http://www.academicinnovations.com/int06.html

Learn about the external evaluation of this academic enrichment program for at-risk students. Staff members also share their insights on why they think this program worked.

Anne Swygert - Greensboro, North Carolina

http://www.academicinnovations.com/int07.html

Learn about Anne Swygert's seven-week summer JTPA program and some of her creative activities and approaches that exposed her students to a world they had never known.

Jessy James - Marshall, Minnesota

http://www.academicinnovations.com/int08.html

Learn about Jessy James's students' significant gains in math and reading and what he credits for these post-testing gains.

Joe Werner - Monterey, California

http://www.academicinnovations.com/int09.html

Learn about the strategies Joe Werner used with his program for very high-risk youth that, as he says, "puts the needs of the students first." The strength of this program is the individualized attention each of his 78 students received.

John Gill - Hempstead, New York

http://www.academicinnovations.com/int10.html

Learn how John Gill adapted *Career Choices* and *Possibilities* to work with his population of 700 at-risk students with varying abilities.

If you'd like to share how you structure your *Career Choices* program on our web site, call our Technical Support Department to arrange an interview.

Using *Career Choices* as a Catalyst for Restructuring

If your school is restructuring or thinking about restructuring, you may want to consider the experience of Tumwater High School in Tumwater, Washington. Its "integrated, blocked, teamed, and applied English/Technology program" utilizing both *Career Choices* and the anthology, *Possibilities*, received the Washington Education Association's *Leaders in Restructuring Award* for 1994.

"Alarmed by a lack of motivation among freshmen in previous years," the school's application letter reads, "we aimed to develop a comprehensive, student-friendly, motivational, curriculum-intensive block that would begin each student's high school academic course on the very best foundation possible. We believe that we succeeded."

By bringing together English and technology classes, instructors hoped to make both more interesting and relevant to their students. The new program superseded the old freshman English trilogy of grammar, composition and literature, using *Career Choices* and *Possibilities* as its texts for one trimester (twelve weeks, one hour a day) of the year-long program. The books were funded through general curriculum funds. The model was part freshman orientation, part Tech Prep, and part language arts. Students completed all exercises in the *Career Choices* text.

The following is taken from the letter of application: "Essentially, the team of six teachers (three for the English department and three from the business department) determined that new technology resulting from a recent bond levy could be of maximum effectiveness only if thoroughly integrated into a core subject area. English was a natural choice due to the extensive writing required of students in that arena. Technology teachers wanted students to work with substantive material while learning essentials of technology. Our goal would be maximum integration—each day's technology lessons would reinforce learnings from English. That concept provided the basis for our design which evolved to include so much more.

"Incoming freshmen were placed into a two-hour morning block to provide a home base where friendships could develop. English and technology rooms were realigned into pairs with a door punched in the adjoining wall to allow a flow of students between rooms in addition to hall access. Freshman lockers were relocated so that students' lockers were near their morning block location. Standard expectations of behavior were developed for all classes, and reality therapy and control theory were taught by counselors early in the year to encourage freshmen to take control of their destiny from their first day at the high school.

"Essays now look and read beautifully. Editing is a snap. Graphics provide a special flair for student-created poetry. Book reports have become tri-fold brochures publicizing the novel. The classroom has become a workplace from which professional looking letters could be drafted and mailed to the editor of the local paper, to the manufacturer of a gender-biased toy, or to a pen pal in a high school across the nation. Using many of the Applied Communications Modules, we dovetail with the objective of our Student Learning Improvement Grant which is to help students experience an effective school to work transition. Students quickly have surpassed their English teachers' knowledge of software and showed their expertise with pride. English is revitalized; technology has substance. Color technology-produced posters, newspapers, and spell-checked and grammar-checked essays replace the drudgery-laden, hand-written daily English assignments.

"Our six-member team churns out creative and meaningful assignments week after week. English teachers accomplished more than ever before, due to the efficiency of technology and the block of time. We still teach traditional material such as *Romeo and Juliet*, and *The Miracle Worker*. We also teach the fundamentals of communication, units on success, units on careers, units on business fundamentals, and units on diversity. Most importantly, the curriculum has cohesive organization based on our three-trimester system. We address personal communication in the fall, business communication in the winter, and creative communication in the spring. The program has re-invigorated the at-risk students due to the hands-on environment and professional-appearing results of their efforts. Next year, portfolio assessment will allow all freshman students to see their tremendous progress and keep their best efforts for posterity.

"Our program brings community members into the classroom to emphasize relevance of the curriculum to the world of work, makes education dynamic and interactive, displays innovation conceptually and on a daily basis, was developed based on district outcomes from the 'bottom up' in a site-based setting, involves integration and teaming, and has been a huge success." (Special thanks to English instructor Scott Hess for allowing us to share this information with you. We thought you'd rather hear from your peers than from us.)

We believe the Tumwater High School program is worthy of its success and can serve as an admirable restructuring model for other schools. Here is a unique guidance curriculum, competency based, truly interdisciplinary in both scope and sequence, that makes integration of academics easily possible. What's more, using this model will save you hundreds of hours of planning time! We recommend that, like Tumwater, you set up a pilot program to demonstrate the effectiveness of interdisciplinary teams. The *Career Choices* curriculum offers an excellent vehicle for efficiently and effectively doing this. From there, you can expand your efforts, and other grades and departments can also follow your model.

The Guidance Curriculum for Tech Prep and School-to-Work Programs

A cutting edge curriculum....It is an outstanding and unique example of how core academic subjects can work together with vocational-technical education to create a new and exciting synergy in education.
– American Vocational Association

In an effort to better serve the 75% of students who will not graduate from college and to provide a more skilled workforce for the nation, the U.S. Departments of Education and Labor are encouraging schools to put Tech Prep and School-to-Work programs in place as never before. The programs have much in common—both are designed to prepare students for skilled, high-paying jobs. Both require cooperation between educators and employers. And both ask students to make important decisions about their future at an age when many do not have the level of maturity or self-knowledge necessary to choose wisely.

As the movement gathers momentum, it is clear that a comprehensive guidance component in the beginning of these programs is essential for success. Fifteen minutes with a guidance counselor or two to three hours with a computerized interest inventory or career exploration software is not enough to help young teens make sophisticated choices that will affect their entire lives. And, since many students are often not educationally motivated to begin with, they also need assistance that demonstrates the relevance of their academic subjects and motivates them to put forth the effort required for them to succeed.

The *Career Choices* curriculum provides a quality comprehensive guidance program that works because:

1. **It is classroom based**, providing 45 to 90 hours of activities, discussions, and research opportunities in a sequential format.

2. **It has scope and sequence**, modeling a self-discovery and decision-making process students can use over and over again throughout their lives, whenever they need to make important decisions.

Career Choices *offers teachers unique and engaging ways of allowing students to explore career interests and opportunities while concurrently meeting life skills required of all students and productive workers. I commend these materials for use in high schools and/or community colleges...I particularly like that the curriculum is grounded in a specific academic discipline and that it is competency-based.*

– Dale Parnell
Author, *The Neglected Majority*
Father of Tech Prep

3. **It helps students develop self-awareness** and to answer the questions: Who am I? What do I want? How do I get it? And why do I need a good education? It helps students become "identity achieved," learn progressive decision-making techniques and skills, become critical thinkers in relation to their future lives, complete quantitative plans, and discover reality-based options for their adult lives.

4. **It exposes students to the skills of personal success**, such as goal setting and decision making, overcoming fears and personal resistances, budgeting, and resource management.

5. **It exposes students to the realities and responsibilities of the adult world.** *Career Choices* offers opportunities to discuss and explore various aspects of adult life so young people can better define the kind of life they want, and thereby make wise educational decisions today.

6. **It helps students learn to project themselves into the future and understand the consequences of their actions today.** Studies show that if students can visualize their future and understand how their choices today impact their future happiness, they are far less likely to drop out of school, become a teen parent, or abuse drugs.

I am using the **Possibilities** *anthology in the English component of the Automotive Integrated Curriculum at my school. This is the material that I have been waiting for. In the past, I would spend many hours analyzing materials for school to work applications. Thanks for a useful, innovative tool.*

– Rosetta B. Tetteh
English Teacher
Senn Metropolitan Academy
Chicago, Illinois

We have 23 sites using this curriculum with great success. As we focus more and more on School-to-Work, this curriculum will become even more essential.

– Lynn Porter
Coordinator of High School Diploma Program
Santa Monica-Malibu Unified School District
Santa Monica, California

For Use with College-Bound and Even Gifted Students

Career Choices allows instructors to personalize the academic rigor of the language arts curriculum for gifted students. These high achievers and academically motivated students are often as socially insecure, unhappy, and unsure about their future as other students. What's more, they may be reluctant to admit their insecurities and talented enough to conceal them.

Before you begin, you might want to hold a parents' meeting (with your principal's permission). Reassure them that you know the importance of the academic mission. These students, however, are probably capable of carrying on much of that work on their own. As parents and teachers, you want to be sure that they also have the personal skills they need to be happy and satisfied individuals. By discussing the importance of problem solving, decision making, and long-range planning with parents, you should be able to demonstrate that, while their children's academic talents will get them into college, these practical skills will determine whether they stay there and thrive.

Studies clearly show that students who enter college with a specific career or career area in mind are far more likely to graduate four years later. It is the strongest indicator of success in college and in an individual's future work life.

Gifted students are often programmed to believe their talents should be applied in a particular direction. Or, because they are used to having things come easily to them, they may tend to give up at the first sign of difficulty. They may also be overwhelmed by the sheer number of choices available to them. It is very important, therefore, that they develop the skills and attitudes (decision making, anxiety tolerance, overcoming fears, and so on) needed to be their own best and happiest person.

I've been reading all your information on career development on the web for the past half hour and must admit I am impressed with your correct approach to today's unmotivated youth. Unfortunately, I can identify with those without direction all too well. I am a 23-year-old recent college graduate and have little motivation towards a specific career path. With each passing day, I increasingly yearn for a passion in some specific vocation but am continually lost.... I can relate to your claim that a person must know themselves before they can correctly choose a career and felt that I never achieved this identification when I should have many years ago.

– Response to web site via e-mail

For Use with JTPA Youth Programs

Some of the most rewarding reports we've received about the *Career Choices* curriculum are from Job Training Partnership Act (JTPA) summer and year-round youth programs. When the federal government requested that an academic component be added to the summer jobs project, most coordinators were caught off guard. They didn't have an academic enrichment program, and there was little time to prepare one.

Most JTPA summer youth want jobs, not school. By the time June comes, they are ready to leave classrooms, books, tests and teachers behind. They are no different from the majority of other youth their age—except that these young people are more frustrated and turned-off by education. While there are many reasons for their frustration, some are directly related to the type of learning they experienced in school. The results are reflected in lower basic skills levels, higher drop out rates, lower self-esteem and more hostile behavior. Summer academic enrichment programs should look different from school.

Although these issues are not the case with all JTPA summer youth, the design of academic enrichment programs should not add to what is already a major challenge for so many of these young people. In other words, if the summer academic program is just a warmed-over English or math class, the frustration of your participants will surface, even if they are being paid to sit in a seat.

The *Career Choices* curriculum, coordinators found with relief, fit nicely. It not only met federal guidelines, it was a big hit with employers, instructors, and the young people themselves. We began to receive amazing reports from big cities, small towns, and isolated rural areas across the country. Where it had not previously been unusual for large percentages of the participants to drop out or attend class only sporadically, nearly everyone was coming nearly every day. Attitudes changed, as did plans for the future. It was not unusual for reading and math abilities to increase by up to several grade levels. And instructors who saw these same students back at school in the fall found that the changes were real and seemingly permanent.

Two words: Common sense.
— Coordinator John Gill on why JTPA youth
benefit from *Career Choices*
Hempstead, New York

The children that we started with seven weeks ago are not the kids we have now. They look different, they act differently, they hold their heads up, they speak distinctly. . . [and it all happened] in seven weeks.

– Anne Swygert, coordinator
Greensboro, North Carolina

We had kids from two different sides of town, two different ethnic backgrounds, two different gang mentalities. We had not one fight.

– Deb Mumford, coordinator
Denver, Colorado

The program did provide 90 hours of quality instruction for the youth which produces significant improvement in academic Basic Skills as well as positive attitudinal changes towards learning. The vast majority of participants did connect academic learning to practical life skills and the majority of participants' self-concepts as learner did improve.

– report by Dr. Charles Branch
external evaluator for Denver JTPA

Sixty-four percent reported they would be or probably would be in the program even if they were not being paid, and 93 percent of the 42 subjects interviewed would recommend the Academic Enrichment Program to friends.

– Dr. Branch's report

They did some wonderful math they weren't supposed to be able to do. [While pre-tests in math and reading showed students performing at levels from fourth grade, fourth month to sixth grade, seventh month] when we finished the program I had quite a few of them jump all the way up to the 12th grade level.

– Jessy James, instructor
Marshall, Minnesota

For Use with At-Risk Students

Career Choices is the ideal central text for an integrated career education/language arts program targeting at-risk students. It makes education relevant to students who have been turned off by academics and allows them to see themselves as important individuals with potential for satisfying lives.

The career education/language arts combination provides ample opportunity for cooperative, hands-on learning, self-analysis, autobiographical reading and writing, and role-playing activities that strengthen academic skills as well as self-awareness. It teaches decision making, problem solving, and overcoming obstacles, critical skills for this population. In addition, the career education component teaches such essential job preparation skills as filling out job applications, writing resumes, and being interviewed for work.

To make the program most effective, instructors should focus on the question "Where do you want to be in ten years?" From that vantage point, it's not difficult for students to determine what might stand in the way of achieving that goal or if the possibility of reaching it makes staying in school worthwhile. It's important that classes for at-risk students be kept small, so that they can be known as individuals who matter, and who have a future.

Journal writing is also essential. When young people are crying out for help, you may learn more about them and their special needs or problems from this ongoing activity than from other sources.

At-risk students also benefit greatly from getting out into the world, as they do with the shadow program prescribed on pages 218-224 of this *Guide*. You might wish to take this one step further by having students become unpaid interns for longer periods of time. This program not only allows students to observe or take part in work that might interest them, but it also validates what is taught in school: the importance of being on time, getting along with others, following directions, and so on.

In Great Falls, Montana, one local business has "adopted" an alternative education high school. Using the Personal Profile System test (mentioned on pages 38-43, 162-165 of the text) for its own workers, the employer first helps the students identify their work behavioral styles, and then places them in intern positions that match their strengths and work styles. The employer believes that this process gives students better opportunities for success and they will therefore be more motivated to apply themselves as a result of the assessment.

Who Is at Risk?

Traditionally, it has not been difficult to recognize the students who are at risk. They are the ones who are failing or dropping out of school, the substance abusers, the ones who can't read, among other obvious signs. We would like to broaden this definition to include anyone who is not living up to his or her full potential. The young woman who sits quietly in the back row using her 140 IQ to earn B's and C's is at risk. So is the student who's attended six different schools in as many years. The abused student is at risk, and the troublemaker, and the one who lives in poverty or whose family is going through an emotional or economic crisis, and the young woman who is pregnant or already a mother. Everyone with physical or emotional problems is at risk, as are all those who can't seem to get their act together, or who lack the discipline to make use of their abundant talents.

Like everyone else, students need to experience success and feel empowered. Success follows self-esteem, and empowerment follows success. Those who can only succeed at failure will fail. We believe that the strength of this curriculum is that it empowers students to feel in control of their lives and motivates them through this empowerment. It provides for a learning environment that focuses on individual strengths rather than weaknesses, allowing students to succeed at what they do best. It speaks to those students who need just a little more support and attention to see how they fit in and how education is relevant to their lives. Together, we can give them what they need. And we will all benefit.

For Use within the Juvenile Justice System

Today, more young people than ever before are out of control, in trouble with the law, or in some other manner limiting their own chances for future satisfaction. Many people who aren't succeeding tend to think of themselves as victims. Something has been "done" to them, and there is nothing they can do about it. In some cases, they are partially correct—youngsters who are abused or neglected are victims. Disadvantaged children have little recourse concerning their plight. But, having come to an age where they are able to make their own decisions, all these young people have choices to make. They can continue to be victims, or they can choose to get on with their lives.

With its emphasis on accountability, problem solving, and decision making, *Career Choices* is valuable in demonstrating that the past doesn't matter. Students must take responsibility for past decisions, but they are working with a fresh slate and are in a position to make choices that will determine their future satisfaction.

HINT: Federal money is available for juvenile justice programs. You may wish to take advantage of this situation by having someone from juvenile justice work with teachers on this project.

For Use with Pregnant Students or Teen Parents

In schools with a comprehensive high school program for pregnant teens or parenting teens, *Career Choices* can be used successfully within the language arts curriculum. In other schools, it can be the core of a child care, future planning, career skills, or life preparation course. It should be offered for credit.

With these materials, students are able to look at their current situation objectively. The course encourages them to believe that obstacles can be overcome, that doors are not permanently closed to them because of a single mistake. It encourages them to ask what they want now, and how they can go about reaching those goals, rather than dwelling on the past.

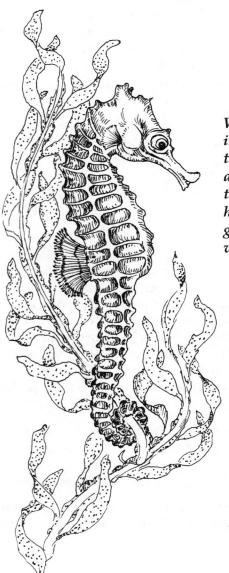

Working with a group of pregnant/parenting teens in a program called "Young Families Can – Jobs," the groups became bonded and shared hopes, fears and dreams for their futures…. They didn't want the program to end. This group of young women had transformed from street smart, tough, gang-girls into talking about freedom, justice and wanting to be president.

– Tamara Luckett
Career Educator
Parents Anonymous
Phoenix, Arizona

One student talked another student (who had dropped out of school) to come back because of what she learned in the program.

– Tim Bridges
Social Studies Career Education Teacher
Lanesville Community School Corp.
Lanesville, Indiana

I am gratified to see an awareness of the girls' self-worth. Low self-esteem is the norm for our students. They really have trouble seeing past their pregnancy. We have had some students who just blossomed here, and as a result, went on to college and earned a degree.

–Jean A. Granger
  Career Exploration Teacher
  School Age Parents Program
  Waukesha, Wisconsin

How Do I Choose?

All the activities and exercises outlined in this guide could easily fill a one-year course, but perhaps you want to be more selective. Let's say you can only devote a nine-week quarter to this topic. We suggest you photocopy this sample worksheet for your planning process.

As you tailor your plan to meet the needs of your particular population of students, keep these points in mind.

1. The text has been written in a sequential order with the activities building on skills learned earlier in the unit. You will need to follow the chapters in order, although you may choose to use only a portion of the curriculum (for example: Section One or Sections One and Two).

2. If you complete the text using only the presentation suggestions in this guide and exclude most of the supplemental activities, you should be able to complete this unit comfortably in a nine-week quarter.

Specialized Lesson Plans

Academic Innovations has available a variety of lesson plans designed for specific disciplines and varied student populations. For more information, contact our:

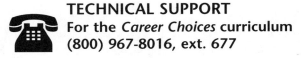 **TECHNICAL SUPPORT**
For the *Career Choices* curriculum
(800) 967-8016, ext. 677

We'd love to receive copies of your plans so we can share them with other educators. You may send them to Academic Innovations' Technical Support Department, 3463 State Street, Suite 267, Santa Barbara, CA 93105.

WORKSHEET FOR LESSON PLAN WEEK OF _____

Monday's Objective(s) _____

_____

Text assignment page(s) _____ Workbook assignment(s) _____

Class discussion _____

Activity _____

Resources _____

Homework assignment _____

Comments _____

Tuesday's Objective(s) _____

_____

Text assignment page(s) _____ Workbook assignment(s) _____

Class discussion _____

Activity _____

Resources _____

Homework assignment _____

Comments _____

Wednesday's Objective(s) _____

_____

Text assignment page(s) _____ Workbook assignment(s) _____

Class discussion _____

Activity _____

Resources _____

Homework assignment _____

Comments _____

Thursday's Objective(s) _____

_____

Text assignment page(s) _____ Workbook assignment(s) _____

Class discussion _____

Activity _____

Resources _____

Homework assignment _____

Comments _____

Friday's Objective(s) _____

_____

Text assignment page(s) _____ Workbook assignment(s) _____

Class discussion _____

Activity _____

Resources _____

Homework assignment _____

Comments _____

Follow-up _____

_____

_____

_____

_____

_____

_____

_____

Grading

Grades can be assigned for this course in a number of ways.

In language arts classes, grades may be based on reading comprehension and composition skills, along with exams on other reading assignments for the course.

Some exercises can be graded on the basis of how much effort went into completing them. You may wish to offer points for class participation or for attendance, if that is a problem at your school.

The 10-year plan in Chapter 12 makes a good final exam. We recommend it be a take-home exam with at least a week to complete. Grades can be based on how thoroughly the plan is completed and how well goals and objectives are defined.

Whatever you decide to do, it's helpful to let the class know on the first day how they will be graded, what they must do to earn an A, B, or C, and so on.

On the first day of class, hand out a grading sheet outlining the total graded assignments for the class and how the points are broken down in A's, B's, C's. This allows students to keep a running tally of their own grades and know exactly how they are doing. A sample grading form for a nine-week quarter class is included on pages 70-71.

Since the main goal of this course is to get students actively involved in planning a satisfying future for themselves, anyone who shows enthusiasm, participates in classroom activities, and completes the assignments should do very well.

My students' semester exam grade was their career research papers. Each unit complemented the stage of their paper. For example, Chapter 5 helped them make their choices of topic; a unit on using resources helped them with their bibliography cards; Chapter 6 helped them with their rough draft and composition; Chapter 7 helped them process their information and decide if it was a good career choices for them; Chapters 8 and 9 helped them implement a proper plan.

– Julia S. Forbus
Occupational Specialist
Fort Pierce Westwood High School
For Pierce, Florida

Sample Grading Form

	Total Points

Attendance – You will earn 5 points per day for a total of 45 days or a total of 255 points. To receive points for the day's attendance, you must also participate in the class discussion, complete appropriate assignments in the workbook, and be supportive of the class goals and rules.

225

Text assignments – Assignments for a total of 150 points

Complete Chapter 2 and the chart on page 27 =	30 points
Budget Process (pages 77-96) =	30 points
Your Personal Chart of Job Characteristics = (pages 126-134)	10 points
Career Interest Surveys (pages 150-155) =	30 points
Decision Chart (page 177) =	10 points
Goals and Objectives (pages 189-190) =	10 points
One Step at a Time (pages 218-221) =	10 points
You're the Boss (pages 238-241) =	10 points
Writing Your Resume (page 253) =	10 points

150

Your journal –   75 points

75

Writing – Three writing projects at 25 points each for a total of 75 points.

75

Reading assignments – Two outside reading assignments and book reports at 50 points each for a total of 100 points.

100

Exams – Five vocabulary quizzes at 10 points each and the final exam at 100 points for a total of 150 points.

150

___

775

```
TOTAL OF 775 points
     A = 698 points
     B = 620 points
     C = 543 points
     D = 504 points
```

Sample Grading Form

	Total Points Possible	Your Points
Attendance	225	
Text assignments —		
Complete Chapter 2 and the chart on page 27	30	
Budget Process *(pages 77-96)*	30	
Your Personal Chart of Job Characteristics *(pages 126-134)*	10	
Career Interest Surveys *(pages 150-155)*	30	
Decision Chart *(page 177)*	10	
Goals and Objectives *(pages 189-190)*	10	
One Step at at Time *(pages 218-221)*	10	
You're the Boss *(pages 238-241)*	10	
Writing Your Resumes *(page 253)*	10	
Your journal —	75	
Writing projects —		
a.	25	
b.	25	
c.	25	
Reading assignments —		
a.	50	
b.	50	
Exams — Vocabulary		
One	10	
Two	10	
Three	10	
Four	10	
Five	10	
Final	100	

775

Course Evaluation

One of the questions asked most often is "How do we know if we're succeeding?" There are many ways to measure and evaluate. We've listed some possibilities throughout Section Five, beginning on page 128, and below.

Before you begin, review the stated goals and objectives and the evaluative criteria on pages 10 and 11. If you are using the English/language arts curriculum and/or the math program, you'll find learning objectives for them on pages 22 and 31.

With these in mind, you may also want to consider such behavioral and attitudinal changes as:

1.   **Retention rates.** Are more students staying in school and graduating? Is the dropout rate for those students who have completed the curriculum lower than that for students with similar backgrounds and ability in your school? Do the students who go on to college stay there and graduate? (Remember, only 50 percent of those who start college complete their course of study.)

2.   **Setting higher or more realistic goals.** Upon completion of the course, do students' 10-year plans reflect higher or more realistic personal, educational, career and life goals?

3.   **Engagement.** Do students become more engaged with their education? Are they more motivated? Do they seek out new opportunities and ways to better prepare themselves for the future? Are they signing up for special programs such as School-to-Work and Tech Prep? Are they actively seeking assistance with getting into college? Are they giving the process more attention and energy?

4.   **Academic achievement.** Are test scores and/or grade point averages rising? As students understand the relevance of reading, writing, speaking and computing, are they becoming more proficient in these important academic areas?

5.   **Self-esteem and self-reliance.** Is students' self-esteem high enough to cope with the challenges that lay ahead to them as they enter adulthood? Do they feel competent to move into the adult world as emotionally and economically self-sufficient individuals?

For the really adventuresome, you may wish to do a more thorough class evaluation. If so, you will also need to:

- Survey the students themselves as they go through the course and for the remainder of their high school career.

- Survey each student's teachers for as long as he or she is a student at your school.

- Get feedback from students' parents.

- Document the education and career histories of students for several years or even a decade beyond high school.

This long-range evaluation would take lots of time and effort. Perhaps the education department of a local university would be interested in undertaking this project.

Innovative Assessment of Students' Progress

Madeline Noakes of Patrick Henry High School in San Diego, California, has developed an innovative way to measure her students' growth during her semester-long "Introduction to Careers" class. During the first week of class, students complete, in writing, the Envisioning Your Future exercise on page 14 of the *Career Choices* text. Then, during the second week, as students are working on assignments, Madeline videotapes students individually reading or presenting their paper.

At the end of the course, she again videotapes students presenting their 10-Year Plan and their Mission Statement (pages 278-81). When the first video is compared with the second, Madeline reports, the differences are astounding. Not only are the students more grounded in realistic expectations and plans by the end of the course, but even their demeanor and attitude have changed. The students present themselves in a more professional and serious fashion once they understand how critical a professional image is to their future success and satisfaction in life.

This project is one you might like to try. School Improvement Committees and School Boards would undoubtedly be interested in and impressed by seeing the results.

Not only are the students more grounded in realistic expectations and plans by the end of the course, but even their demeanor and attitude have changed.

– Madeline Noakes
Careers instructor
Patrick Henry High School
San Diego, California

Vocabulary Lists

Included in the 128-page consumable student workbook are vocabulary lists for each chapter. These are words that appear in that chapter, and knowing their definitions will help the student understand the text.

Students should be encouraged to investigate the meaning of these words because by doing so they will better understand themselves, their futures, and the workforce.

The words are listed in the order in which they appear in the text.

Chapter 1	Chapter 2	Chapter 3	Chapter 4
elaborate	aesthetic	self-actualization	privacy
gamut	forthright	esteem	commitment
vision	forceful	survival	profile
realization	authoritative	capable	widow
frustration	influencing	necessity	aristocrat
security	spontaneous	satisfaction	affordability
discrimination	amiable	hierarchy	variable
achievement	methodical	legacy	extensive
fanatic	analytical	acknowledgement	liberal
excess	meticulous	epitaph	reallocate
flaunt	diplomatic	lifestyle	poverty
prima donna	systematic	sociology	conscious
integrity	submissive	psychology	traits
humility	charismatic	component	minimum
intuition	empathy	contemplation	windfall
impulsive	innovative	spiritual	arrogant
procrastination	perseverance	recuperate	persistence
compliant	versatile	external	dividends
rational	synthesize	internal	inducement
interchangeable	negotiate	priority	interpretation

Sharon Hurwitz, English teacher/Technology Facilitator, Bethel High School, Hampton, Virginia, suggests:

There are many computer software packages that enable teachers and/or students to easily create crossword puzzles based on vocabulary lists. Use the vocabulary words to create a crossword puzzle and then have students work in pairs to complete it. Once completed, discuss the meanings of the words as a class.

Chapter 5

category
characteristics
environment
frequent
acquaintances
isolation
variety
compatible
flexible
potential
incentive
option
composite
free-lance
sequential
anxiety
tolerance
entrepreneur
capital
status

Chapter 6

artistic
accommodate
protective
humanitarian
occupation
tentative
excursion
attributes
visualization
typical
mesh
consult
accurate
explicit
decisive
gregarious
contagious
patient
conscientious
prominent

Chapter 7

alma mater
automatic
issue
logical
evaluate
differentiate
essential
gratification
long-term
pro
con
probability
analyze
apprenticeship
certification
expedite
agonize
fret
avoidance
tendency

Chapter 8

opportunities
flatter
courage
reputation
motivation
technique
temporary
abstract
postpone
struggle
joyous
temptation
wishful
privy
discipline
destructive
goal
objective
diagram
beliefs

Chapter 9

detour
challenge
ironic
affliction
paraplegic
debilitate
orator
serenity
solution
median
consideration
obligation
valedictorian
ambition
evidence
obstacle
concentration
confront
confident
progressive

Chapter 10

attitude
pretend
affirmation
effective
reverse
capable
excellence
expectation
enthusiasm
prophecies
livelihood
enterprise
efficient
ethic
aggression
tardy
elapse
global
enormous
dignity

Chapter 11

principles
publication
résumé
summary
original
chronological
honesty
references
draft
polite
impression
vaccination
misdemeanor
felony
appropriate
rejection
mentor
inspirational
tragedy
negotiable

Chapter 12

overwhelming
alternative
misfortune
alienate
despotism
solace
chasten
virtue
duration
perspective
patience
surmount
muff
fantasies
impress
genius
niche
respect
appreciation
success

Successful Group Discussions

Successful group discussions are likely to depend on the class environment. Every student must feel important, cared for, and supported. It is also helpful if students can see each other. Therefore, arranging desks in a circle or having students take seats around a table is desirable.

Before you begin, set out a few simple guidelines for the class. The essential ones are:

1. Every student must be allowed to speak and to give his or her own opinion on a topic.

2. No one is allowed to interrupt or discount anyone else's opinion.

3. Since some topics are extremely personal, everyone is allowed to "pass" if called on in discussion.

The personal nature of some of the discussions may lead some students to reveal serious problems calling for professional help. In these situations, it is best to show concern, but avoid giving the impression that there's anything "wrong" with the individual. You may instead suggest where the student can get help and then offer any assistance he or she may need.

Make certain you are available after each class or after school. That way, students who are reluctant to speak before the entire class have access to share their concerns, if they wish to do so. Likewise, if a student seems to be upset during class discussion period, suggest that he or she see you after class. Students should know that you are available for such support whenever necessary.

Just as there are sensitive subjects, there are sensitive students who will not feel comfortable sharing their innermost thoughts with the class or even with you. Their privacy should be respected. Those who prefer to hand in written work rather than participate in group discussions should be allowed to do so. On particularly troubling points, they may indicate that you are not to read an assignment by turning it in folded in half or by folding down those pages in the workbook. As you establish an atmosphere of trust in the class, these students gradually should become less fearful.

The curriculum is appropriate for team teaching with the school guidance counselor. You may ask him or her to participate, in particular, with your presentation of Chapters 2 and 9.

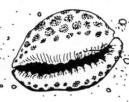

Effective Group Facilitation

For those instructors who have been involved with more traditional, lecture-style teaching in recent years, we offer the following review on the basics of effective group facilitation:

1. Group participation is essential, but students must be motivated to participate. In general, they will be motivated by student input on topics for discussion; seeing the topics of discussion or exercises as relevant to their own lives; solving a problem or making a decision as a group; having an opportunity to voice and hear a variety of opinions; and completing tasks with a definite beginning and end.

2. An informal atmosphere is key. Students should be able to see each other. Desks or chairs should be arranged in a circle rather than in rows.

3. Peer pressure can stifle expression. It is important to build a cohesive group in which others' opinions are validated and accepted.

4. Practice active listening skills, and instruct the group to do the same. You may want to devote at least one class session to discussing and practicing this communication tool. In active listening, the person who is not speaking also takes an active role in the dialogue. He or she never interrupts the speaker, but paraphrases what's been said when the speaker has finished. In his way, the speaker knows that he or she has been heard.

Example:

Speaker: "I like this book very much. I can really relate to the main character."

Active listener: "You like the book very much because the main character is someone with whom you can identify."

It is also appropriate for an active listener to ask about the speaker's feelings.

Example:

Speaker: "I don't like stories with unhappy endings."

Active listener: "How do they make you feel?"

In short then, active listening involves the following skills:

1. Repeat what's been said.

2. Ask how the speaker feels.

3. Let the speaker complete his or her statement without interruption.

4. Address students by name. They need to know that they are important, that you are interested in them. The class might agree to address everyone in the group including you in the same way (either by first name, or by Mr. or Ms. Jones).

5. Ask questions, rather than lecturing, which isn't effective with teens. Before offering an opinion, ask students if they want to hear it. Establish a dialogue.

6. Give students your full attention. Make eye contact with everyone in the group.

7. Use humor in appropriate situations.

8. Establish an atmosphere of trust within the group. Be consistent. Respect students' privacy. Be honest. If you make a mistake, admit it.

9. Be clear about classroom rules, and insist that they be honored. State the consequences for breaking these rules and enforce them actively. Threats are not effective.

10. Point out cause and effect. Hold students accountable for their actions. Ask them to think of consequences, both immediate and long term. This will increase their sense of autonomy and responsibility.

11. Ask for and listen to students' opinions to increase their self-esteem (something that often needs to be done). Use their suggestions when you can. Let students know that you believe in them. A smile or a private word to an adolescent often means a great deal.

12. Celebrate the accomplishments of the group or individuals within the group.

13. Let the group get to know you, too. Be aware of your feelings at the beginning of each class period and, if you are angry or distracted about something, let the group know that they are not the cause of your negative feelings.

14. If you sense too much tension in the room, try changing the subject for a while, or take a short break before resuming the conversation.

15. When a student does or says something that pleases you, let him or her know with a word, look, smile, or nod. Communicate your approval.

16. If one or more students tend to be judgmental or to try to impose their values and ideas on the group, speak with them outside the group and remind them of the ground rules regarding everyone's right to speak without fear of ridicule from others. You might note that learning to get along with others and to work effectively within a group will be a valued skill when they enter the workforce.

17. If a student is particularly difficult, try to mention some positive trait he or she has exhibited.

18. Recognize students' growing sense of self-identity by noting that they are becoming more mature and independent, that they are developing their own values and plans for the future, and so on.

19. Attitudes are contagious. Expect students to be enthusiastic about the course, and they probably will be.

20. Group learning often proceeds in a "two steps forward, one step back" fashion. Be patient when the inevitable setbacks occur.

21. The students with the least apparent skills and positive attributes need your support most. They will appreciate knowing that you care.

22. Never concur with a student's disparaging remarks about parents, siblings, or friends. His or her ties to these people are still very strong, and your remarks will not be well received.

23. Teens often need to practice empathy. Take advantage of opportunities to have them imagine how other people feel. Through your example as an empathetic facilitator, students will understand the importance of empathy.

Typical Problems and What To Do about Them

No matter how well you facilitate your group, some students are likely to have problems. We've listed a few of the most common ones below, along with some suggestions for dealing with them.

IF A STUDENT DOESN'T GET AN OPPORTUNITY TO TALK
To make sure everyone gets an opportunity to be heard, break the group into pairs and have each duo come up with a certain number of ideas, answers, or whatever. Bring the class back together and have team members take turns stating their responses.

IF SOMEONE ELSE HAS ALREADY PRESENTED A STUDENT'S IDEA OR ANSWER
Ask him or her to state the response in another way, or to elaborate on it if the idea has already been voiced.

WHEN SELF-CONSCIOUS STUDENTS ARE EMBARRASSED TO SPEAK
Again, working in groups of two or three can help these students feel safe enough to speak up. As they gain confidence, they should be able to participate in larger group discussions. Don't push it, but encourage shy students with words, smiles, or nods.

WHEN THE CLASS ISN'T PAYING ATTENTION
A less formal atmosphere may encourage some students to act up while others will need time to adapt to the new rules. We suggest confronting the problem by stating your own feelings of frustration or recognizing the situation and discussing students' feelings and possible ways to make the group feel more comfortable.

WHEN THE CLASS IS BORED
Boredom is often a sign that students don't understand the material, or that they don't find it relevant. The better you know your group, the better able you will be to tailor the class to its needs and goals. Breaking into smaller groups is another way to get more students active and involved.

WHEN NO ONE SEEMS ABLE TO CONCENTRATE
Lack of concentration may be due to tension or fatigue. A short stand-up break might be helpful. Or you could ask students to sit quietly, close their eyes, and concentrate fully on the source of their distraction for two or three minutes. When you bring their attention back to the classroom, ask them to note what they see, hear, and feel. This will help them return their attention to the present.

WHEN THERE ARE CONFLICTS OR BAD FEELINGS IN THE CLASSROOM
Conflicts between individuals should be settled out of class. It might be helpful to place these students in different groups, however. The student who simply wants to complain about something should be asked to elaborate on his or her feelings and explain what, exactly, should be done about it.

Evaluating Your Group

Is your group operating effectively? Take time periodically to consider this question. The following checklist may be helpful.

In an effective group:

Members participate somewhat equally.

Members are involved and stimulated by group discussions.

The environment is warm and supportive.

Ideas and emotions are effectively communicated and accepted by others.

Stated tasks are completed (or not completed by group agreement).

Group accomplishments are easily discernible by all members.

Group Size

Whatever the size of your class, there will be times when dividing into smaller groups can be advantageous. The desirable number of students in a group varies with the task to be completed. In general, we've discovered the following:

PAIRS OF STUDENTS   These are ideal for sharing personal information or for encouraging students to voice personal opinions or ideas.

GROUPS OF THREE   This is a great size for discussion, especially at first, when some students may feel uncomfortable speaking in front of larger groups. Groups of three feel relatively safe. They are also good at accomplishing tasks, especially if group members are not close friends (in which case there tends to be too much socializing, not enough work). If you use trios regularly, assign students to different groups from time to time.

GROUPS OF FOUR OR FIVE   As students become more experienced and confident communicators, they can move effectively into a slightly larger group. This size is good for meetings, making decisions, or completing tasks (make sure the task or goal is clearly understood). It also allows students to gain skills in group problem solving.

GROUPS OF SIX   To be most effective, groups of six need an appointed or elected leader who is a good communicator. It might be helpful, too, to have a secretary or recorder. Groups of this size can easily break down into pairs or trios, which can result in overlooking the assigned task. They are good, however, in situations calling for personal feedback. Another way to keep them focused is to have them break into smaller groups and let these groups compete with each other. It's always helpful for groups of this size to have a chalkboard or easel and pad to keep on track. Generally, they are most effective as the course nears its end.

GROUPS OF SEVEN OR MORE   As groups reach this size, they tend to become less effective. It's too easy for individuals to sit back and let others do the work.

MIXING GROUPS   Depending on the task to be completed, it may be appropriate for group members to know each other well or to be less well acquainted. When you want to mix the composition, you might base groups on numbers or names pulled out of a hat. Or you might give half the class questions written on 3 × 5 cards, and the other half of the class answers to the same. Allow students to mingle until they find the person with the matching question or answer.

Group Strategies and Techniques

As you undoubtedly know, there are many strategies and techniques that can encourage learning by stimulating enthusiasm, motivation, and group participation. Some that seem to work particularly well with the materials in this text are listed below. Use them whenever or wherever you see fit or feel comfortable doing so.

BRAINSTORMING   A topic is introduced to the group using a phrase such as, "Think of as many ways as you can to…" or "What are some possible solutions for.". Class members then make verbal suggestions that are written on the board. There is no comment or criticism from the group. When all ideas have been expressed, class discussion, ranking, or prioritizing may follow.

BUZZ GROUPS   Groups of six or less get together and share their opinions or reactions to a speaker, a book, a question, or a statement. A time limit should be stated at the outset to stimulate participation and competition.

CASE STUDIES   An actual situation that illustrates a point or problem is presented and analyzed. Case studies are often fascinating, easy to relate to, and can be less threatening than dealing with the same topics on a personal level. (It's always easier to solve someone else's problems than it is to solve your own.) Cases may come from newspapers, magazines, TV shows, movies, books, or students' past experiences.

DEBATES   Debates are valuable for allowing students to express their opinions or for giving them experience in seeing the other side of an argument. (This is a valuable job skill. You might set up a debate in which the participants argue the position opposite to their own opinion.) A debate can match two individuals or two panels of students. Allow each side to present its case and respond to the other arguments, then follow with total class discussion.

DIALOGUES   Two students discuss a particular topic in front of the class. Class discussion follows.

EXERCISES   These can be done individually or as a group to stimulate discussion or teach skills.

FISHBOWLS   A small group of students (six or less) discusses an issue or case study while the rest of the class observes.

INTERVIEWS   Asking questions of people outside the class allows students to collect and synthesize data and reach conclusions concerning their topic of investigation.

JOURNALS   This is an important ongoing activity for use with *Career Choices*.

LECTURES OR PANELS An outside speaker or group of speakers can offer detailed information, new perspectives, personal experiences, and opinions on a topic. Time should be allowed for questions from the class.

MODELS Models aid understanding with visual representations of certain concepts, processes, or events.

PEER LEARNING GROUPS This is an advanced technique utilizing the leadership skills of peer leaders. Leaders must be trained for their tasks. Then they lead teams of their peers through an exercise.

ROLE PLAYING Students are asked to act out the roles in a particular situation, saying what they think their character would say under the circumstances. This can be an emotional experience for some individuals, so be sure to ask each role player how he or she feels both before and after the exercise.

SKITS Groups of students prepare, practice, and present short plays dealing with a given situation.

We presented a play based on the **Prince of Tides** *selection in* **Possibilities,** *and the students loved it. Many wanted to be "Luke." While not totally professional, everyone dressed as a character. We even made a dolphin and stuffed it.*

– Julie Delrusso
SLD instructor
Lake Brantley High School
Altamonte Springs, Florida

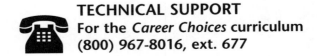

TECHNICAL SUPPORT
For the *Career Choices* curriculum
(800) 967-8016, ext. 677

Examples of Group Learning

To get you started planning cooperative learning experiences for your class, we've listed some examples of activities and exercises that lend themselves to the Group Strategies and Techniques discussed on pages 85 to 86. This list is by no means complete and you may even want to use a different group technique for an activity listed below.

What we've heard over and over again is that it is important to use different strategies and techniques to maintain the students' interest. Try not to get stuck in the rut of using only brainstorming techniques and small work groups.

Brainstorming

Lifestyle Math: page 31, Raising a family on one income

Possibilities: page 213, Question 6, How not to give up your dreams

Career Choices: page 270 in the *Instructor's Guide*

Buzz Groups

Lifestyle Math: page 38, Questions 4 & 5, Would you pay cash or use your savings?

Possibilities: page 224, Questions 1, 2, 3, 4

Career Choices: page 244 in the *Instructor's Guide*

Case Studies

Lifestyle Math: page 42, Case Study

Possibilities: page 85, Menu of Activities

Career Choices: pages 204–205, Detours and Roadblocks in *Career Choices*

Debates

Lifestyle Math: page 83, Making Choices

Possibilities: page 22, Formal Debate

Career Choices: page 160, in the *Instructor's Guide*

Dialogues

Lifestyle Math: page 89, Computing Salaries Quickly in Your Head

Possibilities: page 209, B. Make up dialogues from *The Prince of Tides*

Career Choices: page 162 in the *Instructor's Guide*

Exercises

Lifestyle Math: page 60-63, Planning a Party

Possibilities: pages 279-283, Your 25th High School Reunion Booklet

Career Choices: page 154 in the *Instructor's Guide*

Fishbowls

Lifestyle Math: page 26, Question 4, Would you choose Los Angeles or Oklahoma City?

Possibilities: page 88, Question 4

Career Choices: page 148 in the *Instructor's Guide*, Gender equity activity

Interviews

Lifestyle Math: page 52, Stretching Your Food Dollar

Possibilities: page 215, Question 10, Overcoming Obstacles

Career Choices: page 158 in the *Instructor's Guide*

Lectures and Panels

Lifestyle Math: page 92, Budget Comparisons

Possibilities: page 31, Question 10

Career Choices: page 191 in the *Instructor's Guide*

Models

Lifestyle Math: pages 102-106, Developing an Action Plan

Possibilities: pages 44-45, Acrostic Poetry

Career Choices: page 27, Bull's Eye Chart in *Career Choices*

Peer Learning Groups

Lifestyle Math: pages 98-99, What is Your Math Education Worth to You?, Working As a Team

Possibilities: page 248, Writing a Children's Story

Career Choices: page 244 in the *Instructor's Guide*

Role Playing and Skits

Lifestyle Math: pages 95-97, Developing Charts and Graphs

Possibilities: page 269, Create a Dialogue

Career Choices: pages 228-231 in the *Instructor's Guide*

Getting Acquainted

If most of your students are unacquainted, you may want to use a group warm-up exercise on the first day of class, or even daily for the first week. We suggest dividing students into pairs and having them interview each other for a total of five minutes. Bring the class back together at this point, and have students introduce their interview subject to the others. If the group seems unsure of what to ask, you might suggest some of the following questions:

If you could have any job in the world, what would it be?

If you could be any age, what would it be, and why?

Where would you most like to live, and why?

What would you consider the ideal vacation?

Who is your hero, and why?

What do you like most about school? What do you like least?

What are your favorite hobbies? Books? Movies? Sports?

Speakers' Bank

The topics for discussion in *Career Choices* raise many opportunities for guest speakers to come into the classroom. It is up to the individual instructor, of course, to decide who to use and how to use them. But, to make things a bit easier, we have compiled a chart listing possible speakers for the entire course. Since you are unlikely to be personally acquainted with experts and resource people in all these areas, tracking them down could be time-consuming. Therefore, we recommend using this chart to get some help.

You might simply want to make photocopies of the chart and pass them around to friends and co-workers who might be able to supply some names and phone numbers. If you belong to community organizations such as the Kiwanis, Soroptimists, or the Rotary, you might pass a chart around at the next meeting. If you enjoy public speaking, you could make a presentation about your class to some of these organizations, and then ask for help from the members. Or you might get community people involved by bringing your request before the school improvement team. The list can be easily tailored to reflect community needs or the needs of your students.

On page 220 we have outlined a description of a "Director of Mentors." Perhaps, the person who holds this volunteer position could be enrolled to assist in locating and scheduling guest speakers.

If you conduct this class many times throughout the day, it may be difficult to find individuals who can devote that amount of time. We suggest scheduling your guest speakers in the morning, a half hour to forty-five minutes before the school day begins. Most working adults are used to breakfast meetings, and it should not interfere with their work day. Therefore, it should be easier to get guest speakers at this hour. While students may groan about the earlier hour, you could point out that schedule adjustments are common in the work world and that flexibility of time is a mandatory requirement of most jobs. The expectations should be clear and this should be seen as part of their homework.

Arrange for the presentations to be held in the school theater so many classes can be accommodated. Be sure to advise the other faculty members of your scheduled presentations. Perhaps they would like to attend.

If the school has a video recording service, arrange for a student to video the presentations. This way you can keep the better ones on file and can share them with the counseling office for individual counseling situations.

It might be helpful to lend each speaker a copy of the text *Career Choices* so he or she can review the appropriate section and be familiar with the concepts the students are studying.

Guest Speakers Make Career Planning More Real

At Plantation High School in Broward County, Florida, the most popular part of English teacher Mary Ellen Fowler's Career Decision-Making class is the extensive use of guest speakers.

When asked which part of the class was most beneficial, students responded unanimously: meeting real people who were doing jobs and having careers they were interested in. Using the *Instructor's and Counselor's Guide for Career Choices* to set up a Speaker's Bank, Mary Ellen invited over 30 people from the community to address the class.

"I tried to include people from all walks of life, and that race, color, gender are not necessarily limiting factors," she says. The guest list included a professional soccer player, a 28-year-old journalist who had traveled all over the world, a woman mortician, a goalie on the Women's National Water Polo Team, a Navy Seal, and a lawyer, among others.

"It was amazing—there were no absences!" Mary Ellen told us. "Students actually like coming to school because they find the material relevant and are doing something they really want to do: discovering themselves and exploring their opportunities."

Speakers Bank Recruitment Form

Please list resource people below who could be contacted to make a presentation to a

class on careers at _____.
                                                                  (name of school)

Speaker required	Name	Day phone	Evening phone
Successfully retired individual	_____	_____	_____
Real estate professional	_____	_____	_____
Travel agent	_____	_____	_____
Insurance agent	_____	_____	_____
AFDC parents	_____	_____	_____
Person who gave up an opulent lifestyle to do something meaningful	_____	_____	_____
Psychologist	_____	_____	_____
Entrepreneur	_____	_____	_____
Handicapped individual who copes well	_____	_____	_____
Individuals who overcame adversity: High school dropout	_____	_____	_____
Teen mother	_____	_____	_____
Recovering substance abuser	_____	_____	_____
Individuals still struggling: High school dropout	_____	_____	_____

Speaker required	Name	Day phone	Evening phone
Teen mother	_____	_____	_____
Recovering substance abuser	_____	_____	_____
Women successfully mixing: Career and family	_____	_____	_____
Professional	_____	_____	_____
Blue collar	_____	_____	_____
Immigrant entrepreneur	_____	_____	_____
Community social service resource specialist	_____	_____	_____
United Way staffperson	_____	_____	_____
Bank manager	_____	_____	_____
Stockbroker	_____	_____	_____
Personnel specialist	_____	_____	_____
Career counselor	_____	_____	_____
Vocational counselor	_____	_____	_____
College placement officer	_____	_____	_____
Military recruiter	_____	_____	_____
Union director	_____	_____	_____
Employment development director	_____	_____	_____
Owner of recruiting firm	_____	_____	_____

References for Speakers' Bank

* Be sure they meet the criteria of the exercise.

After hearing the insurance speaker, one boy asked, "If I have to pay this much for insurance, how can I afford gas for the car?"

— Phyllis A. Stewart
Vocational Director
Lincoln High School
Vincennes, Indiana

Getting the Community Involved

Career Choices is an ideal vehicle for getting community members and organizations involved with your school. Many people are particularly interested in helping young people prepare for their future, while employers are interested in the education and preparation of their future workforce.

Some suggestions for community involvement projects include:

Recruitment and involvement of a volunteer "Director of Mentors" *(see pages 218-224)*.

The recruitment of community members to speak to your students about their career/work experiences *(see pages 90-94)*.

Cooperation with local business or industry for a mentorship program.

Formation of a Students Speaker's Bureau offering presentations prepared in class for local community service organizations (such as Kiwanis, Soroptimist, Rotary, Business and Professional Women, Lions, union and industry associations and so on) *(see pages 123-127)*.

Involvement in a student-directed Career Fair.

Community Help with Funding

More and more large businesses and corporations are funneling corporate donations into education. Because of the nature of this curriculum, it makes sense to approach a local business, industry, or community service organization for funding assistance for this program. Grant requests might include funding for books, resource materials, personal profile system assessments for each student, teacher attendance at a *Career Choices* workshop in Santa Barbara, California, a stipend for the director of mentors, or costs of a career fair. If you would like to brainstorm this idea and receive assistance with your grant request, contact the Technical Support Administrator at Academic Innovations at (800) 967-8016.

See pages 116-127 for a variety of funding resources and assistance.

Video Book Club

*...by its very nature, T.V. viewing, unlike reading, will always
be a basically passive exercise since analytical skills are not
required. "What might help," says Marc Miller, Johns Hopkins
University media professor, "is a program to help interpret what
teens look at. Teachers and parents...should teach kids to
read between the pictures, as they are taught to read between
the lines."*

**Newsweek Magazine Special Edition
"The New Teen: What Makes Them Different"
Summer/Fall 1990**

As we expand our forms of communication, moving from a reading, writing, speaking society to one that includes electronic communication (video, audio, computerization), it is imperative that we teach the same analytical skills required in traditional communication forms for use with the new electronic forms. Today's youth must be media-conscious consumers.

While it may be difficult to get some adolescents to read a book, most are willing to watch a movie. Why not hold Video Book Club once a week, or less frequently. Of course, you will need to make sure that all students have access to a VCR. Assignments should be made far enough in advance so that all students will be able to see the film. You might pass out a list early in the course with film titles and dates of discussion so students can schedule accordingly.

You may need to sponsor a showing of the film after school or during the lunch break for those students who do not have access to a VCR or who cannot rent the film.

Like a traditional book club, the purpose of Video Book Club is to introduce and analyze literary themes and to encourage lively discussion.

The movies listed center around the identity questions raised in the text. They should lead to some lively discussions. Many are based on novels or plays that could also be assigned or read for extra credit. Many of these choices have been recommended by instructors teaching the course. Feel free to supplement our list with your own choices.

After discussing several videos, you may assign reading a novel for the next meeting. Students are more likely to complete the assignment enthusiastically and participate in the discussion once they have experienced success in Video Book Club.

At some point you will want to discuss how the book and the movie were different and which was better. (Be sure to assign reading the book first and then the movie.) Usually people will prefer the book. Ask students why.

Video Suggestions*

IT'S A WONDERFUL LIFE
1946 Starring James Stewart and Donna Reed

This sentimental Frank Capra film is usually regraded as a tearjerker about the rewards of helping others. But there is another way to look at it. George Bailey, the main character, has sacrificed all of his passions and dreams in order to uphold his commitments to his family and community. As the movie begins, he is about to commit suicide. The movie concludes that his sacrifices were noble and that he should be a very happy man. What does the class think? How does one balance responsibility for others with responsibility to oneself? Can the class think of ways that George might have been able to incorporate some of his own passions into his life?

This movie was made immediately following World War II, which came on the heels of the Great Depression. These major, unforeseen events disrupted the lives of millions of people like George Bailey. You may also want to discuss how such impersonal factors can affect any plans for the future.

IRRECONCILABLE DIFFERENCES
1984 Starring Ryan O'Neal and Shelley Long

A comedy about a child who "divorces" her parents, this is a provocative starting point for a discussion of the definition of success, both personal and professional, as well as on the importance of taking responsibility for who you become.

THE TURNING POINT
1977 Starring Shirley MacLaine and Anne Bancroft

A drama about two dancers who made different choices for their lives, this film points out that every career involves sacrifices and rewards, and effectively demonstrates the depth of commitment required to achieve excellence.

DEAD POETS SOCIETY
1989 Starring Robin Williams

Based on a novel by Tom Schulman, this film about an unorthodox English teacher at a private boys' school illustrates the difficulties adolescents face in finding and maintaining their identity. The teacher, Mr. Keating, implores his students to "seize the day," "suck the marrow out of life," and "make your lives extraordinary."

*** Please preview selections before showing them to your class to be assured they are appropriate for your students and your class goals.**

A THOUSAND CLOWNS
1965 Starring Jason Robards and Barbara Harris

Based on the play by Herb Gardner, this comedy concerns a single, unemployed writer, Murray Burns, who is also the guardian of his nephew. Authorities threaten to take the nephew away unless Murray gets a job, but his need to "know what day it is, you've got to own your own days and name 'em" makes it difficult for him to stay employed. The film is a good basis for a discussion on identity and compromise as well as how having a child limits freedom.

AMADEUS
1984 Starring Tom Hulce and F. Murray Abraham

Based on a play by Peter Schaeffer, this film about Mozart and the court composer, Salieri, has much to say about passion, commitment, and the creative process.

AMERICAN DREAMER
1984 Starring Jobeth Williams and Tom Conti

When American housewife, Cathy Palmer, wins a contest for writing a mystery story in the manner of her hero, the fictional detective Rebecca Ryan, she is flown to Paris to accept her award. She is hit by a car on her way to the ceremony, however, and when she comes to, she thinks she is Rebecca Ryan and begins to live this dream. This is a film about becoming the person you dream of and about taking control of your own destiny.

BREAKING AWAY
1979 Starring Dennis Christopher and Dennis Quaid

Based on the novel by Steve Tesich, this is a story about four working-class boys trying to decide what to do with their lives after graduation from high school. One boy's passion for and commitment to bicycle racing helps them all take responsibility, gain self-confidence, and experience success.

BABY BOOM
1987 Starring Diane Keaton

When a high-powered businesswoman inherits a child, she discovers the difficulties of mixing career and family and experiences some changes in her own values. This is a good film to illustrate personal definitions of success, creativity, and entrepreneurship.

MY LEFT FOOT

1989 Starring Daniel Day-Lewis and Brenda Fricker

Based on Christy Brown's autobiography, this film about the Irish writer and painter with cerebral palsy makes a convincing argument for refusing to let real or perceived handicaps stand in the way of living up to one's potential.

LEAN ON ME

1989 Starring Morgan Freeman

This story of Principal Joe Clark and his tough-love philosophy of education should lead to some spirited discussions. Does the class agree or disagree with his methods? What motivates students to learn? Who is ultimately responsible for an individual's education?

THE ACCIDENTAL TOURIST

1988 Starring William Hurt, Kathleen Tuner, and Geena Davis

Based on Anne Tyler's Pulitzer Prize-winning novel, this film deals with self-definition and self-discovery, changing direction, and learning to take risks.

STAND AND DELIVER

1988 Starring Edward James Olmos and Lou Diamond Phillips

This true story of a remarkable math teacher at a high school in the Los Angeles barrio is a good basis for a discussion of overcoming familial expectations and societal messages. It demonstrates how some people overcome many obstacles to success, the necessity for hard work, and the importance of mentors.

THE COLOR PURPLE

1985 Starring Whoopi Goldberg and Danny Glover

Alice Walker wrote the Pulitzer Prize-winning novel on which this film is based: the story of Celie, a woman who suffers through a brutal childhood and marriage, but goes on to acquire self-worth and build a satisfying life for herself.

The movie **Cool Runnings** *to be used in conjunction with the work in* **Possibilities,** *"If" by Rudyard Kipling and "The Road Not Taken" by Robert Frost.*

– L. Taylor
9th and 10th grade teacher
John Handley High School
Winchester, Virginia

A RIVER RUNS THROUGH IT
1992 Starring Craig Sheffer and Brad Pitt

Based on the book by Norman Maclean, this is a story of two brothers growing up in a frontier Montana, their passion for fly fishing, and their different paths through adult life.

THE REMAINS OF THE DAY
1993 Starring Anthony Hopkins and Emma Thompson

The story of Stevens, head butler at an English country house, and the personal costs of his extraordinary devotion to his job. Based on the novel by Kazuo Ishiguro.

THE JOY LUCK CLUB
1993 Starring Rosalind Chao and Tamlyn Tomita

From the novel by Amy Tan, this wonderful film explores the lives of four Chinese-American women and their daughters. How does identity reflect personal history, and what strengths can be gained through misfortune?

SCHINDLER'S LIST
1993 Starring Liam Neeson and Ralph Fiennes

This Academy Award-winning film about the Holocaust, based on the book by Thomas Keneally, offers a wealth of important topics for discussion. Identity, values, passions, risk taking, problem solving, and anxiety tolerance all come into play.

Butter Cream Gang, Part I and II
Part I ties to the Maslow Triangle. I have my students evaluate where each kid in the movie is on the triangle and explain why. Part II works with Chapter ten, Attitude is Everything.

–Ann Dabb
Careers Teacher
Wahlquist Junior High School
Ogden, Utah

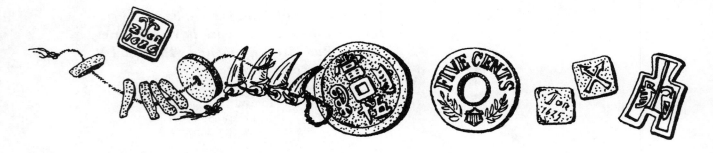

HOWARD'S END
1992 Starring Emma thompson and Helena Bonham-Cater

A beautiful film based on the novel by E.M. Forster, this is the story of two sisters living in Edwardian England and struggling to live independent and worthy lives in a class-conscious and repressive society.

COOL RUNNINGS
1993 Starring Leon and John Candy

A warm-hearted comedy based on the true story of the first Jamaican bobsled team who overcame obstacles to compete in the 1988 Winter Olympics. Great film for encouragement and self-esteem.

SISTER ACT 2: BACK IN THE HABIT
1993 Starring Whoopi Goldberg

Whoopi Goldberg returns as a former lounge singer hiding out as a nun who takes a group of disadvantaged, inner-city youth in San Francisco and turns them into an award-winning choir. Themes include the importance of self-esteem and self-awareness.

RENAISSANCE MAN
1994 Starring Danny DeVito

A group of army slow learners discover Shakespeare and themselves under the guidance of Danny DeVito as Bill Rago, a big-time ad executive who lost his job. He is recruited by the Unemployment Office to teach this group comprehensive skills. Themes include self-esteem, mutual respect and righting wrongs.

RICHIE RICH
1994 Starring Macaulay Culkin

A rich kid played by Macaulay Culkin has everything money can buy except what he most desires, friends. Great film for What Cost This Lifestyle, chapter 4 of *Career Choices.*

THE MIGHTY DUCKS OR D2: THE MIGHTY DUCKS
1992, 1994 Starring Emilio Estevez

Emilio Estevez plays a yuppie lawyer and hockey coach for kids who were told they could never play hockey. Good motivational movies.

LITTLE GIANTS
1994 Starring Rick Moranis and Ed O'Neil

Rick Moranis plays an unlikely football coach to an underdog football team whose members, including his daughter, were not picked for the town team. The town team is coached by his brother, a Heisman Trophy winner, played by Ed O'Neil. Good motivational movie.

IN THE ARMY NOW
1994 Starring Pauly Shore, Lori Petty and David Alan Grier

Pauly Shore plays a slow-witted sales clerk who joins the Army Reserves to receive money for an electronic venture and ends up going to the middle east and becoming a hero.

HOOP DREAMS
1994 With William Gates, Arthur Agee and Steve James

A documentary following the athletic careers of two promising basketball players. Success would provide a means to escape their poverty-stricken environment. They struggle with academics, coaches and families along the way. Both players end up in the real world, not the NBA.

THE AIR UP THERE
1994 Starring Kevin Bacon and Charles Gitonga Maina

Kevin Bacon plays Jimmy Dolan, a restless assistant basketball coach who travels to Africa in search of a new recruit and finds there are more important things in life than basketball. Good self-discovery movie.

FORREST GUMP
1994 Starring Tom Hanks, Sally Field, Robin Wright and Gary Sinise

Tom Hanks stars in this drama about the adventures of life seen through the eyes of a simple man who has a passion for life and an enduring positive perspective. In spite of his low I.Q., Gump becomes an unforgettable hero.

APOLLO 13
1995 Starring Tom Hanks, Kevin Bacon and Ed Harris

A true adventure in problem solving, this film also dramatically illustrates a number of exciting jobs available to those who excel in math and science.

EMMA
1996 Starring Gwyneth Paltrow

CLUELESS
1995 Starring Alicia Silverstone

By watching both the videos of the classic Jane Austen novel and its updated version, students should come to realize that the problems of youth haven't changed all that much in 200 years. This may make them more open to reading classic literature and gaining the wisdom it has to offer.

Your Favorite Videos:

List:

1. _____

2. _____

3. _____

4. _____

5. _____

6. _____

Please send us your suggestions!

I incorporate film as much as possible. For example, after reading "The Secret Life of Walter Mitty" in **Possibilities,** *we viewed the film and then contrasted the two. Before reading "Growing Older," we viewed the first half of* **Driving Miss Daisy.** *We then completed the journal and poem prior to completing the film. The students were very responsive.*

– Kathryn T. Harcum
English Chairperson
North Caroline High School
Ridgely, Maryland

I showed the Australian movie **My Brilliant Career** *at the end of the unit. The movie is hard to find but is about a spirited young girl who is being pushed by her father to get married. She refuses a proposal at the end, from a man she deeply cares about, in order to be a writer. None of my students had seen the movie, and we discussed opportunities for women in the past and present. This worked very well!*

– Tania Lyon
10th grade English teacher
Pequot Lakes School
Pequot Lakes, MN

SECTION THREE

Technical Support

We Want to Help You Be Successful

Technical Support Department

Academic Innovations provides technical support in a variety of ways to schools using *Career Choices* or considering adoption of the curriculum. Choose the one that is right for you.

☑ Telephone support   **(800) 967-8016, ext. 677**

☑ On-line support   **techsupp@academicinnovations.com**

☑ Web page resource files   **http://www.academicinnovations.com**

☑ On-site workshops
and consulting   **Call or e-mail us for information**

☑ A community of
Career Choices users   **CareerChoicesNet@silcom.com**

Through these various forums our staff, consultants, authors, master teachers and certified trainers can provide a variety of services that will help you make your *Career Choices* program exciting and productive.

Our resources and services include:

- ☐ Strategies for curriculum integration
- ☐ Strategies for developing teaching teams that work
- ☐ How to use *Career Choices* with special populations
- ☐ Sharing new ideas from the network of teachers using the curriculum
- ☐ Referrals to other educators using the curriculum
- ☐ Curriculum enhancement ideas (movies, songs, etc.)
- ☐ Strategies for funding your program (using federal, state, local and private sources)
- ☐ Soliciting help from Community Service organizations
- ☐ How to set up a mentoring/shadow program
- ☐ Suggestions for customized lesson plans
- ☐ Information on an array of staff development opportunities and in-service opportunities
- ☐ Information on how to sponsor a *Career Choices* workshop in your district or school
- ☐ Information on Academic Innovations' Staff Development allowance
- ☐ A variety of print resources you'll find helpful to your *Career Choices* program (newsletters, funding guides, success stories from schools, specialized lesson plans)
- ☐ Other products and services available from Academic Innovations
- ☐ Arranging an interview with an author of the textbooks
- ☐ Information about Tech Prep, School-to-Work, SCANS and NOICC
- ☐ You tell us what you need and we'll do our best to meet your request

You'll want to start by either calling our Technical Support Administrator or e-mailing our Director of Technological Customer Service. We stand ready to help you in any way we can.

Our Web Site

Question	Go to URL:	You'll find:	Helpful hints & tips
What other resources and technical assistance are available? How can I contact your technical support department?	http://www. academicinnovations.com/ ccres.html	A listing of the extensive services available to Academic Innovations customers	*Scroll down the page and contact the Technical Support Administrator on the e-mail response form.*

Fax this page to (805) 967-4357

Request for Information

Please send me the following:

- ☐ Information on the *Career Choices* curriculum to share with my peers
- ☐ A *Career Choices* Workshop/Training packet (dates, cost, etc.)
- ☐ Sign me up for a free subscription to *Focus on the Future* newsletter
- ☐ Information on how my district/school can sponsor a *Career Choices* workshop in our locale
- ☐ Sample Student Surveys and course evaluation techniques
- ☐ Interviews of educators using *Career Choices*
- ☐ I'd like to be interviewed for an upcoming edition of *Focus on the Future* newsletter
- ☐ A copy of our Guide to the Academic Innovations' Web Page
- ☐ _____
  _____
- ☐ _____
  _____

Name _____

School/Agency _____

Address _____

City _____ State _____ Zip _____

Day phone (_____)_____ Evening phone (_____)_____

Fax (_____)_____ E-mail _____

- ☐ Please call me as I have questions. Best time to call _____

Telephone Support

PHONE CONSULTATIONS WITH ONE OF OUR TECHNICAL SUPPORT SPECIALISTS

Academic Innovations has Technical Support Specialists with a wealth of experience available to help you implement your *Career Choices* program.

With their finger on the pulse of career education nationwide, our Specialists can answer your questions on how to use *Career Choices* in settings such as Tech Prep, School-to-Work, college prep, career guidance, integration/interdisciplinary models, and applied academics. They have resources for effective restructuring strategies, information on funding, and new lesson plans from other classroom teachers.

Also, if you are interested in staff development, they can help you determine the best plan for training. Our Technical Support Specialists are available to speak with you at (800) 967-8016, 9 am to 3 pm PST.

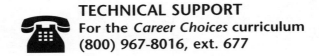

TECHNICAL SUPPORT
For the *Career Choices* curriculum
(800) 967-8016, ext. 677

On-line Support

Help is just a keystroke away!

Simply send an e-mail message to: techsupport@academicinnovations.com.

Give us your name, question and your return e-mail address, and one of our technical support staff can answer your questions or direct you to the resources you need.

Question	Go to URL:	You'll find:	Helpful hints & tips
I have lots of questions about the particular applications of the Career Choices curriculum. Where can I easily find the answers?	http://www.academicinnovations.com/ccres.html	A list of a variety of resources and services offered by our Technical Support Department.	*To request information, e-mail our Tech Support Department using the hyperlink at the bottom of the page or call at (800) 967-8016, ext. 677.*
AND...	http://www.academicinnovations.com/faq.html	A variety of frequently asked questions and the answers as you scroll down this page.	*Print out for later study. This is a wealth of information. You may want to visit this page several times to hyperlink to other sites referenced here.*

Question	Go to URL:	You'll find:	Helpful hints & tips
I'd like to ask the authors a question about one of the exercises. How can I do this?	http://www.academicinnovations.com/ask.html	A hyperlink to an e-mail dialog box in which you can type your question	*Allow up to one week to get a response. If you need help sooner, contact our Tech Support Department by phone at (800) 967-8016, ext. 677.*

Visit our Web Page

http://www.academicinnovations.com

You can't open a newspaper or a magazine these days without reading about the Internet. Reporters, politicians and social commentators are singing its praises. And for good reason. Finally, we have the technology to link diverse populations and make information accessible to everyone.

In the technological age, information is power. And with the advent of the World Wide Web and its user-friendly software, the learning curve has been reduced to minutes versus days. People all over the world are getting online and in touch.

We at Academic Innovations pride ourselves in attempting to stay on the cutting edge of educational strategies. *Career Choices* is the first turnkey interdisciplinary curriculum using a thematic approach to teach core academic subjects.

We've worked hard to provide an Internet site filled with resources for classroom teachers dedicated to improving the lives of their students. Your first surfing expedition will provide immediate rewards.

You'll discover a variety of resources:

- See how other teachers are using the *Career Choices* curriculum.
- Review or share specialized lesson plans for the *Career Choices* curriculum.
- Become part of an online discussion group of *Career Choices* users and share enrichment ideas.
- Meet the authors of our books, and ask them questions online.
- Explore funding strategies and preview sample grant proposals.
- Survey our calendar of *Career Choices* workshops in Santa Barbara, California, and in various cities across the country.

You'll want to visit the Academic Innovations web site often. Our Director of Technological Customer Services is adding new material daily. Teachers from all over the country are sharing their experiences with us and we hope you will soon join them. Future plans include special lesson plan enhancements for *Career Choices* using the Internet, along with an area where students can publish *Career Choices* assignments such as the acrostic poem activity from pages 44-45 of *Possibilities*. *Career Choices* students from all over the country will be able to discuss their futures and share ideas. And as the video capabilities of the Internet increase, we hope to sponsor guest speakers and mentors representing a variety of careers. The possibilities are endless.

So let's create a "virtual community" of *Career Choices* users. By sharing our experiences and resources, students across the country will benefit.

See you on the 'Net!

Focus on the Future Newsletter

We produce a free quarterly newsletter that shares classroom ideas generated by teachers across the country who use these materials. We are learning of many exciting projects, so if you want to join our network, drop us a note stating you'd like to be on the *Focus on the Future* newsletter mailing list. Mail your requests to Academic Innovations, 3463 State St., Suite 267, Santa Barbara, CA 93105.

 Our Web Site

Question	Go to URL:	You'll find:	Helpful hints & tips
I'd like to sign up for a free subscription to your newsletter, Focus on the Future.	http://www.academicinnovations.com/news.html	A form to request a free subscription to our newsletter	*Complete the form with your name, title, school, mailing address and e-mail address.*

Question	Go to URL:	You'll find:	Helpful hints & tips
I'd like ideas on creative ways other teachers are using the Career Choices curriculum. Where can I find them?	http://www.academicinnovations.com/ideas.html	A list of articles from past newsletters	*You'll want to surf the hyper-links. In particular, note articles from North Dakota, Washington, the one about the multimedia ideas and innovative assessment. E-mail us your ideas so we can share them.*

I am so excited at the discovery of your web page and WONDERFUL links! Thank you so much for providing such wonderful information. Now I have substantial information to be able to deliver to several departments on the campus which is sorely needed. Those departments include Tech Prep directors and the technical/industrial division chair at the college. We have all been working on ways to integrate academia and technical studies. Now at least for me, I have found a source of excellent information (that is CURRENT) and extremely applicable to where we are. Again, thanks so much for providing a wonderful, informative, and well-constructed site for "one-step shopping" for academic and technical instructors alike!

– Response via e-mail

Staff Development Opportunities

Remember when cooperative learning meant that no one talked without permission, and team teaching was something the football coach did from the sidelines at the Friday night game? Over the past few years, the education community has come face to face with new terms, new approaches, and new challenges as America struggles to find better ways to help its children learn.

But what about you? When do you get the opportunity to explore new learning strategies, gain insights, exchange ideas, evaluate approaches, develop plans, and create the kind of models that will work best in your school, for your students?

Academic Innovations sponsors two-day *Career Choices* Workshops several times per year in our hometown of Santa Barbara, California. In addition, independent Certified Trainers are available to conduct workshops on site in your district or school. We also co-sponsor workshops with various divisions within state Departments of Education at different geographical locations around the country. Join other educators to learn about interdisciplinary team teaching strategies, School-to-Work integration models, and a variety of proven lesson plans and activities. Discover how to engage your students with career planning activities while they practice their basic skills of reading, writing, mathematical computations and speaking in the academic classroom.For more information on our Staff Development Opportunities, call our office.

The workshop was an excellent first step for those of us who will initiate new career programs in our areas.
– Jan Knight
Counselor
Horn High School
Horn Lake, MS

The most valuable [aspect] was the practical hands-on modeling of how to present materials and lessons.
– Bonnie Morris
Business/Career instructor
Anacortes High School
Anacortes, WA

Our Web Site

Question	Go to URL:	You'll find:	Helpful hints & tips
I'm interested in attending a Career Choices workshop in my area. Where can I find the dates and locations of upcoming workshops?	http://www. academicinnovations.com/ tpwork.html	Text about the Tech Prep and School-to-Work workshops along with hyperlinks to specific information on such topics as fees and agenda.	*Print out the text along with the text from the hyperlinks found at the bottom of the page. You'll want to check to see if a workshop is scheduled near you.*
AND...	http://www. academicinnovations.com/ wcal.html	The dates and locations of upcoming workshops around the country.	*Scroll down the page to request more information on a specific workshop in the boxes at the bottom. We'll send you a brochure with specifics for that particular workshop and a registration form.*

Staff Development Allowances

Academic Innovations customers may qualify for an allowance on our workshops and staff development opportunities. To receive a copy of our *Staff Development Allowance Policy*, call our office at (800) 967-8016, or go online for our current policy.

Question	Go to URL:	You'll find:	Helpful hints & tips
I'd like to attend a two-day Career Choices workshop in Santa Barbara, CA, but require financial assistance. How do I find out about your Staff Development allowance?	http://www.academicinnovations.com/staffdev.html	Our policy for administering our staff development allowance.	*Print out a copy of this page and the Staff Development Allowance Request Form. Contact us by e-mail or phone to request an accounting of your school's allowance to date.*

Borrow a Video of the Two-Day Workshop

We realize that it is not always possible for educators to travel to California to participate in one of our two-day training workshops or to sponsor a training in their own region. Therefore, Academic Innovations has a six-hour videotape highlighting one of our two-day workshops conducted by author Mindy Bingham. Whether you are unable to attend a workshop or just want to preview one prior to attendance, this video is available for loan. If you wish to borrow a copy, please contact our office. Due to demand, please allow up to one month for delivery.

How to borrow a copy of our two-day workshop video   http://www.academicinnovations.com/wvideo.html

Join the *CareerChoicesNet* Discussion Group

Now, thanks to the Internet and technology, networking with other teachers can be easy and fun. At last, there's no need for you to feel isolated as you pioneer and innovate new ways of educating and motivating your students.

What is CareerChoicesNet?

CareerChoicesNet discussion group is a closed and moderated on-line list of teachers, administrators and counselors from across the country who are currently using the *Career Choices* curriculum in their schools and classrooms. This is known in Internet parlance as a "virtual community." The goal of CareerChoicesNet is to provide a nation-wide forum for educators that will foster open-minded discussion of issues important to the educational community as well as the sharing of ideas and classroom resources.

How does CareerChoicesNet work?

Once you have been accepted for membership, your name and e-mail address will be added to a "mailing list" under CareerChoicesNet. Then, messages sent to CareerChoicesNet will be sent automatically to you via e-mail. By remaining selective as to who can join the list, we have ensured that all posts to the list are relevant topics for discussion.

When you check your e-mail box you'll find questions, discussions and resources from other members of the list. Certain topics will be of particular interest to you and you can choose to join in an "electronic" dialogue about that issue. The "mailing list" format allows you to be as active as you like. You can choose to remain a passive participant of current discussions by just reading the dialogues delivered to your e-mail box (known as lurking). Or you can get actively involved by participating and answering queries, sharing ideas and providing resource suggestions, either to the complete membership or back to the person sending the original message.

Two ways to subscribe:

You can subscribe to the CareerChoicesNet directly from the *Career Choices* Discussion group page on the Academic Innovations' web site. Enter the URL http://www.academicinnovations.com/usrgrp.html Fill out the form, click on "send form" and your subscription will be processed.

Or send an e-mail message to usrgrp@academicinnovations.com. Be sure to indicate that you want to join CareerChoicesNet and include the following information in your message to us: your name, e-mail address, title, department, school, address, phone and fax numbers and a brief description of your program.

Master Teacher Program

The Master Teacher program is designed to provide a system that will allow educators across the country to share their experience and expertise with each other and at the same time provide a method to recognize and reward excellence in the classroom.

If you become a Master Teacher, we will enter your listing on our Internet web site and in our database for referral, so teachers across the country seeking help can contact you for guidance and benefit from your years of experience.

Perhaps you remember how challenging it was to change from a traditional method of teaching (lecture) to the one required for *Career Choices* (facilitator). How did you convince your administration to try a thematic approach to academics? How do you supplement the suggested lessons? If working in an interdisciplinary team, how do you coordinate your lesson plans? These are just some of the types of issues other *Career Choices* teachers will want to talk about.

As a *Career Choices* Master Teacher you will be eligible for a variety of special services and programs.

- Master Teachers receive a discount off the registration fee of any *Career Choices* workshop/conference they attend.

- Master Teachers are eligible for free phone training by our Director of Technological Customer Service as they learn the Internet.

- Master Teachers will automatically receive complimentary review copies of new classroom extensions for *Career Choices* or new curriculums in development.

- Master Teachers are eligible for the special conference stipend program when they present at an approved state or national educational conference.

- Master Teachers can tap the expertise of the Academic Innovations Production Department for assistance in developing custom overheads or PowerPoint computerized presentations for conference workshops.

- Master Teachers can join a special Peer Review Editorial Team to comment on future curriculums or *Career Choices* extensions.

- Master Teachers can apply to become a Certified Trainer for *Career Choices* to be hired by Academic Innovations or referred to school districts as a freelance consultant for one-day staff development workshops.

For more information, contact our Technical Support Department.

Question	Go to URL:	You'll find:	Helpful hints & tips
I'd like to talk with other teachers using the Career Choices curriculum. How can I contact these volunteer Master Teachers?	http://www. academicinnovations.com/ master.html	The names and addresses of educators who have volunteered to share their expertise with others using *Career Choices*	*Locate one or two who have a similar program and contact them to share information and support. If you'd like to be considered as a Master Teacher, use the hyperlink to contact us.*

Funding Your *Career Choices* Textbooks

From the responses we get via the phone and e-mail, finding funding for a *Career Choices* program is probably one of the most challenging aspects of starting a course. The following pages *(117 to 127)* are included to help you start this process.

You'll find information on:

- Federal programs (Carl Perkins funding in particular)

- State funding

- Corporate funding

- On-line resources to help with writing your grant

- Information on student-funded workbooks

- Funding from community organizations

But you probably won't want to stop here. Because the domain of funding and grants is an ever-changing area, particularly when it comes to federal programs, you'll want to visit our web site periodically to gather the newest information on available grants that will fund a *Career Choices* program.

Funding Information   http://www.academicinnovations.com/funding.html

By going online you'll also have access to computer files of sample text you can download and use for your first draft or as the backbone of your written proposal *(see pages 120-121)*. This will save you hours of research and writing time.

Remember, our Technical Support Department stands ready to help you with this empowering process. Please don't hesitate to call.

*Many students commented that this class (vocational studies using **Career Choices**) was their favorite class. The reasons included their ownership of their workbook and questions and activities about themselves.*

– Deborah Back
Vocational Studies Teacher
Carr Creek Elementary
Litt Carr, Kentucky

Carl Perkins Funding Guide Available

🖱 Carl Perkins Funding Guide   http://www.academicinnovations.com/calperk.html

To assist you in writing Carl Perkins grants, Academic Innovations has prepared an easy-to-understand guide. You will find that virtually every component of the Perkins Act addresses the need for career counseling, either as a requirement or recommended program. Whether your area is special populations, Tech Prep, gender equity, single parent, or another Perkins initiative, *Career Choices* may be purchased with these funds. Included in this guide are:

- Samples of goals, objectives and outcomes, important requirements for funding programs.
- Strategies to help you identify resources and information needed to understand funding opportunities in your state.
- Suggestions for developing strong proposals by eliminating common weaknesses.
- Potential sources of funds beyond Perkins.

Whether you are an administrator, counselor, supervisor or teacher, this resource will save time and help you write a successful proposal.

It is important to mention that each state allocates Perkins funds differently. Before you spend valuable time writing a proposal, determine whether funds are available for your program. This grant writing process will, nevertheless, be appropriate for obtaining funding from a variety of other sources such as foundations, community organizations, PTA's and local businesses.

As education becomes more responsive to the needs of the workplace, more groups will respond and fund effective programs. Therefore, if you find the doors closed with Carl Perkins, change your proposal slightly and submit it to your local Rotary, Kiwanis, or even a progressive business owner in your community (see the following pages). As noted in this guide, there are many opportunities for funding from community businesses and service organizations. If they see a project can produce results, identifying individuals or groups willing to help young people focus on their education and their future is not difficult.

The information and recommendations in this guide are directed to classroom teachers or department heads who are beginning the grant writing process. Unfortunately, far too many good projects go unfunded because of the perception that the funding process is difficult. In some areas, and for some projects, that may be the case. But in most school districts, proposals for Carl Perkins funding are not overwhelming if you have a strategy and a fundable program.

This guide will help you with the strategy and *Career Choices* will provide the fundable program.

State Funding

How to Research State Funding for your Program   http://www.academicinnovations.com/statefun.html

Each state has different mandates and different priorities for allocating funds to new and innovative programs. The best place to start your research is with your principal. You'll want to be sure to advise him/her of your plans. Ask for the names of individuals at the district office who are responsible for grant writing. Contact them to discuss your project and find out what opportunities there are in your state. Ask what special funding is available for:

1. Career and vocational programs
2. Tech Prep and/or School-to-Work
3. Restructuring and model programs
4. Guidance and career planning
5. Working with at-risk or drop-out prevention
6. Gender equity or teen pregnancy prevention

Be sure your district grant writers are familiar with your program and its goals. "Requests for Proposals" (RFP – documents soliciting grant applications) come across their desks daily. If the grant writers are familiar with your program and a suitable RFP arrives, they will be much more likely to contact you and write a proposal for your program. It's a good idea to write a brief summary of what you'd like your program to accomplish and send it to the district office.

How to Build a Strong Proposal   http://www.academicinnovations.com/cppropo.html

Funding Decisions are Personal   http://www.academicinnovations.com/cpfun.html

Defining the Need, Purpose and Goals of Your Program   http://www.academicinnovations.com/cpdef.html

Fundable Projects - Team and Cluster Concept   http://www.academicinnovations.com/cpproj.html

Example of a District Plan and Objectives   http://www.academicinnovations.com/cpex.html

Suggested Narratives for Proposals   http://www.academicinnovations.com/cpnarr.html

Corporate Funding

🖰 Corporate Funding Ideas   http://www.academicinnovations.com/corpfun.html

Many companies today are focusing their corporate philanthropy efforts on education. They are very aware that they will need educated and motivated workers in the future. The *Career Choices* program is a wonderful vehicle for soliciting corporate sponsorship. Here's one plan for researching and executing a corporate funding campaign.

First, find out what corporations are prominent or do business in your community. The best place to start your research is with the Chamber of Commerce or the Better Business Bureau. Watch the paper to see what companies are in the news. Don't be shy. Remember you are not asking for a lot of money by most corporate standards. Let's say you request funding for 100 copies of the *Workbook and Portfolio*. This costs about $700, or the price of a good size advertisement in your regional newspaper.

Once you've narrowed your choice to two or three prospects, use your own network of peers, parents and friends to see if you can get an introduction to either the CEO, Director of Public Relations or Director of Community Relations. If you cannot get an introduction, make an appointment to see the Director of Community Relations anyway.

When you pay your first visit, take along a complete set of the *Career Choices* textbooks. They make a wonderful "prop" for your presentation. Besides talking about the program, be sure to ask questions and listen carefully to what the funder has to say. You'll want to incorporate his or her ideas into your written proposal, which should arrive within a few days of your interview.

Remember, most businesses and corporations make donations not only to do good but also to get publicity and generate good will from the public. So it is imperative that you solicit media attention for your program throughout the year (newspaper articles, TV news stories, etc.). Anywhere your *Career Choices* program is mentioned, be sure to add the tagline "Funded by the *XYZ* Corporation." The more you do this, the more likely the business or corporation is to fund your program year after year.

Some of your presentation strategies will parallel what we suggest for Community Service Organizations in this section.

On-line Resources for Your Grant Proposal

The following resources should help as you begin seeking funds for your *Career Choices* program. Review the charts below to find the areas on our web page that best meet your needs.

Besides helping you understand how a variety of funding sources work, these web pages contain a variety of documents that can be downloaded to your computer hard drive and used as the backbone of your proposal. Naturally, you will want to edit them to fit your school's program methodology, but using some of the text will save you hours of researching, creating and keyboarding.

If you don't find what you need on-line or you do not have access to the Internet, be sure to contact our Technical Support Department at (800) 967-8016, ext. 677. They can help you.

Our Web Site

Question	Go to URL:	You'll find:	Helpful hints & tips
I've never written a grant proposal for funding before. Where do I start?	http://www. academicinnovations.com/ cppropo.html	Information that will help you begin your proposal process	*Explore the other hyperlinks on the Corporate Funding Ideas page. Print out or download appropriate sections.*

Question	Go to URL:	You'll find:	Helpful hints & tips
I'd like to approach a community service organization for help funding our workshops and to recruit mentors the students can shadow. Give me a step-by-step plan.	http://www. academicinnovations.com/ cso.html	An extensive plan on how to get funding from your community service organizations	*Print out and review this easy-to-follow plan. Return to surf the funding hyperlinks recommended on this page.*
AND...	http://www. academicinnovations.com/ comminv.html	Ideas of how to get community members actively involved with your *Career Choices* program	*Hyperlink to Career Exploration Brainstorming Session and Job Interview Night for details on how to run these community activities.*

Our Web Site

Question	Go to URL:	You'll find:	Helpful hints & tips
I need help writing a grant proposal for my Career Choices program. Where can I find sample text?	http://www.academicinnovations.com/cpex.html	Text of an example of one district's plan	*Print out the text for future reference or download to your hard drive for later word processing.*
AND...	http://www.academicinnovations.com/cpnarr.html	Text for a variety of proposals.	*Choose the most appropriate narrative for your program and print or download it for later inclusion in your proposal.*
AND...	http://www.academicinnovations.com/expert.html	A series of short articles on the special needs of adolescents.	*Choose the articles that help to justify your program. Download that text to your hard drive for later editing, customizing and inclusion into your proposal.*
AND...	http://www.academicinnovations.com/ccphilo.html	More text that can be partially incorporated into your proposal.	*Download to your hard drive for later editing. You may want to use part of this essay in your cover letter.*

Question	Go to URL:	You'll find:	Helpful hints & tips
How would I approach a business in our community for help with funding our Career Choices program?	http://www.academicinnovations.com/corpfun.html	A detailed explanation of how to approach the business community for funding	*Print out this page plus the text from all the hyperlinks in this section. Form a committee to strategize a plan using this information.*

Student Funding

 Student Funding   http://www.academicinnovations.com/studfun.html

Many states allow schools to require students to purchase "consumable" supplies. Some California schools, therefore, have students purchase the *Workbook and Portfolio*. If your state has a similar provision, you might use this strategy to fund part of your *Career Choices* program.

You can seek special funding for students who can't afford to buy their own workbook. This is a small project for a Community Service Organization and one that members can decide on quickly.

Working with Community Service Organizations

Mentors and role models are very important for young people, especially at-risk adolescents. Shadowing and internship opportunities are very meaningful but finding volunteers can be difficult and time consuming. Yet many people in business are interested in helping young people prepare for the working world. So, if you haven't already, why not consider recruiting one of the service organizations in your community to sponsor your school's program.

FINDING THE RIGHT SERVICE ORGANIZATION TO APPROACH

If you aren't familiar with the different service organizations in your community, contact your local Chamber of Commerce to get a list. They will have the names and phone numbers of the president and the program chairperson for each organization in your community.

Some of the organizations you should consider contacting include:
- Altrusa
- American Association of University Women
- Business and Professional Women
- Kiwanis
- Lions Club
- Rotary
- Soroptimist
- Zonta International

These organizations are made up of professional and career-oriented individuals who will probably be particularly interested in helping young people become ready for the work force.

Do some homework before you contact someone within the organization. Try to find out which organizations within your community are particularly interested in supporting either youth or education. Use your network of friends and professional acquaintances to research this information. If you have an advisory board, it will be helpful with this task.

RECRUITING THE SERVICE ORGANIZATION

Once you have determined which organization(s) would be most interested in becoming involved with your school's program, contact the program chair and offer to give a presentation at one of their meetings. For the organizations which have weekly meetings (usually at lunch), program chairs are constantly on the lookout for interesting presentations about the community. Your call will be most welcome.

YOUR PRESENTATION

Once you have scheduled a presentation, plan and practice what you want to say. Be sure to ask the program chair how much time you have and be careful not to go over that limit. Leave time for questions. The following suggestions might be helpful as you plan your presentation:

Tell success stories about students you have graduated. If you have graduates who like to speak in front of groups, you might bring them along to give a short presentation.

Give the Startling Statement Quiz on page 201 of *Career Choices* to warm up the audience, or use the statistics on page 202 to support your presentation.

The following pages of the *Career Choices Instructor's and Counselor's Guide* may have material, quotes and statistics you will want to incorporate into your presentation: Pages 3, 4, 7-9.

If you have display material, supporting videos or articles, be sure to bring these along and set up a display in the back of the room.

Be sure to take along at least one copy of *Career Choices* to pass around the audience while you are speaking.

YOUR PRESENTATION: "ASKING FOR SUPPORT"

Toward the end of your presentation, be sure to ask for support or assistance from the members. As their name implies, community service organizations are dedicated to giving service to the community. They organize primarily for that purpose and are usually looking for projects in the community that will make a difference. Working with students who need special attention to become productive citizens should have a high appeal for members.

WHAT KINDS OF SUPPORT CAN YOU ASK FOR?

Speaker's Bureau
At the minimum, be sure to take a copy of pages 92-93 in the *Instructor's Guide*. Ask the audience to help you identify individuals who would be good guest speakers for your group. Pass the form around the room as you speak

Shadowing Mentors
Also, have a number of copies of the Shadow Program Mentor Survey form from pages 222-223 of the *Instructor's Guide* with you. Ask for individuals to volunteer as mentors for your program. Be sure to add your name and address at the bottom of the form so people can fill it out later and send it back.

Director of Mentors

If you are looking for a Director of Mentors (see pages 220-224 of this *Instructor's Guide*) mention that fact and ask any interested individuals to see you after the meeting. There will probably be retired individuals in the audience who are interested in quality volunteer placement (activities where they see that they are making a difference) and who have good contacts in the business community.

Funding for Books

If the service organization provided the funding, each student could have their own copy of *Career Choices* instead of the *Workbook and Portfolio*. This would encourage the students to work more diligently.

FUNDING FOR BOOKS

Most community service organizations raise funds throughout the year for projects in the community. If, after your presentation, you feel there was a lot of interest your program and the members support the concepts, contact the president of the organization and ask what their procedure is for requesting program funding.

Follow the procedure and suggest that the organization fund a copy of *Career Choices* for each participant. This is something "concrete" that the service organization can take pride in providing.

Once you receive funding for the books, design a sticker that says (for example):

Affix it to each cover of *Career Choices*. Your local instant print shop can arrange for custom stickers.

KEEPING YOUR SUPPORTERS INVOLVED

Book Presentation Ceremony

You may want to ask representatives of your sponsoring community service organization to attend a presentation ceremony where each participant of your class is "presented" their own copy of their book. Consider even putting a ribbon around each copy. When the students see that people care about them, they will work harder to learn.

When given their books, be sure to remind the students that this is a journal that they will want to keep along with their school annuals, family photo albums and keepsakes, because someday they will want to share it with their own teenager. After the ceremony, the service organization might sponsor a luncheon or ice cream social.

At Graduation Time

At a meeting of the service organization, share copies of the students' ten-year plans (*Career Choices*, pages 279-280) and their mission statements (page 281). When service organizations' members see young people making an effort, you'll find they become interested in seeing that these students succeed in getting jobs.

Remember to say thank you throughout the year. Cards made by students or letters written by students are always appreciated. If you get any media coverage, always remember to give credit to your sponsoring organization.

An involved group will become a committed group.

PRESENTATIONS THROUGHOUT THE YEAR

If you keep your sponsoring organization informed and involved, it will probably continue to support you in the future. In coordination with the program chair of the community service organization, schedule two or three informative programs throughout the year. Here are some ideas:

Career Exploration Brainstorming Session

A one- or two-week activity, this session could be scheduled after your students have completed Chapter five in *Career Choices*.

First half hour:

During the first week, make a presentation about the *Career Choices* career decision-making process to the service organization membership. Include a description of the Bull's Eye Chart, the budgeting process and the career characteristics in chapter five. Because you are going to ask them to work directly with students, give them some guidelines and prospective outcomes.

Second half hour:

At the follow-up meeting, bring enough students so that each student can brainstorm career possibilities with a panel of 2 or 3 service organization members. Ask the service organization members to break into panels and assign each student to a panel. The students will provide each member of their panel with a completed copy of the following worksheets from *Career Choices*: the Bull's Eye chart on page 27, a copy of their budget on page 92 and a copy of their desired career characteristics on page 134. Because these business people have real world experience, they can be helpful in presenting career options and strategies for getting a job.

This should be a noisy and lively session that everyone will enjoy. Allow enough time for the groups to report out. Some of your students may receive offers for shadowing or internships from their group members.

You may find that your sponsors enjoy this activity so much they will want to repeat it with more students from your program.

Job Interview Night

Towards the end of the year ask your service organization to sponsor a job interview night. You may want to hold this at the school so you have plenty of classrooms to use for break-out rooms.

The service organization members will break into three-person panels and conduct mock job interviews. Each panel will provide a fictitious job description for the position for which they are interviewing.

Once the 15-minute trial interview is complete, the panel will critique the interviewee and give suggestions of how better to handle the interview.

Students will float between panels and interview with at least three different panels. Suggest that they pay particular attention to the areas which the panel identifies as needing practice and try to improve each time. A social/reception for all participants could be held in the cafeteria at the end of the evening.

You may also want to hold a training session for the interviewers before the activity if you feel they need to be sensitive to certain issues.

Good luck!

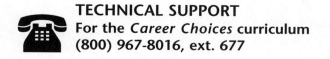

TECHNICAL SUPPORT
For the *Career Choices* curriculum
(800) 967-8016, ext. 677

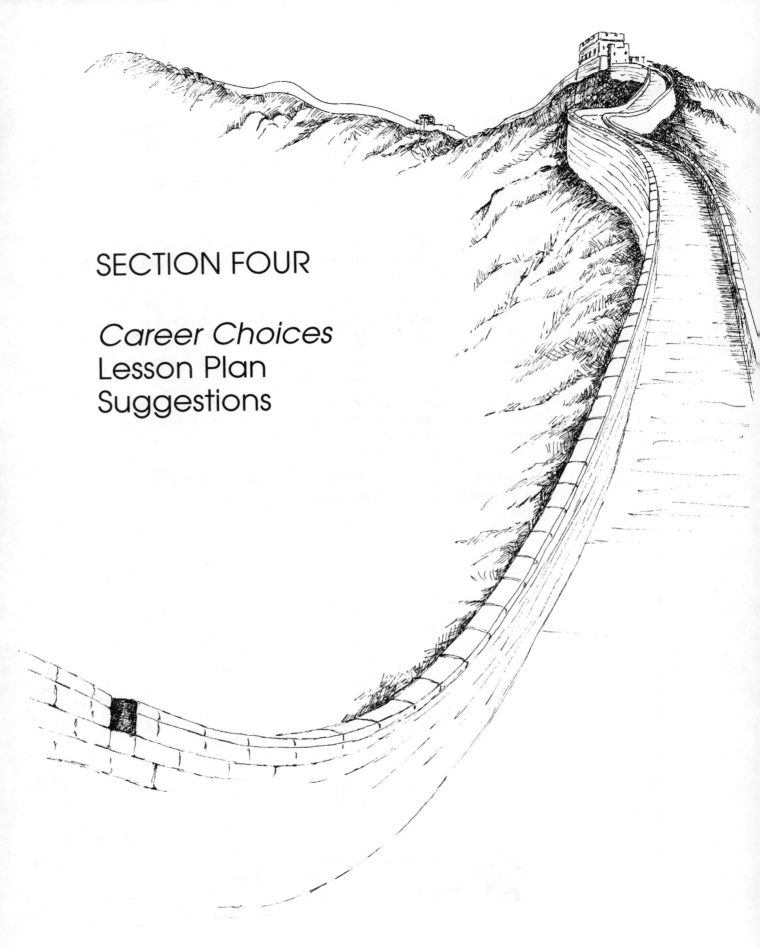

SECTION FOUR

Career Choices Lesson Plan Suggestions

The following chapter-by-chapter, exercise-by-exercise classroom suggestions should be helpful as you develop you own lesson plans. Each exercise has a learning objective with presentation suggestions. In addition, many have suggestions for optional activities, resources, and suggested reading and writing assignments.

The *Energizers* are special activities which students particularly enjoy. Their activity-oriented design facilitates a high level of student participation.

As you experiment with what works best with your population, make notes in the margins of the *Guide*. Please remember to share your ideas so we can consider including them in a future version of this *Guide*.

Introduction

Presentation suggestions:

Ask a student to read the introduction aloud in class. Then ask each student how he or she would have completed the flight assignment. Note the variety of responses.

Emphasize the last paragraph of the introduction. It is not the purpose of this course to have students make a final career choice. They should, however, learn a process for making rewarding life choices in the future.

Activities:

To help the class get acquainted, ask students to write several things about themselves on nametags and then move about the class, silently reading other tags. Students may want to note a particular talent or skill they are proud of, an interest area or favorite hobby, a place they most like to visit, the most important people in their lives, an important achievement, or even something personal no one else in the room knows.

As with all activities of this nature, if an individual does not want to share information, respect that student's privacy.

Chapter 1

Envisioning Your Future

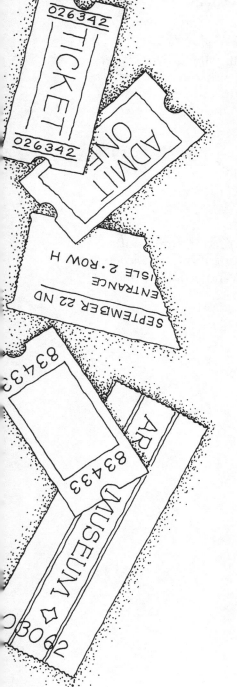

As you move into Chapter 1, have students read the opening stories aloud.

The overall goal of this course is to help each student become aware of his or her own identity and ambitions, and to develop an action plan for realizing these dreams. The basic purpose of the first chapter is to start students thinking about an ideal future. It also provides you with some baseline information on how much thought they have given this topic previously and whether their ambitions are relatively high or low. This information should be taken into account as you plan the remainder of the course.

As you begin, be careful not to step on anyone's dreams. A goal may seem unrealistic for a particular student, but many, many people who demonstrate little potential in high school go on to excel in their future careers. You may need to remind some students from time to time that success requires action in addition to vision. It may also be appropriate to encourage some students to aim higher if you sense they lack confidence in their own capabilities.

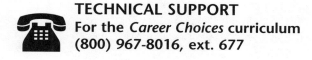

TECHNICAL SUPPORT
For the *Career Choices* curriculum
(800) 967-8016, ext. 677

Vision Plus Energy
Equals Success

Page 13

Page 5

Learning objective:

To help students realize that success does not come just from daydreaming, but from combining a vision with appropriate and necessary actions.

Presentation suggestions:

Discuss the difference between daydreaming and working toward a vision. Emphasize that daydreaming is an important first step, but that it must be followed by action if dreams are to become reality. Can students think of daydreams they've had that they did not work to realize? Did the daydreams come true?

As a class, work through the charts for Sally, Oprah, and Bill. While students can't know what actions these people took, the class should be able to think of some reasonable steps based on their accomplishments.

Activities:

Ask the class to think of synonyms for the words *vision* (dream, imagination, conception, creation, inspiration, invention, fantasy, fabrication) and *energy* (activity, liveliness, spirit, vivacity, eagerness, zeal, vigor). What images do these terms suggest?

I invited a Native American artist to my class to teach my students how to make "Dream Catchers."

– Barbara Muir
Teacher
North High School
Minneapolis, Minnesota

*Distribute short magazine articles on the visions of famous people. (**Newsweek, Parade** magazine, etc.) As a small-group activity, have students write a phrase explaining the vision of each celebrity.*

– Sharon Hurwitz
English teacher/Technology Facilitator
Bethel High School
Hampton, Virginia

Optional

Pages 11-18

The Secret Life of Walter Mitty
by James Thurber
Read after completing pages 10-13 in *Career Choices*

I learned a variety of things. The most important words that I learned were "vision + energy = success." I think those words are very important to a person who tries to figure out his/her own career....I know now that I have to plan my career. I can't just jump into anything, I have to plan out my career first. I have to do research on what job I would like to do.

– Student in Linda Costello's class
ASA Learning Center
San Bernadino, California

The following is a copy of the invitation Arlene Bowman of William Penn High School in New Castle, Delaware, hands out to her 9th grade English students at the beginning of Chapters one and two:

Join the Celebration!!
Let's celebrate ourselves and each other…

Who: Everyone in this classroom
When: Friday, September 8th through Wednesday, September 13th
What: Creating a community of learners

Celebration Preparation:

1. I will bring the balloons, markers, glue, and ideas…
2. You bring your "open mind" and…
   a. Go someplace you've never been before.
   b. Write down the things (at least 10) you feel you would need in this place to feel at home in it. (Bring list Friday).
   c. Bring three symbols to class on Friday that reflect what you value about yourself and your life.

Envisioning Your Future

Page 14

Page 6

Learning objective:

> To have students begin imagining the kind of future they would find most satisfying.
>
> For instructor to use as a pre-assessment survey to establish baseline information that can be used to measure growth and learning.

Presentation suggestions:

> After reading the introductory material for this exercise to the class, ask students to close their eyes and imagine their ideal future lives. Allow several minutes for the vision to appear, then have the class describe in writing what they imagined. You may want to have students share their visions as a way of getting to know each other better (and to help you know what their thoughts are at this point.) You should ask to see everyone's description, whether it is shared with the class or not. This will also help you gauge how much progress individuals are making as they proceed through the class. Realize, though, that this will be a difficult exercise for some people in the class. After they have attempted this task, reassure them that even if they had no vision at all, it's okay. They will, soon enough.
>
> Refer again to the previous exercise, emphasizing that energy must match vision in order to achieve success.
>
> This may be a good time to bring the school counselor into the class as a resource person and facilitator.

I added musical selections to enhance my program.
For example, for Martin Luther King's "I Have a
Dream," I used Garth Brooks' "We Shall Be Free."

— Belinda Boyce
English Teacher
Buckeye Local High School
Rayland, Ohio

Optional

Pages 19-32

A Psalm of Life
by Henry Wadsworth Longfellow
Dreams
by Langston Hughes
I Have a Dream... (speech)
by Martin Luther King, Jr.
Read after completing page 14 in *Career Choices*

Linda Paulson's "Visualizer" Activity

The idea for "visualizers" or "fantasy tuner-inners" came to Linda Paulson, 9th grade language arts teacher in Grafton, North Dakota, one day in class when students couldn't seem to grasp the meaning of James Thurber's story, "The Secret Life of Walter Mitty" (*Possibilities*, pages 11-18). Clearly, the class needed a way to get in touch with its own hopes and dreams.

Paulson asked each student to bring a wire coat hanger to class the following day, and the first "visualizers" were born. The hangers were bent any way the students chose, so long as they could be worn on their heads in order to receive visions of their future. Today, class members plan ahead and bring all sorts of materials to school to decorate their vision receivers, which have become much more sophisticated. Paulson's only stipulation is that only found objects can be used. Nothing can be bought.

Students wear their contraptions for an entire day (they get points for doing so). In Paulson's English class, they get time to fantasize about possibilities for their own lives—living somewhere else, holding a particular job, or whatever— and then write about that fantasy (*Career Choices*, page 14). In other classes, teachers allow five or ten minutes on that day to pose a question related to their subject, and students again imagine a solution and write it down. They receive credit for their work in every class.

Although the hats are formally used only on this day, Paulson keeps them in her classroom, and students have permission to wear them "whenever they feel the need." It gives them "a right to be playful," Paulson says, and also breaks down barriers that can hold a young person's imagination in check.

What a wonderful way to help students begin to get in touch with their own visions of their future. Congratulations, Linda, on a fabulous idea!

Reproduced from quarterly Focus on the Future *newsletter. To be added to our mailing list for this free publication, call (800) 967-8016.*

Why People Work

Page 15   No Workbook
                      Page

Learning objective:

To illustrate that work is not just a way to earn a living, but an important part of most people's identity.

Presentation suggestions:

Review the reasons why people work listed in the book. Write them on the board. Ask the class if they can think of other possible reasons. Why do they think their parents work? Students will probably come to the conclusion that people work for a combination of all of these reasons.

Optional

Work, **an excerpt from *The Prophet***
by Kahlil Gibran
Read after completing page 15 in *Career Choices*

Pages 33-36

Everybody Works

Career Choices

Page 17

Workbook and Portfolio

Page 7

Learning objective:

To allow students to recognize the scope and diversity of every individual's accomplishments on a daily basis.

Presentation suggestions:

Discuss work in terms of the things students do every day and ask them to answer the questions on page 17. Follow with class discussion. How do students feel about their accomplishments (proud, intelligent, resentful, satisfied, talented, lucky, relieved)?

Be sure to emphasize that everything we "do" is work. A student is a worker—unpaid, perhaps, but still a worker.

Activity:

Because students are going to be asked how they "feel" about something throughout this course, define emotions and feelings.

Brainstorm with the class a list of emotions and feelings. Are they adjectives or verbs? You might debate this issue. Noted psychologist Dr. William Glasser argues that emotions and feelings are verbs because you choose them (i.e. you choose to be angry).

Defining Success

Pages 18-19   Page 8-9

Learning objective:

To help students see that individuals have a definition of success and that the only one they need to meet is their own.

Presentation suggestions:

In contemporary American society, success is often seen in terms of money, power, or material possessions. Assure students that while these things may make them appear successful to the rest of the world, they hardly guarantee a life of contentment. Everyone must define success personally. It is only by living up to that definition that people feel truly successful. Have students individually read the statements on the chart and mark whether they strongly agree, agree, are not sure, disagree, or strongly disagree with each definition. There are no right or wrong answers. The point is to help students sort out their own feelings on the topic. They should write their own definition of success on page 21 and sign it.

Allow plenty of time for students to think about the quotations or assign this exercise as homework. In your discussion emphasize, too, that their own definitions are likely to change, depending on what's going on in their life. A new parent who formerly defined success as getting ahead at work may decide that raising a healthy, happy child is far more important. Someone taken seriously ill might redefine success as getting and staying well.

Activities:

Ask students how they think certain well-known individuals [Abraham Lincoln, Shaquille O'Neil ("Shaq") Whoopi Goldberg, Ann Landers, Bart Simpson, Steven Spielberg, Gloria Estefan, Amy Tan, Rush Limbaugh, Steffi Graf] would define success, based on their actions.

Have students view the movie *Forrest Gump* for your first Video Book Club discussion (see page 96). Did Forrest have a vision of success? What energy did he display? How does the class think he would define success for himself? Is Forrest a good role model for the class? Why or why not?

Reading assignment:

Bless the Beasts and the Children, by Glenden Swarthout

This book centers around a group of young "misfits" who have been sent to camp to be "straightened out." The group comes together as one by one they are rejected by the other groups in camp. The boys go on an unusual quest to see a herd of buffalo sentenced to a cruel death by the park service and, in so doing, find a measure of their own worth and freedom. An excellent starting point for discussions on setting and achieving goals and defining and attaining personal success, this book is high-interest reading with a strong message. (Good video available.)

While students are entering the room, have the Simon and Garfunkel song "Richard Cory" playing. Then have the students read the poem "Richard Cory" in **Possibilities** *and answer the questions following the work.*

– Sharon Hurwitz
English teacher/Technology Facilitator
Bethel High School
Hampton, Virginia

The writing activities were most appealing to the students. For example, writing the last page of Richard Cory's diary.

– Belinda Boyce
English Teacher
Buckeye Local High School
Rayland, Ohio

Optional

Pages 37-39

Richard Cory

by Edwin Arlington Robinson

Read after completing pages 18-21 in *Career Choices*

Course Wrap-Up

Ask students to write their own definitions of success entitled "Success Is..." Refer them to the Robert Louis Stevenson quotation at the bottom of page 283 in *Career Choices*.

Throughout the course, there will be a great deal of discussion and debate as to what success is. By the end of the course, each student should have a more complete personal definition of what success means. Allow at least a couple of days from making the assignment to completion so they have time to think about it. This is not an activity that should be done as a group. Explain that the personal nature of the task requires individual contemplation.

Energizer:

Once their expanded definition is complete, turn it into an art project by neatly lettering it on a large piece of art paper. The computer lab can be utilized along with a laser printer to produce high-quality lettering. The italic setting usually adds interest to a quotation. Remind the students to "sign" their quotation similar to the style used for quotes in *Career Choices*.

Ask the students to complete a color border around their quotation using watercolors, felt pens, tissue paper collage, or even color pictures from magazines.

We suggest using this activity as a celebration. Perhaps some students will bring in refreshments. Play instrumental recordings in the background.

Once the projects are complete, post them around the room for everyone to share. If there are appropriate display areas in the school, why not share the project with a PTA meeting, a school board meeting or with other students?

At the time you make the assignment, why not share your own success quotation and art project?

The Stevenson quotation written in calligraphy with completed art would make a lovely classroom decoration. Collaborate with your art department on this.

Making Career Choices

Page 20-21   Page 9

Learning objective:

To help students identify their own decision-making patterns and evaluate their effectiveness.

Presentation suggestions:

Read the stories about the various decision-making patterns aloud in class. Then ask students to evaluate and discuss which patterns are likely to lead to the most desirable results, which patterns are likely to lead to the least desirable results and which patterns they use most often. Let students know they will learn much more about decision making as they work through *Career Choices*.

Instructor's Notes:

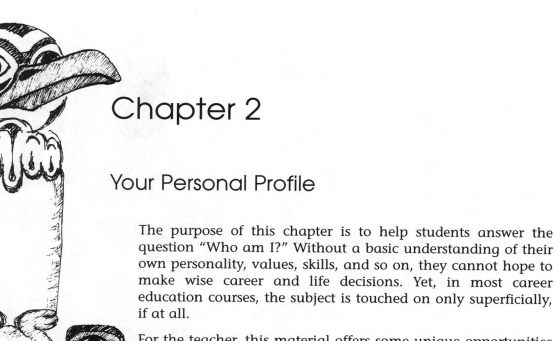

Chapter 2

Your Personal Profile

The purpose of this chapter is to help students answer the question "Who am I?" Without a basic understanding of their own personality, values, skills, and so on, they cannot hope to make wise career and life decisions. Yet, in most career education courses, the subject is touched on only superficially, if at all.

For the teacher, this material offers some unique opportunities as well as a few potential problems. Identity, after all, is a very personal matter. Some students will be reluctant to share their innermost thoughts and desires with the class. These feelings must be respected. It is much more important for the individual to discover his or her own unique qualities than it is for the class to hear about them. On the other hand, some students may need to overcome a bit of discomfort in order to begin thinking about these important concepts. Many young men, for example, will be unfamiliar with identifying and talking about their feelings. Yet, until they can articulate their emotional responses—either verbally or in writing—their lives are likely to be less satisfying.

You are in the best position to judge the activities that will best serve your class. Some groups will be open to lively class discussions. Others may feel more comfortable—or be more honest—in writing. In all cases, students should be assured of confidentiality if they so desire.

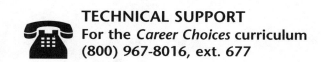

TECHNICAL SUPPORT
For the *Career Choices* curriculum
(800) 967-8016, ext. 677

Bull's Eye Chart

Page 24-27   Page 11

Learning objective:

To help students discover the many layers of qualities and characteristics that make up their unique identity, and to help them appreciate how knowing this identity is a necessary and ongoing part of any rewarding life.

Presentation suggestions:

Before you begin, review the definitions on page 26 with the class. Then, together, try to complete a chart on the board. You may use yourself as the example, if that feels comfortable. Or, you might try to make a chart for a celebrity or historic figure the class feels it knows well (examples: George Washington, Connie Chung, Bill Cosby, Roseanne, Michael Jordan, Eleanor Roosevelt).

Begin with the outer circles of the chart, and work your way toward the center.

Activities:

Ask students to make a collage representing their own passions, values, personality traits, strengths, skills and aptitudes, roles, occupations, and vocations. If you want to do this in class, bring in large pieces of paper or poster board, scissors, glue, and an assortment of old magazines. Have students find images they feel represent their own identity, cut them out, and glue them to the large pieces of paper. You may wish to assign this activity as homework.

Have students "define" themselves audio-visually with a collage of photos and words, songs, or whatever comes to mind. Then, as a class, try to identify which project matches which student.

Energizers:

Ask students to complete their own charts but not to share them with anyone. Then have class members choose a partner they feel they know well and complete a chart for him or her. Ask them to compare the second-party chart with the original. In most cases, students will find it relatively easy to complete the outer rings of the chart. They are unlikely to do as well with the inner ring topics, however.

Follow-up at the end of the course:

When the class has completed the book or the course, ask students to go back and update their charts with new information they have gained. These newly discovered qualities and traits should be entered in a different color ink. Then assign a one-page essay on the topic "Self-Discovery: A Life-long Process." If students are willing to share, you might post charts and essays around the room, allow time for students to read them, and follow with a group discussion.

Reading assignment:

The Diary of Anne Frank, by Anne Frank

The Personality Profile helped them see themselves as well-rounded, complex and unique individuals.

— Bonnie Morris
   Business and Careers Instructor
   Anacortes High School
   Anacortes, Washington

Chapter two was wonderful! The students enjoyed determining their values, passions, and work styles. The activities in the guide were fun and easy to incorporate into regular class discussion and activities. This chapter was a wonderful "ice breaker."

— Kyra Krause
   Special Education teacher
   Lubbock-Cooper High School
   Lubbock, Texas

Identifying Your Passions

Page 28-29   Page 12

Learning objective:

To help students learn to identify and articulate those things that are extremely important to them on an emotional level.

Presentation suggestions:

We thought about substituting another word for *passion* but, after lengthy debate, decided it was the most appropriate term. You are likely, however, to get some snickering from a few students. Be prepared. Use the situation to demonstrate how the things that matter most to an individual can elicit feelings of excitement similar to those usually associated with romantic or sexual passion.

Begin by writing the two definitions on page 28 in *Career Choices* on the board. Then have students brainstorm and write their own definitions and share them with the class. When someone alludes to the romantic overtones in the term, ask him or her to describe the feeling. List these on the board and then use them to help the class identify other passions. "What else makes you grin? What other situations make your heart race? What else do you do that makes you lose track of time?" And so on.

Activities:

As a group, think of words that could be substituted for *passion* or that convey the same feelings. Examples: Rapture, bliss, ecstasy, euphoria, exaltation, something that makes you go "aha!" Learning to recognize the objects, events, or situations that make you feel like this is an important step toward self-knowledge.

English/Language Arts:

Have students use the list of passions they identified on page 29 to write an essay on their ideal day—one that involves as many of their favorite experiences as possible. Letitia's day, for example, might include winning a political debate while wearing her red shoes, hearing "The Star-Spangled Banner" at the start of a Lakers' game, then eating chocolate during a sad movie and walking home in a thunderstorm.

Follow-up:

Throughout the course occasionally ask students at the beginning of class, "Did anyone discover a new passion recently?" Be prepared for blank stares and even giggles the first few times you ask this question. But go on and share an experience or feeling you have had or someone has shared with you. (You might start this conversation in the staff lunchroom to gather stories and examples, being sure to protect confidentiality.) Soon students will start sharing their experiences and ideas. The importance of this is that they will start recognizing the feeling and evaluating what is happening at the time. This simple skill will help with life-long happiness.

When students began to see themselves for what they wanted instead of what other people expected, it was remarkable.

–Lauren K. DeLay
Family and Consumer Science Teacher
Conestoga Public School
Murray, Nebraska

Optional

Pages 40-42

Excerpt from *Sonnets From the Portuguese*
by Elizabeth Barrett Browning
Read after completing pages 28-29 in *Career Choices*

Work Values Survey

Page 31-37

Page 13-16

Learning objective:

To help students clarify which work values are most meaningful in their own lives.

Presentation suggestions:

Read the directions on page 31 aloud. Allow about 45 minutes for students to complete the survey and score their answers. Stress the importance of answering from their own perspective since there are no right or wrong answers. Remind the class that values can change over the course of one's life. Periodic reevaluations are helpful.

To make scoring easier, you may wish to prepare an answer sheet which will eliminate the need to turn pages back and forth.

After students have finished scoring their surveys, have class members identify their top three values. Review the definitions on pages 36 and 37. Remind students that a combination of their values must be considered when choosing a career.

Activities:

In a dialogue with friends and families, students begin to learn their values and passions.

Gender equity activity:

Poll the class to see if there seems to be any relationship between gender stereotypes and values identification. How many males included helping others in their top three values? How many females? How many females had power as their top value versus the males? What about money?

If any trends are evident, discuss why this might be. Young women, for example, are more likely than young men to value helping others. And, quite often, young men will be more comfortable saying they value power than will young women. Why do students think this is so? Is it biological? Societal conditioning?

Is there any relationship between power and helping others? Who would be in a position to help more people, a nurse's aide or a chief surgeon?

To carry this concept further, read the children's picture book *My Way Sally* to the class. Winner of the 1989 Ben Franklin Award, this story is an allegory in which a compassionate foxhound learns that power and leadership can be used to help others. The issues addressed in the Afterward on page 47 of *My Way Sally* would make for lively class discussion.

Follow-up:

Suggest that students have their parents, siblings, or boy/girlfriend also take the work values survey (on a separate piece of paper). Do they have the same work values? Different ones? This can open new fields of communication. It is also interesting to discuss in class how students' values compare to those of these "significant others." Quite often, brothers and sisters have very different work values, even though they were raised by the same parents in the same household. Why do students think this is so?

> *Students created "value totems" and then orally presented their belief systems. Many of the totems were works of art.*
>
> –John Fishburne
> Teacher
> Cascade High School
> Leavenworth, Washington

OF SPECIAL NOTE:

This Work Value Survey is an activity that helps students identify and evaluate the kinds of preferences they have in relationship to career or work choice. For instance, some students will find they value independence, while other may value security. The individuals who value independence will not want to work in an environment that is too restrictive or set-in-its-ways. On the other hand, the student who values security would probably want to find a career where the work is steady and predictable. A Work Value Survey merely helps an individual measure his or her priorities, predictions, and inclinations.

If you are questioned about teaching "Values," the following quote from *Newsweek* magazine may be helpful:

> *For the ordinary citizen, virtue is easily confused with "values." Since personal values differ, Americans argue over whose values ought to be taught. But "values" is a morally neutral term that merely indicates preference and can be quite banal. To choose vanilla over chocolate is not the same as deciding how to raise children though both express values. A virtue, by contrast, is a quality of character by which individuals habitually recognize and do the right thing. "Instead of talking about family values," says James Wilson of UCLA, "everyone would be better off talking about virtues that a decent family tries to inculcate.*

Kenneth L. Woodward
Newsweek magazine, June 13, 1994

Strengths and Personality

Page 38-43   Page 17-19

Learning objective:

To help students identify and understand their work behavioral style as an important trait to consider when evaluating their interests.

Presentation:

You may need to review the definitions on page 39 before students complete that exercise. A number are included in the vocabulary list for this chapter.

Once they have completed the exercises on pages 39, 41 and 42, ask each dominant style to go to a different corner of the room. For example, all the students whose style is (a) are dominant, the (b's) are influencing, etc. Then read the descriptions on page 43 together. Many students will nudge each other as they agree with these very basic descriptions.

Point out that the higher the number of responses in each of the letters the more prominent those characteristics might be. Also be sure to remind the students that there are 19 different profiles in this assessment system. Very few people are pure dominance or pure steadiness. Each person has varying degrees of each of these characteristics. Without taking the actual assessment tool (a self-scoring seven-minute activity) it would be hard to know just what your real profile is. The purpose of the activity is to introduce the student to another dimension of personality that should be taken into account when choosing a career and aiming for the highest level of satisfaction.

For further applications of this theory see pages 162-165 in *Career Choices* and pages 228-231 in this *Instructor's Guide.*

The assessment instruments and training are available through Academic Innovations. For more information, you can contact Academic Innovations (800) 967-8016.

For ordering information on the Personal Profile System see page 351 of this *Guide.*

Resources:

William Moulton Marston, *Emotions of Normal People.* Persona Press, Inc. Minneapolis, MN.

Author's note

In 1983 I attended a week-long training seminar for community agency leaders sponsored by the IBM Corporation. During that week, we were introduced to the latest systems and management techniques that would help us better manage our charitable agencies. Of particular interest to me was the Personal Profile System assessment tool that major corporations use to help them determine what jobs employees will do best.

For more than a dozen years, I have used this instrument with my staff, our local Junior League, and in various consulting and personal situations. It is one of the most usable and powerful assessments I have ever seen.

Of particular interest to me was how people who were dissatisfied in their work were able to change either their job or job description to better fit their work behavioral style. When this took place, I saw greater job satisfaction and therefore higher productivity.

Pretty soon I became somewhat intuitive as to what a person's style was and this impacted who I hired for specific jobs in my agency. Also as I counseled young people on career choice, this factor was an important component when suggesting different careers for possible research.

Therefore, it is an understatement to say I was excited when the Carlson Corporation gave me permission to adapt their research into a simplified evaluation exercise. I feel that this information is extremely important to young people and will give them another means of knowing themselves and making the right choices. Major corporations have used the assessment as an important management tool for 20 years. It is exciting to see it now available to young people.

I recommend that you consider giving the actual assessment to your students. Academic Innovations distributes these. For ordering information see page 351.

I would also like to recommend using the Personal Profile System assessment tool (the one used by corporations) for staff development and team building with faculty and school personnel. It will be one of the most productive staff training and sharing sessions you have ever conducted. As your team begins understanding everyone's strengths (and yes, weaknesses too), task force assignments and committee work will become more productive and satisfying for everyone.

And, yes, I have a dream. It is my hope that once instructors learn their own personal style of working and communicating, they will go on to identify the style of each of their students by using the assessment tool; then they will better understand how each student learns and works and therefore they will be able to nurture and reward those individual strengths in the academic setting.

– Mindy Bingham

Your Strengths

Page 44-45   Page 20

Learning objective:
To help students identify their strengths and, in so doing, raise their self-esteem.

Presentation suggestions:
Review the list of possible strengths, and ask the class to add any other traits. Divide the class into groups of four, and ask group members to help each other identify their strengths. Then have students individually complete the chart on page 45.

Activities:
Write the list of adjectives from page 44 of *Career Choices* and cut them into slips with one word per piece of paper. Have each student draw three slips. Using each adjective, students complete the following statement (in writing):

I am _____ when I _____.
            (chosen adjective)

Examples:

I am decisive when I choose my wardrobe.

I am spontaneous when I play with my little brother.

I am sensitive when my friends have a problem.

Ask students to share one of their statements at the next class meeting. This exercise should help them realize that, in some circumstances, they are capable of displaying almost any character trait. That should increase their self-esteem.

I had students ask adults at home to list their child's strengths and weaknesses, while I wrote each student a letter telling him or her what I thought their strengths and one of their weaknesses were—in a very positive vein, of course. The students seemed to appreciate the interest, and several had a chance for good interaction at home because of this activity.

– Mary Nan Johnson
9th grade English teacher
Lake Brantley High School
Altamonte Springs, Florida

Energizer:

Divide the class into the same groups of four as above. Make copies of the situations on page 154 of this *Guide* and give one copy to each group. Ask them to choose one of the problems described and then, based on their individual strengths, to decide who would play what role and what their solution would be.

Ask each group to report back to the class.

This exercise should be useful for getting across the concepts of (1) how various kinds of strengths have different values and (2) the importance of teamwork—and shared responsibility to occupations in a changing society.

Using Langston Hughes' poem "Dreams," I have the students replace lines 3 and 4 and lines 7 and 8 with their own creations. Then after they've written their Acrostic Poem, I have them place them back-to-back on construction paper; attached to a wire coat hanger with red yarn and we hang them as mobiles around the room.

– Felicity Swerdlow
9th Grade English Teacher
Duarte High School
Duarte, California

Optional

Alice in Wonderland
by Lewis Carroll
Read after completing
pages 28-45 in *Career Choices*

Pages 43-46

Class Exercise

Before choosing a situation, review the four top strengths of each group member.
Record below.

Name   Strengths

_____   _____

_____   _____

_____   _____

_____   _____

Situation 1
Your group is stranded behind enemy lines, and you need to cross five miles of dangerous terrain in order to get back to your side. You are likely to be stopped. The enemy speaks English. What would you do, and what roles would each group member play?

Situation 2
Your boss has assigned your group to develop a new product and a plan for selling it. What would the product be, and who would be in charge of what?

Situation 3
An industrial polluter is dumping the wastes from its factory into the river that flows through the middle of your lovely city. Your group decides to expose the company's illegal activities and force it to stop poisoning the water supply. What would you do, and what jobs would you assign to each group member?

Situation 4
Your group decides to hold a fund raiser for the new homeless shelter in your town. What would you do, and what jobs would you assign to each group member?

Name That Skill

Page 46-47   Page 21

Learning objective:

To help students identify the skills they have developed over the years.

Presentation suggestions:

Be sure that the class understands the difference between an aptitude, an interest, and a skill.

An "aptitude" is best thought of as potential for being able to do something. A "skill" is competence in doing something. An "interest" is a desire to do something. Some aptitudes, however, especially among young people, may not have been tapped. For example, a student may have an aptitude for math, but, if he or she has not taken the necessary classes, that aptitude is probably not yet a skill. An interest is something a person enjoys, but it does not necessarily involve an aptitude or skill. Millions of people, for example, have an interest in professional football, but few have the necessary aptitude or skills to take part.

Divide the class into small groups where individuals can help each other identify their skills following the exercise on page 47.

Students with low self-esteem may have trouble identifying any of their skills or accomplishments. As a class, identify things any class member could accomplish and break them down into the skills involved.

Also point out that each student does excel in some things.

> Example: Getting to school on time may involve coordinating a wardrobe, compiling books and papers, making breakfast or fixing lunch, negotiating a ride with one's older sister, and so on.

If your class is mature and supportive enough, you might try a "hot seat" exercise in which class members take turns voicing the skills of a particular student. Unkind remarks—or deafening silence—can be devastating to the student's self-esteem, so judge your group carefully. It's also helpful to allow a few minutes for the class to consider its answers.

Or bring a rubber ball or bean bag to class. Arrange the group in a circle so the ball can be tossed from student to student. The "pitcher" throws the ball to the person of his or her choice. That person must then say something nice about the tosser, and then throw the ball to another individual, who must in turn say something nice and so on. Again, this exercise requires a supportive group.

Skills Identification

Page 48

Page 22

Learning objective:
To help students identify and understand standard skills categories.

Presentation suggestions:
Write the list of skills on page 48 on the board and discuss them to make sure students understand the meaning of each term.

Have the class try to think of ways in which each of these skills might be used in a certain activity, such as giving a party.

To demonstrate that all skills are necessary and valuable, have the class consider all of the skills that go into a project such as building a house or publishing a newspaper. The plumber and the painter are as essential as the architect. The reporters may get more glory, but where would they be without the typesetters, truckdrivers, and so on.

Remind the class that they will continue to acquire new skills throughout their lives.

Activities:
List the skills of several student volunteers on the board. Then ask the class to think of potential careers for someone with these skills.

Examples:

Drawing, Sewing: fashion designer, architect (sewing is a spatial skill), display artist

Math, persuading: business executive, sales representative, math teacher

Follow-up:
Interest and aptitude tests can be helpful in skills identification. If your school does not provide them, you may at least want to inform students that they are available elsewhere. Young people, especially, can benefit from these tests since they may open up whole new fields for exploration.

Mental aptitude tests usually measure verbal, math, and reasoning abilities. Physical aptitude tests measure such things as finger dexterity and manual dexterity.

The Kuder interest inventory helps determine suitable career categories by asking students to identify which of three items they like most, and which they like least.

The COPs, another interest inventory, asks students to indicate their feelings about given statements ("like a lot" to "don't like at all"). In addition to determining job categories, it lists specific jobs for which the student may be suited.

Resources:

Kuder: Science Research Associates, 1540 Page Mill Road, Palo Alto, CA 94304.

COPs: California Occupational Preference System, Edits, P.O. Box 7234, San Diego, CA 92107.

Other well-known career interest inventories include:

Harrington-O'Shea Career Decision-making System: American Guidance Service, Publishers' Building, Circle Pines, MN 55014.

Ohio Vocational Interest Survey: Psychological Corporation, 555 Academic Court, San Antonio, TX 78204.

Strong-Campbell Interest Inventory: Consulting Psychologists Press, 577 College Avenue, Palo Alto, CA 94306.

Roles, Occupations, and Vocations

Page 49   No Workbook
                      Page

Learning objective:

To help students identify and evaluate their roles, occupations, and vocations.

Presentation suggestions:

With the class, review the definitions for each term on page 49. Point out that this may be the easiest ring to complete on their charts, since what you do is much more obvious than who you are.

Activities:

Divide the group into pairs and have them introduce each other to the class without using roles, occupations, or vocations. Instruct the rest of the class to respond with whistles or boos if any titles (student, sister, basketball player, or whatever) sneak into the introduction. It sounds easy, but it's not. When a hundred highly educated, professional people came together and tried this experiment, they found it extremely frustrating. (If it seems more appropriate in your classroom, you could have students introduce themselves instead of dividing into pairs.)

Even though we usually define ourselves by what we do, it is important that students realize this is only a portion of who we are. It is a measure of self-esteem to be able to identify and value the traits that make us unique. Then, no matter what a person's occupation, he or she will feel confident of holding a special place in the world.

Chapter Follow-up:

Once this exercise is complete, ask the students to turn back to page 27 in *Career Choices* and in a different color ink write the additional characteristics they've identified while working through Chapter 2.

As a homework assignment, ask each student to decide on three heroes/heroines (present-day or historical figures). In class, ask them to choose and complete a bull's eye chart for one figure. When the chart is complete, ask the students to underline characteristics that parallel their own chart and to circle those characteristics on the hero's or heroine's chart they would like to acquire as they mature and gain experience.

Once this is done, write this statement on the board:

> *"The people we admire most are a reflection of our inner selves."*
>
> – Joseph Campbell

Do your students agree or disagree with this statement? If many of the characteristics on their hero's or heroine's charts are either underlined or circled, this could be accurate.

With our theme, "Search for Identity," we use the mandala to show each student's "sun side" and "shadow side." After that search for self, they can better understand characters such as Mitty ("Secret Life of Walter Mitty") and Loisel ("The Necklace"). Also, their identity poems were great and their poetry was so beautiful that some were published.

– Claudia Gerhardt
English Department Chair
Hillside Junior High School
Boise, Idaho

Message Center

Page 50-53

Page 23-24

Learning objective:

To make students more aware of the messages—verbal and otherwise—they get from society and from significant people in their lives, and to help them understand how these messages can affect the way they feel about their future or their potential.

Presentation suggestions:

If students become aware of the messages they are getting from their friends, family, or the world at large, they will be better able to base decisions about their future on their own desires and abilities. Discuss this concept, and then ask students to complete the exercise on their own.

Activities:

Ask a school counselor or psychologist to talk with the class about this topic.

Invite a panel of parents to complete the exercise and then tell the class how the messages they were given had an impact on their career and life choices.

Discuss in class the messages society gives individuals based on their gender, race, age, physical appearance, physical ability, social status, economic status, intellectual capacity, educational achievement, and so on.

Compositions:

"The Person Who Has Most Affected My Life."

"The Brainwashing of the American Mind: How Media Impacts Our Culture."

Debate:

"Does society give girls and boys different messages?"

If you ask a group of students to debate this question, do not put all boys on one side and all girls on the other. Be sure each side is co-ed.

Optional

Pages 61-68

Life
by Nan Terrell Reed
Read after completing page 52 in *Career Choices*

Excerpt from *Self-Reliance*
by Ralph Waldo Emerson
Read after completing page 53 in *Career Choices*

Character Analysis

Activity:

Throughout the course, you might include the Character Analysis Worksheet on page 163 of this *Guide* for each reading assignment. It can be used in a variety of ways:

> Ask students to complete the worksheet for their favorite character.

> Choose three to five main characters and divide the class into small groups to analyze one or all of them using the worksheet.

Writing Fiction:

When asking students to write fiction, suggest they use the worksheet to develop their character(s) before they begin to write.

> *For explanations of each of the concepts on the Character Analysis Worksheet refer to the following pages in the text* Career Choices:

> **Bull's Eye Chart:** *page 27*
> **Question 1:** *pages 15-16*
> **Question 2:** *pages 18-21*
> **Question 3:** *page 20*
> **Question 4:** *pages 66-71*
> **Question 5:** *pages 196-227*
> **Question 6:** *pages 60-61*

For the writer, character analysis is an essential task. However, remind students that it is also a vital skill for everyone as we choose our friends and associates.

Brainstorm which relationships require this in-depth analysis.

Examples:	Employer	Employee
	Spouse	Mentor
	Best friend	Business partner

Energizer:

Divide the class into pairs. Ask each pair to roleplay a dialogue between two individuals considering going into business together. Point out that choosing the right business partner may be as important as selecting the right marriage partner. Suggest that students refer to the Character Analysis Worksheet for ideas about the type of questions to ask. You may want to brainstorm how the questions could be rephrased to elicit a certain response. This could be assigned as a written follow-up assignment.

Another Energizer:

Ask a mature student population to complete a Character Analysis Worksheet for a drug dealer.

Optional

I Know Why the Caged Bird Sings
   by Maya Angelou
Sympathy
   by Paul Laurence Dunbar
Read after completing pages 28-53 in *Career Choices*

Pages 47-60

Character Analysis Worksheet

Character _____ Story _____

```
                    (concentric circles diagram)

                              Name

                            Passions

                             Values

                      Personality and
                         Strengths

                        Skills and
                        Aptitudes

                   Roles, Occupations
                     and Vocations
```

1. Why do they work?

_____

2. How would they define success?_____

_____

3. How do they make decisions?_____

_____

4. How balanced is their lifestyle?_____

_____

5. What limitations, either self-imposed or societally imposed, do they face? _____

_____

6. What is their mission in life?_____

_____

Instructor's Notes:

Chapter 3

Lifestyles of the Satisfied and Happy

The next five chapters of this book are meant to help students answer the question "What do I want?" It's not an easy task. Perhaps that is why most career and life planning books devote more time to getting what you want rather than to determining what that is.

We strongly believe that establishing and consolidating identity and setting goals based on that identity are essential parts of making a career choice. Without these preliminary steps, it is impossible to choose wisely. Students are likely to base their decisions more on what their friends or parents want them to do or what their favorite TV character does than on what will be most satisfying for them.

In this chapter, students are asked to consider their ideal lifestyle. While career, family, leisure activities, friends, and spiritual concerns are part of everyone's lifestyle, which elements are most important is something each individual must determine for him- or herself.

Career choice has a huge impact on the other aspects of lifestyle. In fact, for many people, lifestyle is determined in large part by career. We think it is essential, therefore, that students give careful consideration to the way they want to live before deciding on a career path.

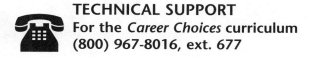

TECHNICAL SUPPORT
For the *Career Choices* curriculum
(800) 967-8016, ext. 677

Maslow's Triangle

Page 56-59

Page 26

Learning objective:
To teach students Maslow's hierarchy of needs and help them understand its impact on their identity and self-esteem.

Presentation suggestions:
Offer an overview of Maslow's triangle, explaining how survival needs must be met before a person can be concerned about safety, how people must feel safe before they can care about social needs, how they seek esteem when their social needs have been met, and how, finally, they can become self-actualized.

Discuss the difference between a *want* and a *need*. Many people, especially those with low self-esteem, do not see anything beyond the most basic means of survival as legitimate needs for themselves. Explain that everyone needs—and has a right to expect or ask for—respect, compassion, companionship, enjoyable experiences, acceptance by others and by oneself.

Activities:
Have students complete the exercise on page 59 on their own. Once they have identified where they are on Maslow's triangle, ask them to begin thinking how they can continue to move up the triangle. What support can they seek? What action can they take? The rest of this course should help them identify possibilities.

Note of caution:
If you are dealing with a high-risk population, it will become very apparent to the learners that they are stuck at the bottom rungs of the triangle. Take extra time with this group or these individuals to talk about possible plans for feeling safe and secure, getting support, and gaining control over their lives. If appropriate, suggest privately that some students might like to see a school counselor.

Since this section has the potential to identify individuals who may need extra counseling and support, discuss how you should handle this with your principal and counselor ahead of time so you can respond to a student's needs immediately.

Reading assignment:
The fable *Pandora's Box*. Afterward, discuss how hope drives us to improve our lives.

How Do You Want to Be Remembered?

Page 60-61   Page 27

Learning objective:

To help students identify an overall goal or mission for their lives.

Presentation suggestions:

Explain to the class that people have a strong need to be identified with something that is "bigger than themselves." Allow students two or three days to think about this assignment. It's something that requires some thought. Remind students that this is a very personal assignment, not something they should decide with a group of friends. Remind them, too, that their goal or mission may change over time.

Activities:

Invite three "self-actualizers" from the community—preferably senior citizens—to talk with the class about their mission in life, how and when they chose it, the sacrifices they've made as a result, how they would advise a young person, and so on. (Be sure to tell the guests what you want them to talk about a few days ahead of time so they can be prepared.) If possible, invite an activist or someone with a high profile in the community, a successful businessperson, and a private person with a satisfying personal life as your guests.

English/Language Arts:

Complete the activity described on page 169. Ask for volunteers to share their letters. Take a poll. What percentage of students wrote about something they did or something they accomplished? What percentage wrote about an accomplishment in a career sense?

One success we have had is with "How Do You Want to be Remembered?" in Chapter 3. In addition to talking about the epitaphs, we have a picture of an ancient Memory Bottle that was discovered in China. After looking at the picture and trying to identify the items in the bottle, we discussed the different ways that different cultures have to remember themselves after their death. Students are then asked to reflect on what they would like their descendants to remember about them. After listing the items vertically on a sheet of paper, they are given the homework assignment to create a memory bottle (either visual or written)…. The "bottles" brought in by most students were far beyond my expectations. Some students used arts and crafts tools to create a masterpiece.

– Sharon Hurwitz
English Teacher and Technology Facilitator
Bethel High School
Hampton, Virginia

Follow-up:

Students will be asked to reiterate their mission in life at the very end of the book. At that time, turn back and again administer the exercise that follows.

I began my unit, "My Dream: Why and How?" by doing a hands-on activity. My students developed huge collages or posters to represent their dreams for their lives, and because I do a unit on aging (using the poem "Warning" from **When I Grow Old, I Shall Wear Purple** *as a springboard) I ask them to project dreams for an entire lifetime. I display these and refer back to them for the entire year. At the end of the year, we discuss these initial dreams and note any changes. The dreams are also identified in terms of the Maslow hierarchy. Are the students closer to self-actualization now? Usually the answer is yes! My students' most common observation: "For the first time, I feel a class actually relates to me. I can use this 'stuff' in my life..."*

– Sarah Marsh
12th grade Applied English teacher
Burley High School
Burley, Idaho

When using "I Shall Not Pass This Way Again" we had our students write their own version as suggested on page 73 of **Possibilities.** *Then the students prepared illustrated posters with their poem and we put them up around the room to remind them of the goals they were setting for the year. We extended the activity by recognizing the uniqueness of each student and the student of the week program.*

– Suzanne M. Reese
Teacher/Gifted Liaison
R.L. Turner High School
Carrollton, Texas

Optional

Possibilities

Pages 69-71

Growing Older
by R.G. Wells

Read as an introduction to the activity on page 169 of this *Instructor's Guide*

I Shall Not Pass This Way Again

Read after completing pages 60-61 in *Career Choices*

Looking into the Future

Allow an entire class period for this exercise. Ask students to have paper and pens on their desks before you begin.

Turn down the lights and close the doors and windows. If your room is unavoidably noisy, try to find a quieter one.

Speak slowly and quietly, pausing where indicated. Your script follows.

Relax and settle into your chair. Place your feet flat on the floor. Close your eyes. Clear your mind by imagining the space between your eyes. (Pause at least 15 seconds)

Pay attention to your breathing. (Pause) Inhale slowly, filling your lungs with air. (Pause) Exhale slowly. (Pause) (Repeat two more times)

Take a few slow, deep, deliberate breaths. As you exhale, tell yourself to relax and let go. (Pause long enough for three or four deep breaths)

Feel your body relax (Pause) from your face all the way down to your legs and toes. (Pause) Feel the pleasant warm and tingly feeling of relaxed muscles. (Pause)

Now project yourself into the future. (Pause) You see calendar pages flipping. (Pause) It's 1999. (Pause) The year 2000. (Pause) 2010. (Pause) 2020. (Pause) 2030. (Pause) How old are you now?

The calender continues to flip. Stop the calendar at the year you plan to retire.

You are there now. Take a look around. (Pause) Where are you? What is the setting? (Pause) Who is there with you? Who are the important people in your life? (Pause) Look in a mirror. What do you look like? (Longer pause)

You hear the doorbell ring. When you go to the door, a mail carrier hands you a letter. You open the letter. It is from someone important to you, commending you, thanking you, and praising you. You feel very good about this letter. (Pause) You feel successful, (Pause) fulfilled, (Pause) and acknowledged. Enjoy that good feeling for a moment. (Pause 30-60 seconds)

What does the letter say? (Pause a minute or two)

Now open your eyes and, without saying a word, pick up your pen. . .(Wait until everyone picks up their pen) now write that letter. Begin now.

NOTE TO TEACHERS: Many writers put themselves into a trancelike state in order to create. They become immersed in the time and place they are writing about and become closely identified with their characters. This exercise may provide your students with their first experience of this "altered" creative state. After the students have turned in their letters, discuss this part of the creative process. Ask students how they felt during the exercise, and whether they have ever experienced this "altered" creative state.

Components of Lifestyle

Page 62-63   Page 28

Learning objective:

To teach students to project into the future and to realize the diversity of lifestyle options open to them.

Presentation suggestions:

The necessity of being able to project into the future and realize how today's actions may have long-term consequences is a key theme of this curriculum. This ability has been shown to be a key factor in preventing teen parenting, dropping out of school, and drug use. The present exercise provides another opportunity for students to practice this skill.

Explain to the class the importance of defining their desired lifestyle before choosing a career because career usually dictates lifestyle. This will not be an easy exercise for most students. (Explain this *after* they have made an attempt to complete it.) Instruct them not to be frustrated if they cannot finish in one sitting. Students may need to come back to this as they work through the remainder of the book, adding elements or readjusting their plans. Stress, too, that it is a good idea to re-evaluate their lifestyle goals throughout their lives.

You may need to remind the students that they'll need to draw on their fantasies and imaginations to complete this exercise. This is the first step in creating a vision. (Remember the formula for success: Vision plus Energy equals Success.)

Composition:

Once the chart on page 63 is complete, ask them to write an essay *"A Day in My Life in _____" (year)*. Choose a year when students will be between the ages of 30 and 45.

Debate:

Which should come first—lifestyle choice or career choice?

Happiness is a Balanced Lifestyle

Page 64-65

No Workbook Page

Learning objective:

To help students identify the components of a balanced lifestyle.

Presentation suggestions:

Discuss the various concepts of a balanced lifestyle as described on pages 64 and 65.

Activities:

The spiritual aspect of lifestyle is, for many people, the most difficult to define. It's an extremely personal matter, and can mean different things to different people. In December 1989, *Lear's* magazine published "Making the Spiritual Connection," which included fifteen short, thoughtful essays on the topic from a variety of well-known writers and thinkers. We suggest having the class read the article (your public library should have the magazine on CD-ROM or microfiche) and then write an essay of their own on the topic.

Reading Assignment:

Having Our Say; The Delany Sisters' First 100 Years, by Sarah and A. Elizabeth Delany with Amy Hill Hearth, Dell Publishing, New York, NY 1994.

In *Having Our Say*, Bessie, age 101, and her sister Sadie, age 103, share humorous and poignant anecdotes of the last 100 years. This inspiring memoir offers a rare glimpse into the early Civil Rights movement and the lives of women of achievement and wisdom.

The Modified Maslow Triangle

Page 66-69   Page 29

Learning objective:

To help students understand and identify their needs and to appreciate the desirability of having a balanced internal and external, personal and professional, private and public life.

Presentation suggestions:

Present the modified triangle as described in the book. If students grasped the meaning of the Maslow triangle discussed earlier, this new concept should not be too difficult. Make sure they understand the difference between external and internal needs. Emphasize that it is quite possible to be at different levels on each side of the triangle. That, in fact, is how to determine if a life is out of balance.

Break the class into small groups and ask them to discuss Emma's and Isaac's problems and try to find solutions for them. Then have the groups evaluate Joanie's lifestyle and discuss what she might do to bring her life back into balance, and the trade-offs she might have to make.

Resources:

Mindy Bingham and Sandy Stryker, *More Choices: A Strategic Planning Guide for Mixing Career and Family.* Advocacy Press, 1987. See ordering information on page 350.

Optional

Red Geraniums
by Martha Haskell Clark
Read after completing pages 66-69 in *Career Choices*

Pages 74-75

What About Your Life?

Page 70-71   Page 30

Learning objective:

To personalize the balanced lifestyle evaluation process and help students realize the effect outside forces can have on a person's life.

Presentation suggestions:

Ask students to review the questions at the top of the page and write a paragraph about their current situation before shading the triangle to represent the balance in their own lives.

Activities:

Have students interview a parent or another adult, then write a paragraph about this person's lifestyle and shade in a triangle to represent the balance.

As a class, talk about the chart for a homeless person. Obviously, he or she must be solely concerned with basic survival needs. What causes homelessness? There are both personal (drug abuse, emotional illness) and societal causes. Have the class discuss some of the latter.

Examples:

Lack of educational opportunities

Welfare "reform"

Scarcity of unskilled jobs

The minimum wage as it relates to the cost of housing

Inadequate facilities or programs to deal with the chemically addicted or the emotionally ill

Decreasing numbers of low-cost rooming houses because they are torn down to make room for office buildings

Can the class imagine how societal issues could have an impact on their lifestyle?

What happens when a pregnant woman works for a company that does not offer maternity leave?

What if a working single parent can't find affordable, competent child care?

What happens if someone who can't afford or doesn't qualify for medical insurance becomes seriously ill?

What if a person working at the best job he or she can find doesn't earn enough to rent an apartment?

English/Language Arts:

After the above discussions, ask students to write a fictional account in the first-person narrative form of a homeless individual's typical day.

Instructor's Notes:

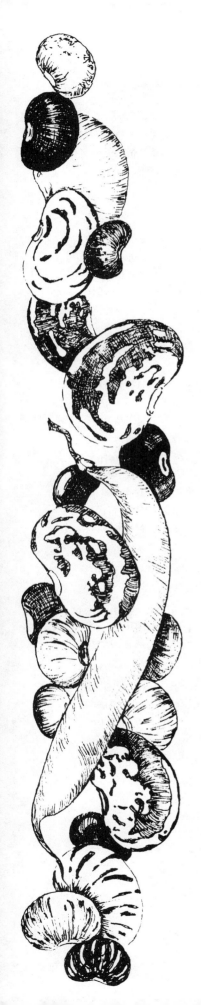

Chapter 4

What Cost This Lifestyle?

Students are likely to know that any given lifestyle has financial costs. Like many adults, however, they have probably not considered the psychological costs or the costs in terms of commitment to a given career. The goal of this chapter is to instill an understanding of *all three* costs. Emphasis should be on the importance of finding the balance that is best suited to each individual.

As they work through the exercises in this chapter, students should begin to see how the different aspects relate to each other. For example, someone wanting a career that will support a lavish lifestyle must usually be willing to make huge commitments in terms of time and/or education.

Similarly, a career that offers a great deal of psychological satisfaction may not always be the one with the biggest financial payoff. As we move into the final years of this century, however, many people are finding that financial success is not all it was promised to be.

Optional

Pages 12-88

An expanded version of the Budget exercise from *Career Choices* **text**

Computerized
Correction Key
for
Lifestyle Math

Optional

Pages 76-79

The Mills of the Gods
Read after reading the Ivy Elms' story on pages 74-75 in *Career Choices*

Your Budget

Page 77-94

Page 32-43

Learning objective:

Before they can make a wise career decision, students must take into account the cost of living. This exercise should give them a realistic view of how many financial considerations will be important when deciding on a career path. It should also start them thinking about their own financial priorities. Do they really want that expensive sports car? How important are exotic vacations? If they had to choose one or the other, which would it be? Are they willing to work hard enough to have either or both?

Presentation suggestions:

This exercise can be approached in different ways. If you have the time, it is well worth spending it to do a thorough, investigative job in which students come up with their own figures. If time is at a premium, however, students can simply use the charts provided to come up with generally accurate figures.

Go over the exercise in class beforehand to make sure students understand what they should do and how to go about it. As an example, it may be helpful to work the complete exercise as a class by choosing a composite family; otherwise known as budget-by-consensus. To do this, complete each section, soliciting input from the class, and try to come up with figures that represent the average lifestyle expectations of the class.

Then as students complete their own budget, you may want to review them section by section, stopping each time to discuss and brainstorm possibilities.

This is an extremely important writing assignment. Budgets are much more realistic and manageable when presented and communicated in written form. Once students have experimented and experienced this written activity, they are going to be much more adept at it as adults.

If you do decide to take the longer route, you will probably want to bring in classified sections from local newspapers and catalogs from major department stores, utility bills, and various other resources for class reference. Students can use these to determine the cost of appropriate housing, transportation, equipment, furnishings, and the like. They may get other figures by asking parents or other adults, checking prices in stores, and so on.

Having calculators available would also be helpful.

Optional

 Pages 12-88 For the most detailed version of the budget exercise, you will want to use *Lifestyle Math: Your Financial Planning Portfolio.*

Author's note

Between 1976 and 1983, I taught evening classes at a local private college for soon-to-graduate seniors. One of the exercises I used with these students was a version of this budget exercise. I was always struck with the response I got from my students. It was usually one of shock and, because they were just completing a degree in a lower paying helping profession, sometimes anger. "Why didn't someone do this with us before?" they'd ask bewildered. They had just completed a degree yet, for many of them, the average salary of their chosen profession could not meet their lifestyle expectations.

This is one of the most critical exercises you can do with your students...the younger the better. We have successfully completed a version of this with sixth graders. Make it interesting, hands-on, and fun. Don't hurry through it. It will probably be one of the favorite activities of the course and perhaps one of the most important.

– Mindy Bingham

Checklist of Resources for Budgeting Exercise

Depending on how extensive you want to make this exercise, the following items will be helpful:

☐ One complete classified section from the newspaper for each student in the class

☐ Sample utility bills

☐ Catalogs of major department stores such as Sears

☐ Sample weekly food bills for families of various sizes

☐ Vacation brochures

☐ Calculator(s)

☐ Internet access

Family Profile

Before they begin to make their budgets, students must project themselves into the future. The exercise is intended to help them make career decisions, after all. Emphasize that this budget should be based on the way they would like to live after they have completed their education and are working at the job of their choice. Students should assume they are at least 29 years old for the purposes of this exercise.

The cost of living also depends to a large extent on the number of people in the household. Do students plan to be married? Will they have children? How many? What ages?

Finally, since costs vary greatly depending on where they will be living (the budget of an executive in Manhattan will be very different from that of a farmer in Iowa, for example), students must also consider this aspect of their future lives.

Encourage students to fantasize a bit here. They should consider the way of life they think would be most rewarding, not simply the lifestyle they think is most probable for someone in their circumstances. Where would they really like to live? What would be their ideal family? What kind of home would they have? Where would they vacation?

A word of caution before you begin. Because the lifestyles of the most visible individuals tend to be lavish, try to encourage students to be somewhat realistic in their projections while at the same time respecting the students who insist they are going to have a lifestyle very different from their family's. One of the purposes of this total curriculum is to show how with education, planning, and hard work individuals can realize their dreams.

Once students decide on their future families, you may choose to introduce a hitch into the planning process. Tell them that for whatever reason they are suddenly single. In most cases, they will find themselves single parents. If they look at you aghast, remind them that nearly 50 percent of today's children are raised in single-parent families at some point in their lives.

This aspect of the exercise is of particular importance to the females in your class. Otherwise many will complete the exercise assuming they will be married when, in reality, a high percentage will be the sole support of their families.

Housing

Ask students to consider their ideal living situation. Would they own or rent? Have a mansion or a modest apartment? Once they've decided, have them go to the classified ads to find something suitable and see how much it costs. The charts on page 79 will be helpful.

To figure utility costs, ask students to brainstorm with you all the expenses that fall into this category. As a homework assignment, ask them to bring in sample utility bills from their own families.

Sample utility categories:

Gas

Electric

Heating fuel

Phone

Water

Trash

Cable

Activity:

Invite a realtor or mortgage broker to speak to the class on the costs of housing in the community and how to finance the first-time purchase of a home.

Optional

Pages 14-31

Transportation

Students should consider their desired mode of transportation in view of their living situation as well as their dreams. If they're planning to live in an area without much public transportation, for example, some kind of vehicle is probably necessary. City dwellers with access to taxis, buses, or subways, on the other hand, might not want or need to own a car.

If they feel the need to own a car, once again refer them to the classified section of the newspaper. Ask them to choose a make and model and figure the monthly payments.

What do they project will be their mileage per month? Once they have an idea of this figure, the chart on page 81 should help with factoring estimated gas and maintenance costs.

We had loan officers from local banks take students through the loan process after they had chosen a car, house, and occupation they'd be interested in pursuing. This was extremely beneficial.

    – Linda Wulff
       Chairperson, Communication Department
       Waupun High School
       Waupun, Wisconsin

Optional

Pages 32-42

Purchasing a Car on the Internet

Curriculum sequence: *(optional)*
After students have reviewed the classified section of the newspaper and have a good idea of the type of car they want to own, new or used.

Internet address/Directions: http://edmund.com
Web site description: This free site provides a thorough listing of all common automobile makes and models in the United States, both new and used, and their wholesale and retail prices. It also provides evaluative and consumer information on most models. In addition, there are a variety of informational articles of interest to the consumer purchasing a car.

Learning objective:
Students will learn how to acquire comprehensive, up-to-date information using the Internet for data retrieval.

Methodology:
Because the topic of car ownership is of such interest to the average young teen, this activity provides a wonderful opportunity to teach a variety of academic and critical thinking skills.

We recommend that students use the classifieds to begin the process of finding a car to purchase because this will still be the medium most available to the majority of them. Also, it provides an experience that is different from their web search and therefore an opportunity to compare and contrast these two experiences.

Ask students to go online and find the cost (wholesale and retail) of the car they want to buy (make, model and year).

Lesson extensions:
How to Surf the Internet: If students have not visited the Internet before, this is an ideal site. It is logically laid out but requires that the student make a variety of choices between hyperlinks to find the information they want.

Compare the Internet with the newspaper: What are the pros and cons of each for collecting data? Ask students as a class or in small groups to brainstorm the pros and cons of using each resource to gather data. Which one are they most likely to use when the time comes to purchase a car?

Project into the future: Ask how the Internet/World Wide Web will change the process of purchasing a car. What impact will this have on you? What impact will it have on your community? What impact will this have on society?

How the age of a car affects its price: Ask your students to chart the retail prices of the automobile make and model they have chosen for the last ten years. In the next column, figure the percentage change from year to year. Decide which year the price drops the most. *This information can also be presented on a computerized spreadsheet with charts.*

> **Discussion:** Then have students compare their findings. Is there a common age (say after three years) when the price ratio of used cars makes it such a good value that serious consideration should be given to purchasing a used car?

Clothing

Students are probably more aware of clothing costs than they are of any other kind. But their present wardrobes may not be appropriate for the kinds of jobs they hope to hold. They must take into consideration whether they'll need a uniform, special work clothes, or professional clothing. They may not have any idea how much children's clothing costs, or how quickly a child can outgrow a pair of shoes. You may be able to provide some of this information, or perhaps students with younger brothers and sisters or nieces and nephews can get figures to share with the class.

For their own clothing, remind students that they will not need to buy an entire wardrobe each year.

Writing assignment:

Ask students to break down their personal annual clothing budget item by item. Have them use either a current budget or their projected budget for this exercise.

Optional

Pages 43-47

Food

Food costs vary widely, depending on the size of the family, ages of children, and personal preferences. You might ask for volunteers from families of different sizes to bring in grocery tapes to share with the class.

Activity:

Ask students to plan a week's worth of menus for their fictional family. Then prepare a shopping list item by item. As a homework assignment ask them to go to the store and cost out this shopping list.

Sundries

Variations are also possible in this category. You might ask students to consider how much they spend now for such items as deodorant, shampoo, and makeup, how often they get their hair cut, and so on. They might ask their parents how often they need to buy toilet paper, soap, laundry detergent, and the like.

Activity:

An activity similar to the one in the food section could be completed for sundries except now complete it for a month's worth of supplies and services.

Optional

Pages 43-63

Entertainment and Recreation

This item can be easily overlooked or carried to an extreme. Ask students to think seriously about the "extras" that they would find most satisfying. What are their hobbies? Their passions?

Optional

Pages 64-67

Vacations

Around this point, students start becoming more cautious as their expense figures begin adding up. So many say, "We don't need a vacation!" This is the time to remind them that vacations are important for their physical and psychological health.

Activity:

Ask a travel agent to visit the class and talk about vacation expenses.

Invite someone to speak to the class about how he or she went to Europe on $40 a day.

Brainstorm as a class ways to have economical vacations such as:

>   Camping

>   Hosteling

>   House swapping

>   Visiting friends and relatives

Optional

Pages 68-70

Child Care

Ask students to research monthly costs for each of the child care arrangements listed on page 88 of *Career Choices*. You may want to divide the class up and give each small group a category to research.

It is important to point out that they should not assume "Grandma" will take care of their children. Failure to budget for this important expense could be disastrous.

Optional

Pages 71-73

Health Care

Refer to the chart on page 94 for average health care costs for families of various sizes.

Invite an insurance agent in to discuss health care costs, pensions, and savings plans.

Optional

Pages 74-75

Many of my female students planned not to get married ("didn't want the commitment"), but they also planned children out of wedlock. After the budgeting exercise many said, "I don't think I can afford to have a baby."

— Linda Fraser
Instructor, Tech Prep program
Edison High School
Minneapolis, MN

Furnishings

Refer students to catalogs of large department stores to get sample costs of furnishings.

Savings

Refer to the charts on page 91 of *Career Choices*.

Ask an insurance agent to share charts that show how tax-free deposits in pension accounts grow, especially when they are started at a young age.

Important: Planning for retirement is important and should be encouraged among young people. You will be doing your students a great service by spending time on this concept.

Miscellaneous

Ask the class to brainstorm other items that might go in this miscellaneous category.

Optional

The Savings Book
by Gary Soto

Read after completing page 89
in *Career Choices*

Pages 80-86

Optional

Pages 76-84

Your Budget Profile

Page 92

Page 42

Students will total their figures from the previous pages to get the average monthly expenses for their desired lifestyle.

Writing assignment:

Have students write a budget narrative describing, explaining or justifying each of their line items. For example:

Housing:

The cost of a three-bedroom, two-bath home in a nice area of the city is $109,000. Amenities include fenced yard, fireplace, and large family room. It is located in one of the best school districts. Utilities are a moderate expense because of the conservation efforts of my family. The only high expense in this category is the phone bill. My best friend and my mother live out of the state.

My favorite unit is Chapter Four, "What Cost This Lifestyle?" Your process is easy to understand with brief explanations, and I found your tables to be very realistic. Because this is an English class, I had the students write a paper at the end of the unit explaining what they had learned from the process. Some were wonderful!

– Dorette Kanengieter
11th and 12th grade English/Language Arts
and Applied Communications instructor
Owatona High School
Owatona, MN

Optional

Page 85

What Salary Will Support this Lifestyle?

Page 93

Page 42

One final step is required so that monthly expenses can be transposed into the salary required to support this lifestyle. Students must factor in taxes withheld from their paycheck.

The last figure on the page will be very important as they continue the career research process.

Spend one or two class periods at the career center so students can research and make a list of all the careers and jobs they can find that will support their desired lifestyle.

My students play a simulation game called "Living On Your Own." They get a job, pay a deposit on an apartment, pay their deposit on utilities, etc. Students clock in each day. A class period is worth eight hours of work. They learn to budget their money because they must pay out-of-pocket, and emergencies each week along with monthly and weekly bills. We devote one day a week to this activity although my students would like to do it every day. My students can't believe these activities are really English. I remind them that the skills learned in English (reading, writing, speaking and listening) are the skills we are using.

– Linda Spriggs
English Department Chairperson
Lithia Springs High School
Lithia Springs, Georgia

Optional

Pages 86-91

Hard Times Budget

Page 96

Page 43

Learning objective:

To learn to budget the more common way—by having a total figure available and allocating that figure among the line items.

Presentation:

Ask students to review the figure they arrived at on page 93. If this seems beyond what they think they will earn in a year, ask them to research that more appropriate figure and enter it on line (b). Now they must figure their net pay (take home) from this figure. The formula is as follows:

$$\underline{\hspace{3cm}} \div 12 = \underline{\hspace{3cm}}$$
(b) monthly salary

$$\underline{\hspace{3cm}} \times 80\% = \underline{\hspace{3cm}}$$
(b) monthly salary   net or take home pay

Depending upon the population you are working with, you might choose to assign this exercise using the figures for the following:

A person earning the minimum wage

A single parent living on AFDC
(Aid to Families with Dependent Children)

A single parent living on unemployment insurance

I do a scenario unit. Students pick a real life situation from a hat which may involve a single parent, a drop out, a college student, or a lawyer. Each must locate a job in the employment listings of a newspaper, prepare a budget, and go through an interview with me. By starting with real life situations, students realize they don't want the handicap of being a single parent or high school drop out.

– Dana L. Mayers
English teacher
Sequoyah Middle School
Edmond, Oklahoma

Optional

Pages 93-94

Some Sample Budgets

Page 97-101   Page 44-45

Learning objective:

To have students learn to budget the way most people do—by taking a given income and deciding how it should be allocated. An added observation will be the impact of career choice on lifestyle.

Presentation suggestions:

The earlier budget exercise gave students a chance to dream about their future lifestyle, an extremely important thing for them to do. In the real world, though, budgets do not determine income. Instead, it is quite the opposite. In this exercise, students can begin doing something they are likely to become very familiar with later in their lives: deciding how to live within a fixed income. We have presented five stories, each representing a fairly common situation.

> Phyllis is a single parent supporting her two children and herself on her income alone.
>
> Will is a single person living in subsidized housing provided, in his case, by the military.
>
> Jeff and Francie are a typical blue-collar couple.
>
> Carl and Ruth head a double-income professional household.
>
> Ben and Lynn represent the "traditional" two-parent, single-income family.

There are two ways to assign the exercise. You could ask students to complete it on their own, or you might break the class into groups and assign a particular budget to each. Group members can spend time discussing how the money should be allotted, doing necessary research, and so on. Then, when the class comes back together, each group can present its budget to the class.

Follow-up:

This is a good time to talk about dual earner families (both individuals work in low skill jobs without a career plan) versus dual career families (each individual has a career plan that focuses on the acquisition of additional skills and therefore to upgrade their desirability as an employee).

190

A Few Words About Poverty

Career Choices

Page 102-103

Workbook and Portfolio

Page 46

Learning objective:

To recognize the causes of poverty and to reduce the chances of becoming a poverty statistic.

Presentation suggestions:

Review the materials presented in the book in class. Then have students study the statistics on poverty. Ask them to select the statistic they found most startling and write a paragraph suggesting why this condition exists. Have students share their writings with the class. On the board, list any statistic mentioned by a student to see if there is a consensus concerning which facts are most disturbing.

Ask students to answer the questions on page 103, Could You Become a Poverty Statistic.

A word of caution: Be particularly sensitive to students who may be living in poverty. If you think this might present a problem, ask the school counselor to help facilitate this discussion. The important theme of the follow-up discussion should be that planning, energy, and a vision can enable individuals to work their way out of poverty.

Activities:

At the beginning of class, ask students to list the factors they think cause poverty. (Examples: lack of education, too few jobs, high cost of housing, inflation, the changing economy, lack of opportunity to succeed, inability to budget or to live within one's means)

Gender equity activity:

Ask a single parent on AFDC or a panel of single mothers living in poverty to talk with the class about such things as what they thought they were going to be when they were growing up, how they got into their present situation, and, if appropriate, what their plans are for the future.

This activity could be especially powerful for young women in the class who do not think it's necessary to prepare for a career because there will always be someone else willing and able to support them. Students of both sexes may feel that poverty is something that happens to other people, never to anyone they know. This activity could be both a cautionary tale and a lesson in empathy.

Composition:

Poverty Is Only a Divorce Away: A National Crisis for Women and Children.

Ask students to come up with recommended solutions.

After this assignment, brainstorm the reasons men usually end up as poverty statistics. One example is that they are replaced in industry by automated machinery or robots.

Debate:

Do men and women experience poverty differently?

Optional

Pages 95-97

Optional

Pages 87-94

Miss Rosie
by Lucille Clifton

Christmas Day in the Workhouse
by George R. Sims

Read after completing page 103 in *Career Choices*

Money Isn't Everything

Page 104-105   No Workbook
Page

Learning objective:

To explore the myth that money can make you happy.

Presentation suggestions:

It's a very common perception among young people that their lives would be perfect if only they were rich and famous. Statistics and anecdotal evidence, however, indicate that this is not so. Present the information to the class and have them discuss why they agree or disagree with the evidence. Ask students to list rich people or celebrities who have been in the news in recent years because of personal problems that would seem to indicate they are not entirely happy. Examples: Kelsey Grammer (chemical dependency), Darryl Strawberry (chemical dependency), Princess Stephanie of Monaco (divorce), Prince Charles and Princess Diana (adultery and divorce), Elizabeth Taylor (alcoholism and divorce), Kurt Cobain (suicide), Leona Helmsley (felony conviction), and so on.

Activities:

Bring in magazine articles or ask students to research and write a short paper based on an interview with a wealthy person who has recently had problems. Have them share their reports in class. The same phrase will probably turn up in interview after interview: money isn't everything.

If you know of a wealthy person in your community who has had to overcome personal tragedy, or who has given up "life in the fast lane" to do meaningful but unglamorous work, you might ask him or her to talk on this subject with the class.

Reading assignment:

The Gift of the Magi, by O. Henry

In this story of a young couple who sacrifice their most precious possessions for each other, how is happiness defined? Students will argue this one!

Optional

Pages 95-102

Gift of the Magi
by O. Henry
Read before you assign *Money Isn't Enough* on pages 104-105 in *Career Choices*

Psychological Costs — Sacrifices Versus Rewards

Page 106-110   Page 46-48

Learning objective:

To help students learn that there are sacrifices as well as rewards associated with every job and every lifestyle. This exercise should help them evaluate both aspects of any career they are considering and to decide whether or not it would be a wise choice.

Presentation suggestions:

Discuss the material presented in *Career Choices*, using Bert's story as an example. Ask the class to add to the answers provided if they can. Then break the class into small groups, and assign each to discuss Juan, Vincent, Sara, or Rose's story and then to answer the questions that follow. Bring the class back together, and have the groups summarize the story and report their answers to the questions. Allow discussion time for other students to disagree with a group, or to add to its answers. In summing up, be sure to emphasize how important it is for each student to evaluate his or her own values in conjunction with the careers presented. Students should see that, depending on a person's values, some sacrifices would be devastating, others not too hard to accept. Similarly, some rewards would be well worth any sacrifice for certain individuals, while for others the same rewards would be less than satisfying.

Activities:

Ask students to write a paragraph about the situation of a well-known professional person they know something about and to answer the questions from this exercise for that individual. Suggested individuals might be the president of the United States, governor of your state, or the mayor of your city.

Have a panel of people in different professions discuss the rewards and sacrifices involved in their jobs and what values are reflected in both areas. (Be sure to let your guests know what you want them to talk about ahead of time. They may not have given this much thought.)

Have students interview a parent or other adult on this topic.

Encourage students to watch some of the celebrity interview shows on TV, or bring in tapes if you can. In-depth interviews of the Barbara Walters or Mike Wallace variety often bring out this kind of information.

You Win Some,
You Lose Some

Page 111   Page 49

Learning objective:

To help students recognize the rewards and sacrifices of specific careers as they relate to values.

Presentation suggestions:

Have students complete the exercise individually, or break the class into small groups to discuss and come to agreement concerning which values would be rewarded and which would be sacrificed in each of the careers listed. Follow with class discussion.

Then have students go back and circle any careers that are compatible with their own values. That is, careers in which at least one of their top values matches the rewards, while none of their top three is listed as a sacrifice.

Students are now beginning to relate their own values to specific career choices.

Activities:

Have students list five careers they have considered for themselves in recent years and identify which values would be rewarded or sacrificed in each job.

The students are beginning to see that a career offers more than just an income. The psychological rewards are a new concept for many of them.
– Linda L. Poznanter
Careers Teacher
Oasis High School
Fallbrook, California

After-hours Rewards

Page 112-113   Page 50

Learning objective:

To demonstrate that values not satisfied on the job can be met with appropriate after-hours activities. This is an important concept, since few careers will be a perfect fit with a person's top values.

Presentation suggestions:

After presenting the materials and going over the examples, have students—individually or in pairs—complete the exercise. Discuss as a class. There is likely to be some disagreement. That's okay. The individual's perceptions are likely to be valid for her- or himself.

In the examples presented, a social worker would, of course, meet her or his need to help others. Creativity, too, would come into play through creative problem-solving in crisis situations. To meet a need for power, a social worker might consider being an officer in a community organization or political group.

A computer assembly worker might feel secure about working in the high tech industry. He or she is likely to work with many potential friends. A need to help others might be met through community volunteer work.

As for the rest of the exercise —

A carpenter might satisfy a need for adventure with vacations in the wilderness or with hang gliding or similar sports as hobbies.

A traveling sales representative would need to make a point of being available to his or her family when home, calling in nightly from the road, and perhaps taking family members along on a trip from time to time.

A homemaker might satisfy a need for power by taking a leading role in community activities.

A museum guide might find adventure spending a vacation working on an archaeological dig.

A professor might get recognition from publishing books and articles.

A farmer might find friendship in his or her community or religious groups.

A psychologist might satisfy a need for aesthetics by collecting art or find adventure learning to pilot an airplane.

An accountant might find power by starting his or her own firm or find a creative outlet in painting or piano lessons.

A chemist might gain recognition by giving demonstrations (*á la* "Mr. Wizard") to groups of school children.

A writer might find friendship in a writers' group or workshop.

A veterinarian could find power by taking a leading role in a campaign to save an endangered species.

Activities:

Perhaps the same panel that spoke about rewards and sacrifices could address the question of how they meet some of their other values outside of the work setting.

Discuss the concept that leisure activity is really work—unpaid work perhaps—but indeed work. These endeavors meet the human need for meaningful work when that need isn't fully realized in paid employment.

An Investment In Education – Yields Dividends For A Lifetime

Page 116-117   Page 51-53

Learning objective:

To demonstrate the financial payoff—over a lifetime—of an investment in education.

Presentation suggestions:

Review the chart on page 116. Does a common theme run through the data presented? One obvious one is that more education usually means increased earning potential. Be sure to remind the students that this is not a hard and fast rule—there are lots of exceptions—but in the majority of circumstances, education and training usually correlate with earnings.

Ask students to complete the math on page 117. What is their response to these figures?

A student who expects to be in the workforce 38 years between the ages of 18 and 65 (taking time out for schooling and raising a family) would have a chart like this:

How many years do you plan to work between the age of 18 and 65?

<u>38</u> years in workforce

Multiply the number of years you plan to be in the workforce by each of the annual salaries listed below to find out how much you would earn over the course of your working life.

$10,000 x <u>38</u> years in workforce = <u>$380,000</u> lifetime earnings

$15,000 x <u>38</u> years in workforce = <u>$570,000</u> lifetime earnings

$20,000 x <u>38</u> years in workforce = <u>$760,000</u> lifetime earnings

$30,000 x <u>38</u> years in workforce = <u>$1,140,000</u> lifetime earnings

$50,000 x <u>38</u> years in workforce = <u>$1,900,000</u> lifetime earnings

What is the difference between a $10,000 and $15,000 annual salary over a lifetime? <u>$190,000</u>

What is the difference between a $10,000 and $20,000 annual salary over a lifetime? <u>$380,000</u>

What is the difference between a $10,000 and $30,000 annual salary over a lifetime? <u>$760,000</u>

What is the difference between a $10,000 and $50,000 annual salary over a lifetime? <u>$1,520,000</u>

Have the students complete the Bar Graph on page 118. What do their graphs show? Comments should suggest that time spent on the remainder of their education is short compared to the years they'll spend in the workforce.

Now ask the students to complete the worksheet on page 119 using the information from the chart.

Discuss the ratio between years spent in post-high school training and education and years in the workforce. Do the energy and time spent in training seem worth it in the long run?

Careers are listed on index cards along with wages. Students are to calculate how many hours/weeks/months they must "work" to afford something on a "wish" list that they brought to class from the previous day. Later they learn that the cards were color coded by education levels. They quickly see that wages are directly proportional to education.

—Judy F. Miller
Teen Living Teacher
Clinton Middle School
Clinton, Tennessee

One student, who was doing the grocery shopping required for the budget, saw a woman with her child at the store. The student's scenario, chosen in class, seemed similar to this woman. As they both shopped for bargains, the student became aware that the scenario was real. The next day she shared the experience and cried in class. She described the clothing and attitude of the woman. She said she never wanted that scenario for herself, therefore she was never quitting school or having children too soon.

—Dana L. Mayers
Sequoyah Middle School
Edmond, Oklahoma

Optional

Pages 98-99

Ask Someone
Who's Been There

Page 120

Page 54

Learning objective:

To help students gain specific information about the costs and rewards of various jobs from people they know. This is likely to be more meaningful and to stick with them longer than any information they read in a book.

Presentation suggestions:

While making the assignment, be sure to remind students of the etiquette of interviewing. When asking for the interview, they should clearly indicate its purpose and how much time it will take. If they are interviewing people outside their immediate family or visiting people on the job, it is essential to be punctual, and not to stay any longer than they said they would. After the interview, they should send a brief, handwritten thank you.

When students have completed their interviews, ask them to share what they learned.

Follow-up:

Encourage students to keep these questions in mind and to continue to ask them of adults working in other fields as they proceed with their career planning process.

My students interviewed a person who doesn't like his/her job so that they understand [the effect on a worker's morale and] what that can do to one's spirit over the years.

– Lynn Porter
Coordinator of High School Diploma Program
Santa Monica-Malibu Unified School District
Santa Monica, CA

Easier Said Than Done

Career Choices

Page 121

Workbook and Portfolio

Page 55

Learning objective:

To help students realize that in order to meet long-term goals they will have to make some short-term sacrifices, and to provide a decision-making model that will help them keep their goals in mind.

Presentation suggestions:

As a class, discuss long-term and short-term goals in relation to the examples presented. In each case, ask students to circle the long-term goal and underline the short-term goal, and then to make a decision about the best course of action for each individual to take. Complete the chart at the bottom of the page.

Then ask students to turn back to Chapter 3 and identify two or three of their own long-term lifestyle goals. Have them use the model provided to make some decisions about their own current activities.

Activity:

In class, consider what might have happened if certain historical figures had sacrificed their long-term goals in favor of the short term. (First you must decide what those long-term goals were.) For example, what if Thomas Jefferson had decided to stay home and work in his garden instead of going to Philadelphia and writing the Declaration of Independence? (His long-term goal: to help his country gain independence. His possible short-term goal: to get rid of the crab grass.)

Resources:

Robert Fritz, *The Path of Least Resistance: Principles for Creating What You Want To Create.* New Hampshire: Stillpointe, 1986.

Optional

Possibilities

Pages 103-107

A Legacy for My Daughter
by James Webb

Read after completing pages 114-121 in *Career Choices*

Instructor's Notes:

Chapter 5

Your Ideal Career

It's important for students to take a look at the general characteristics they hope to find in a job before they begin considering a specific career. Since there are more than 12,000 job titles to choose from, narrowing down those choices at the outset will save a great deal of time. In this chapter, students are asked to choose their most important considerations in terms of the physical setting of a job, the working conditions, the kinds of relationships they would like to have in their career, the psychological rewards they hope to achieve, how they want their career to relate to their family responsibilities, the financial situation they would find most comfortable, and the type of work they can do or are capable of learning.

Preparing for a career takes a great deal of dedication and energy. If young people can identify career choices that meet their personal needs and values they are more likely to commit the time and resources to staying in school and getting the education and training required.

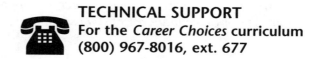

TECHNICAL SUPPORT
For the *Career Choices* curriculum
(800) 967-8016, ext. 677

Your Ideal Job

Page 126-134   Page 57-62

Learning objective:

To help students narrow their career choices by first considering the general job characteristics that are most important to them, and then by being creative in thinking of jobs that meet their requirements.

Presentation suggestions:

In class, discuss each of the general classifications presented in this exercise to make sure everyone understands what is involved. Then have students individually go through the lists, checking *all* the items they find appealing.

Once they have completed this process, ask them to go over their lists again, this time choosing only one or two items from each classification that they think are most essential to career satisfaction.

Circle the boxes in front of these statements. When they have narrowed down their lists, have students enter their preferences on the chart on page 134, as illustrated by Gena's chart. Remind the class that this chart is important and that they should refer to it often as they consider different career options.

After your students have completed their charts, begin brainstorming possible careers that meet their most essential career characteristics.

To get the class in a creative mood, discuss Gena's chart, trying to come up with as many other job titles as possible that fall within the range of her preferences (architect? advertising copy writer? public relations specialist?).

Depending upon the population of your classroom, encourage students to brainstorm careers from many educational training levels. Categories would include:

College educational

Vocational school

High school graduate

Blue collar

White collar

Professional/Certified

Example:

Gena: furniture refurnisher, antique restorer, art appraiser, cabinetmaker, or office manager of a museum or gallery

Then break the class into focus groups of four or five students each. Have each student share his or her chart and then brainstorm possible careers with the group. Students will always come up with the obvious, but encourage them to be as creative as possible. Bring the class back together and ask students to share their most creative ideas.

Energizer:

Offer a prize, extra credit points, or privileges to the group that comes up with the most creative ideas that fall within the range of its participants' charts. Let the class vote. This should encourage energy and creativity.

Resource:

Edward de Bono, *Lateral Thinking Creativity Step by Step*. New York: Harper & Row, 1973.

A previous student, now at the community college, started the program wanting to be an auto mechanic but realized he didn't want the lifestyle and environment, so he has gone into computers because of the class.

–Jean Anne Conlor
English Teacher
South Tahoe High School
South Lake Tahoe, California

Consider Your Options

Page 135-137   Page 63

Learning objective:
   To give students an opportunity to consider job preferences in terms of structured or unstructured employment, and to analyze their level of anxiety tolerance in relation to working.

Presentation suggestions:
   Review the terms defined in the text to make sure students understand them. Then, as a class, list examples of jobs that fit each definition. Can the class think of individuals who have had composite careers? Sequential careers? (Examples: Emma Thompson has a composite career: She has won Academy Awards for her work as an actor and as a screenwriter. Former President Bush's political career was sequential. He has been a congressman from Texas, ambassador to China, head of the CIA, vice president, and president.)

   Then ask students to circle the most appealing job characteristics on the chart provided. When they finish, bring up the topic of anxiety tolerance. This is an important issue, although students may never have thought about it. Since anxiety is a part of everyone's life, learning to deal with it and tolerate it is essential. That is not possible, however, until students can identify anxiety as normal. Unless they can do that, they are likely to see this uneasy feeling as something to be avoided at all costs. Point out that running away from anxiety means denying themselves many of the things they hold most important in life. If something isn't important to a person, he or she is unlikely to feel anxious about it. For example, someone with low anxiety tolerance who dreams of attending a highly selective college probably would not even bother to apply for admission because the anxiety level, the fear of rejection, would be so great. Similarly, the aspiring actor or actress will not audition for the school play if he or she thinks a knot in the stomach means it would be wise to stop and reconsider that goal.

   Discuss these and other examples with the class to make sure they thoroughly understand the topic. Then relate anxiety tolerance to job selection. As the chart shows, the most flexible careers, the ones offering the greatest amount of control and freedom, also call for more anxiety tolerance. Students need to be able to judge how comfortable they are with ambivalence and ambiguity in order to make a satisfying career choice in this regard. Point out, though, that with practice they can hope to increase their tolerance levels. Again, assure them that the feeling is normal, but that they must learn to trust themselves enough to go after what they really want.

Activities:
   Ask a school counselor or psychologist to talk with the class about anxiety tolerance.

Employee or Employer?

Page 138-139   Page 64-65

Learning objective:

To help students evaluate whether their attitudes, characteristics, and skills are more consistent with those of an employer or of an employee.

Presentation suggestions:

Have students mark the checklist, score, and then discuss.

To total a score, add up all the checked numbers. A number 1 has the weight of 1, a number 2 scores a 2 and a 3 equals 3. If your total score is between 12 and 16, you are a good candidate and should consider starting your own business at some time in your career.

Point out that this is not a question of whether it is "better" to be an employee or an employer. It is simply a matter of what fits an individual's personality. Students should understand, too, that an employer can be anything from a self-employed individual to the owner of a huge corporation. Self-employed people don't necessarily have to invest a huge amount of money (another common misconception). Anyone with a skill that fills a need for someone else can do it. (Examples: carpenters, writers, child care providers, housekeepers, gardeners, hair stylists, caterers, plumbers, electricians, exercise trainers, and so on.)

Brainstorm the *pros* and *cons* of entrepreneurship: Out of this activity should come the realization that most people first entering the workforce are not prepared financially or in experience for starting their own business. Point out that owning your business might be a future goal.

Activities:

Invite an entrepreneur to talk with the class. (It's best if this is someone whose achievements are realistic enough to your class to identify with him or her.)

English/Language Arts:

Students write a short paper about the kind of business they would most like to start and why.

Gender equity activity:

The class debates which worker would have the most options for parenting, someone in a structured job or someone who is self-employed.

Energizer:

If your class shows a lot of enthusiasm for entrepreneurship, a long-term project such as the one offered by the Junior Achievement Program might be appropriate.

With an "applied" approach to keyboarding, students now practice on reports and exercises generated in English, instead of meaningless keyboarding exercises. They do everything from acrostic poems to reports on careers.

Using the computer program PowerPoint, each student created a series of 12 slides about a chosen career. By incorporating graphics, word processing, and other elements in the process, a colorful, sound and motion "advertisement" was displayed. The programs became personal and interactive when students viewed and evaluated the displays. They then wrote positive comments in a formal business letter to send to the students whose work was chosen.

– Scott Hess
Applied English and Technology teacher
Tumwater High School
Tumwater, Washington

What About Status?

Page 140-141

Page 65

Learning objective:

To help students sort out their own feelings about status as it relates to job selection.

Presentation suggestions:

Review the material presented and discuss the questions on pages 140-141. Then have students decide individually how they feel about the statements on page 141.

English/Language Arts:

First, debate in class: Who should have more status, a teacher or a rock star?

Then ask your students to write an essay on why they would or would not consider teaching as a career.

Point out that in Japan teaching is one of the highest paid and most respected professions. Also point out that until recent decades, teachers and professors were given high status in the United States.

Reading assignment:

Good-bye, Mr. Chips, by James Hilton

Optional

Pages 108-111

I Decline to Accept the End of Man
by William Faulkner
Read after completing Chapter 5 in *Career Choices*

209

Instructor's Notes:

Chapter 6

Career Research

In this chapter, students complete a three-step process in order to arrive at a career decision they will use for the remainder of the book. Be sure to emphasize that this is a tentative selection, one that can—and probably will—be changed a number of times. There isn't just one perfect occupation. Today's youth will change occupations several times during the years they are in the workforce.

The process we present here is based on the old saying "Tell me, I forget; show me, I remember; involve me, I understand." For many of us, career research involved only step one of this process. That stops far short of the goal: allowing students to get a real feeling for a career before they invest years of their lives preparing for it.

TV Worth Watching

It's not often we can recommend a TV show without reservation, but CBS's award-winning *Sunday Morning* is a treasure trove of materials you can use in your classroom. You'll find wonderfully written and produced segments on exceptional individuals working in the humanities and sciences. These are excellent resources for career exploration. Or, you might use John Leonard's weekly critique of the popular media as a source for new vocabulary words. Segments on social issues can help launch lively and meaningful debates and discussions.

Check your local TV listing for the broadcast time in your area. The show runs for 90 minutes each week. Videos of selected segments from particular shows can be purchased by calling (800) 242-7747.

Reproduced from quarterly Focus on the Future *newsletter. To be added to our mailing list for this free publication, call (800) 967-8016.*

Career Interest Areas

Page 145-146   No Workbook
                           Page

Learning objective:
> To help students understand the twelve career interest areas and the types of jobs in each area.

Presentation suggestions:
> Review each of the career interest groups presented and ask the class to think of additional careers that might fit each category. (It would be a good idea for you to have a copy of the _Guide for Occupational Exploration._ If your library doesn't have one, it can be ordered from any government bookstore for about $15.)

Resource:
> William Hopke. _Encyclopedia of Career & Vocational Guidance._ J.G. Ferguson Publishing Co., 1987.

Students enjoyed interviewing adults in the community who were already working in a career field of interest to them. Some were even offered part-time jobs or the opportunity to "shadow" an adult.

> – Mary Turella
> 8th grade English and Communications teacher
> North Royalton Middle School
> North Royalton, OH

Optional

The Boys' Ambition, excerpt from
Life on the Mississippi
  by Mark Twain
Read after reading page 146 in _Career Choices_

Pages 112-117

Bring in Your Identity

Career Choices

Page 147

Workbook and Portfolio

Page 67

Learning objective:

To help students make some tentative career choices based on their own personality traits.

Presentation suggestions:

At this point, students are ready to select some specific careers for more in-depth examination. Before they complete the exercise, make sure they understand that all of the work they have done up to this point must be considered in making these choices. A quick review of Chapters 2 to 5 might be helpful now. In particular, have students review their bull's eye chart on page 27, their required annual salary on page 93, and their job characteristic chart on page 134.

Optional

Possibilities

Pages 118-123

Lego

from *The New Yorker Magazine*

Read after completing page 147 in *Career Choices*

Career Interest Survey

Page 150-155   Page 68-73

Learning objective:

To help students learn library and research skills as they begin to gather information about potential careers.

Presentation suggestions:

Discuss basic career research methods and review the questions on the career interest survey to make sure everyone understands. We strongly suggest that you take the class to the school library and allow students to do their research and complete their surveys during class time. (It should take about three hours.) This is an ideal opportunity for you to demonstrate research techniques and introduce students to the library and all the benefits it can offer them. Since the information they are looking for is of personal importance to them, they are likely to target what is available. If your school library doesn't have an adequate career research section, try to arrange a field trip to the career center at a nearby college or junior college.

If your school or community has a computerized career research system, this is also an excellent resource.

Be sure to consult your school counselor on appropriate resources.

Activities:

Guest speakers can be very helpful at this point. Before choosing them, however, consider the careers of greatest interest to students. If no one seems to be a potential electrical engineer, for example, there's not much point in bringing one in to speak. Try, too, to have an appropriate mix of blue- and white-collar speakers, depending on the class's aspirations. Students seem better able to relate to younger presenters.

Ask speakers to discuss not only the tasks involved in their jobs, but what they like and dislike about them, how they got interested in them, the necessary training, and so on. Allow time for questions from the class.

If you decide against having guest speakers, you might form committees of students interested in a particular career area and ask them to report their research findings regarding this area to the class.

Resources:
Books:

Richard Bolles, *What Color Is Your Parachute? A Practical Manual for Job-Hunters & Career Changers*, Ten Speed Press.

John Wright, *The American Almanac of Jobs and Salaries, 1990-91*, Avon Books.

Robert O. Snelling and Anne M. Snelling, *Jobs! What They Are. . .Where They Are. . .What They Pay!* Fireside Book, Simon and Schuster.

Beatryce Nivens, *Careers for Women without College Degrees*, McGraw-Hill Book Company.

Jo Ann Russo, *Careers without College*, Betterway Publications, Inc.

Paul Phifer, *College Majors and Careers: A Resource Guide for Effective Life Planning*, Garrett Park Press.

Joyce Lain Kennedy and D. Laranore, *Joyce Lain Kennedy's Career Book*, VGM Career Horizons.

Video:

"Follow Your Dream," 6 minutes, 30 seconds. YWCA, 9440 W. 25th Avenue, Phoenix, AZ 85021. (602) 944-0569.

We used most of Chapter 6 during our Career Research paper assignment. In addition to writing a research paper, students are also required to present with a computer-generated multimedia presentation.

– Sharon Hurwitz
English Teacher and Technology Facilitator
Bethel High School
Hampton, Virginia

Parents came in to speak to classes about how they started in their chosen field. They brought slides, videos, etc. Since many students knew these speakers personally, it was highly relevant and interesting to them.

– Mary Turella
8th grade English and Communications teacher
North Royalton Middle School
North Royalton, Ohio

Seeing in the Mind's Eye*

Career Choices
Page 156-157

Workbook and Portfolio
Page 73-74

Learning objective:

To help students begin thinking about—and actually experiencing—what it would be like to spend a typical day at the job of their choice.

Presentation suggestions:

Review the concepts of visualization and "seeing in the mind's eye" (SCANS) with the class. Then take them through the exercise.

Allow an entire class period for this exercise. Ask them to choose one of the careers they researched for the career interest survey. Have your students open their books to this exercise on page 157 and have a pen on their desks before you begin.

Turn down the lights and close the doors and windows. If your room is unavoidably noisy, try to find a quieter one.

Speak slowly and quietly, pausing where indicated. Your script follows.

Relax and settle into your chair. Place your feet flat on the floor. Close your eyes. Clear your mind.

Pay attention to your breathing. (Pause) Inhale slowly, filling your lungs with air. (Pause) Exhale slowly. (Pause)

Take a few slow, deep, deliberate breaths. As you exhale, tell yourself to relax and let go. (Pause long enough for three or four deep breaths)

Feel your body relax (Pause) from your face all the way down to your legs and toes. (Pause) Feel the pleasant warm and tingly feeling of relaxed muscles. (Pause)

Now project yourself into the future. (Pause) You've completed your education. (Pause) You've found a job in the field of your choice. (Pause) This is the beginning of a typical working day. (Pause) How do you feel as you get ready for work? (Pause) What are you wearing? (Pause) Are you looking forward to the day? (Pause)

You're on your way to work. (Pause) Are you in a car or some type of public transportation? (Pause) Is it a long commute? (Pause) Or do you work at home? (Pause)

You walk into your office. (Pause) What does it look like? (Pause) Who else is there? (Pause) How do they greet you? (Pause) How does your morning pass? (Pause) This is a typical day. What kinds of tasks do you see yourself doing? (Pause) Take a minute and do those tasks (Pause for two minutes).

It's lunch time. (Pause) Where are you eating lunch? (Pause) Who is with you? (Pause)

Back at work, you find some special challenges. What are they? (Pause) How do you deal with them? (Pause)

Work with those challenges for a few minutes (Pause) As you finish your day on the job, how do you feel? (Pause) What are you thinking about? (Pause) Do you have plans for this evening? (Pause) What are they? (Pause)

Now open your eyes and pick up your pen and without saying anything complete the exercise on page 157 in your book. Begin now. (Don't say anything more.)

Follow-up:

You might ask students to share any revelations they had during the exercise. For example, a future waiter or waitress may have realized how tired he or she would be by the end of the day.

Suggest the students complete this exercise for each of the three careers they researched.

* One of the foundation skills recommended by SCANS is "seeing in the mind's eye." This skill is used by many successful people as they visualize how to complete a project at work or develop a new product.

The Shadow Program

Page 158-159   Page 75

Learning objective:

To give students practice in writing a business letter and conducting an interview, and to allow them to see firsthand what it might be like to spend a day at a particular job.

IMPORTANT NOTE: In order to complete this exercise, students will miss an entire day of school. Check with your administration office and the parents for permission before proceeding. Also solicit the support of your career counselor.

Presentation suggestions:

This is an extremely valuable exercise, but it requires a great deal of research to locate the workers who will consent to being "shadowed." We strongly urge that you get help from a volunteer. Many community professional associations (Kiwanis, Lions, Soroptimists, Business and Professional Women, and so on) are supportive of such projects. These organizations are also a good starting point for locating the individuals who will take part in the exercise. Your Chamber of Commerce should have a list and contact phone numbers of all the groups active in your community.

Don't be shy about calling. This is exactly the kind of program most professional and community organizations love to support. The secret is to ask up-front for a liaison to mentor and monitor the project. The right person will take 95 percent of the responsibility. All you need to do is supply him or her with complete copies of the student survey that follows, beginning on page 221.

Activity:

Make sure students understand that this is called the Shadow Program for a reason: shadows do not say anything, they do not do anything, they are just there. Emphasize the need for students to be as unobtrusive as possible, except during the agreed upon interview time.

Energizer:

If appropriate, some students could shadow their mentor beginning early in the morning at breakfast. It is a valuable lesson to observe a working parent and see how he or she mixes career and family.

English/Language Arts:

Use this exercise as an opportunity to review the components of a good business letter. Make the letter itself an assignment that will be graded on the basis of correct form, grammar, spelling, neatness, and so on.

Ask students to write a short essay on what they learned from their day as a shadow.

One girl (in our Career Choices program) shadowed a medical surgeon into surgery, looked through a scope, then held some tissue.... She's still talking about it two years later and has been accepted to nursing school!

– Megan Schroeder
Vocational/Workplace Readiness Teacher
Cascade High School
Leavenworth, Washington

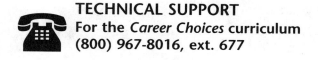

TECHNICAL SUPPORT
For the *Career Choices* curriculum
(800) 967-8016, ext. 677

How to Find Your "Director of Mentors"

Call the president of one of the service organizations whose members are career-oriented. Explain your project and ask for names of individuals who might be interested or suggest you come and give a presentation at one of their meetings. This is ideal. You can generate a lot of interest plus meet prospective volunteers. Be sure to take a couple of copies of *Career Choices* to pass around the audience as you speak. This visual prop will help them better understand what you are doing.

What to Look for in Your "Director of Mentors"

1. *Someone who has lived in your community long enough to have plenty of contacts.* A senior member of one of the professional service organizations mentioned above is ideal. A recently retired professional will have more time.

2. *Someone who likes to be responsible and follow through on a project from beginning to end.* The more the Director of Mentors does, the less responsibility you will have to assume. But remember that you have to let this person do his or her job. Give your director of mentors the necessary tools (completed, legible student surveys) and turn him or her loose. Provide support, praise, and appreciation!

This person could become a community liaison to your class. He or she could assist in finding guest speakers or perhaps be a guest speaker. Your volunteer might even be willing to mentor students with special needs. Many community members are vitally interested in working with young people. You can give them the opportunity to get involved. Be sure to share this *Instructor's Guide* and a copy of *Career Choices* with your volunteer. She or he might have great ideas.

Photocopy the survey on page 221 of this *Guide* and have each student complete it. Pass these on to the director so he or she can begin the process of finding appropriate mentors.

Also supply your volunteer with a copy of the Mentor Survey on pages 222 and 223 of this *Guide* to use in locating mentors and matching students.

Hint: Ask the volunteer to share these completed forms with you. Keep a growing file for future years along with a file of guest speakers.

Shadow Program Student Survey

Name _____ Age _____

High School _____ Grade _____

Teacher _____

Class Title _____ Period _____

Three careers of interest:

    1st choice _____

    2nd choice _____

    3rd choice _____

When I can shadow: (circle any restrictions)

    Any time   Evenings only

    Weekdays only   Weekends only

    Other _____

Explain any time restrictions such as employment or after-school activities from which you cannot be excused:

_____

_____

Do you plan to attend college? Yes   No   Maybe   Undecided

Do you plan to attend trade school? Yes   No   Maybe   Undecided

Why are you interested in these career areas? _____

_____

_____

_____

Shadow Program Mentor Survey

We are seeking volunteers for a Student Career Shadow Program. This important activity links young people with someone in a career field in which they have expressed an interest. For a day or a portion of a day, they "shadow" that individual. They have been coached not to be obtrusive or to interrupt your work time. All we ask is that you grant 15-30 minutes for an interview at the end of the day.

If you are interested in allowing a student to "shadow" you for a day or a portion of a day, please complete the following survey and return to:

_____

_____

The student assigned to you will contact you directly by letter and phone, so the two of you can arrange a convenient time.

Profession _____ Title _____

Name _____

Address _____

_____

Day phone _____

Evening phone _____

Company _____

Address _____

_____

A brief description of your job duties _____

_____

_____

Your educational background _____

_____

(Over)

Restrictions on shadowing times (days, times, etc.) _____

_____

_____

Any preference on ability and motivation of student?   (check one)

_____ Please send me only motivated students.

_____ I am willing to work with an at-risk or undermotivated student.

_____ I am willing to work with a handicapped/learning disabled student.

_____ I would be especially good with _____

_____

_____ Undecided

Are you a working parent?   Yes   No

Optional: Would you consider allowing a student to come to your home an hour before you leave for work to observe how you mix career and family?   Yes   No   Perhaps

Optional: Would you consider speaking to a high school class on your area of career expertise or other professional experience?   Yes   No   Perhaps

Comments:

Shadow Program Referral Form

Referral for _____

Profession _____ Title _____

Name _____

Address _____

_____

Day phone _____ Evening phone _____

Company _____

Address _____

_____

Restrictions on shadowing times _____

_____

Comments _____

_____

_____

_____

_____

If you have questions contact:

_____   _____
              Name   Phone

Involve Me and I Understand

Page 160-161   Page 76

Learning objective:

To allow students, through paid or unpaid employment, to observe people working in their chosen career field over a period of time.

Presentation suggestions:

Review the material presented in the text and, as a class, try to think of paid and unpaid jobs for people wanting to work at the careers listed on page 160. Add to the list the careers students in your class are considering. Emphasize that the jobs may not be fun or interesting and may offer little or no pay. The purpose is simply for the students to get into a position where they can observe people performing jobs that interest them. Instruct students to be especially observant—both of what is happening around them, and of how they *feel*.

Follow-up:

Some students may want to do volunteer work with their shadow mentors. Please advise the students that it is not appropriate for them to do this on the day of their shadow assignment. Suggest that they follow up their visit with a thank you letter and a request for a volunteer position. It is not appropriate for them to request a paid position unless it is offered by the mentor.

Again, your Director of Mentors can help. Finding these types of jobs, both paid and unpaid, usually takes someone with contacts.

Making It Real
Internet Enhancement

Internet Search of the Jobs Posted in the Classified Ads of the Nation's Largest Newspapers

Curriculum sequence: *(optional)*

Assign after students complete Chapter 5 of their *Career Choices* workbook.

Internet address/Directions: http://www.careerpath.com

Web site description: CareerPath.com posts more than a quarter million new jobs on the Internet every month and is updated daily by over 25 large national newspapers. It is the most visited job-related site on the Internet. Once students log on, they can search each newspaper by industry/position/key word(s) to find career opportunities that match their ideal jobs.

Learning objective:

To investigate real careers in real time. Students will learn to conduct a computer search of actual career opportunities by industry, position, functional competencies and geographical location. This is a powerful skill that will help them further envision a future in the workforce.

Methodology:

You'll want to give students plenty of time to complete this activity. Depending on the availability of Internet access in your classroom or school lab, each student could spend from 30 minutes to three hours online gathering the data they seek. This is an engrossing activity and because it is based in reality, very motivational.

Once students log on to the URL http://www.careerpath.com, direct them to read the first page and then click on the hyperlink Jobs. This will begin their search of the *Help Wanted* databases by newspaper, job category and key word.

Next, it is important that the students click on the HELP logo and then print out the three or four pages of directions. While most students will be able to figure out the process of searching the databases without this help, these directions give them valuable information on how to get the most out of their searches and how to customize their searches to save time. You may want to review these directions in class before having the students begin, or you may want to make the assignment, advising the class that the next midterm will include questions from this document.

Ask your students to search for actual jobs that meet their interests, lifestyle requirements and educational commitment: jobs they feel they will be qualified for when they are 28 years old (10 years after high school and/or 4 to 6 years after college). Advise them to print out the classified ads they find and include them in their guidance portfolio. Ask them to search *at least* six different newspapers in six different areas of the country.

> Additional *Making It Real* activities are available through the Academic Innovations home page on the World Wide Web. For more information on how you can access these Internet enhancement activities, see pages 36 and 37 of this *Instructor's Guide.*

Synthesizing their Data

Lesson extensions:

From the data they have collected, you may want to assign any or all of the following activities:

Investigate different areas of the country in which to live. Students may find intriguing jobs in areas of the country that are far from home. Now, because of the Internet, they can easily research what it would be like to live in a particular community, from the cost of housing to the amenities the community and area offer. *See page 264 of this Guide for a detailed lesson.*

Create a career ladder that visually shows the sequence of jobs within a career path in an industry. After your students choose an industry, have them draw a five or six rung ladder on a large piece of construction paper. Beginning at the bottom rung, ask them to place (glue) a classified ad for an entry level job within that industry. Beside the next rung up, have them place an ad for a job representing the next "step" toward their chosen career. Continue up the ladder until, at the top, they have placed a classified ad for their ideal job. This could be assigned as a group activity for individuals who are interested in similar careers.

Write a paper that describes the research methods used in their search. This is an excellent opportunity to discuss and practice technical writing skills.

Have your students write a classified ad for their ideal career based on ads found on the Internet. Direct them to include job title, job duties, skills required, experience and education required and salary information. Advise them that the salary must accurately represent the data collected. This advertisement should be at least 150 words long. *This could be done in conjunction with the Energizer activity described on page 228 of this Instructor's Guide.*

Ask students to analyze the skills required for desirable jobs in their chosen industry. Have them make a chart that outlines the skills for each job. (Students will have to use the longer classified ads that go into more detail as their research base.) From this chart ask them to project into the future and describe how they intend to acquire these skills over the next 10 years. *This assignment might be made while they are completing their 10-year plans on pages 278 to 280 of Career Choices.*

The Chemistry Test

Career Choices
Page 162-165

Workbook and Portfolio
Page 77-78

Learning objective:

To help students decide whether the careers they are considering are good matches for their personalities and working styles.

Presentation suggestions:

As a class, read the story on page 162 and discuss the four personality styles described. This might be a good time to turn back to Chapter 2, pages 38-43 for a quick review. Students might be interested in a more complete personal profile. For more information, see page 351.

Ask students to recall any occasions in the past few years when they've worked on a committee like this one. How did things work out? Can the students relate the results (either good or bad) to the personality styles of the people involved and the jobs they were assigned?

Have students complete the rest of the exercise either individually or in small groups. Encourage students to come up with their own solutions before they look at the answers which are provided.

Energizer:

Have students identify their work behavioral styles either from the exercise on pages 38-43 or by actually taking the assessment using the Personal Profile Instrument. See page 351 for ordering information.

Forming heterogeneous groups that include at least one of each personality type:

Once they have identified their predominant style, ask all the Dominance (D) to go one corner of the room, Influencing (I) to another, Steadiness (S) to another, and Compliance (C) to another.

Then ask each group to count off. Therefore, each group will have one 1, one 2, one 3, and so on.

Now ask the ones to form a group, the twos, the threes, and so on until you run out of numbers for the smallest group.

Assign the students who are left to the existing groups (which now have one of each of the DISC's) so that each group has five to seven members. Be sure to have no more than two of each work style in a group.

The assignment for each group:

Design a company and assign job titles to each member of the group based upon the strengths and interests of the group.

First ask the group to review the exercises on pages 163 and 164. As a warm-up, choose one of the companies, for example, a factory, and list other jobs that each of the work styles might find matches their personality.

Example:

D's – union organizer, office manager, head custodian, plant manager.

I's – salesperson, trainer, personnel director, child care director

S's – mechanic, heavy equipment operator, clerical worker, department specialist

C's – auditor, bookkeeper, research and development director

Once you feel the groups understand the process, let them begin brainstorming their company. This could take one to three class periods depending upon the enthusiasm of the group.

It may be easiest to outline the assignment for them this way:

First – Identify an industry or company that everyone in the group finds of interest. The larger the company or industry, the better.

Second – Brainstorm all the possible job titles for each of the predominant work behavioral styles – D's, I's, S's, C's – in that company or organization.

Third – Have each person choose a job title based on the charts they completed on pages 27 and 134 in *Career Choices*.

Fourth – As a group, write a job description for each person. Use the form on page 231 of this *Guide*. The job description should include the following:

Job title:
Experience, skills, and training required:
Job duties:
Hours and working conditions:
Annual salary:

Ask the students to make the conditions as realistic as they can. For example, there should be no inflated salaries just to meet personal budget requirements.

Groups may need to spend one day in the library researching appropriate jobs, but this is not necessary unless you have a lot of C's in your class who want everything very precise and correct!

Once the groups have completed their assignment, ask the group to present their project.

After they have introduced their company and staff open up the brainstorming to the rest of the class to complete the lists of possible job titles in that company.

Then ask all members of the staff to make a presentation about their job, why they chose it, and how it fits their personality.

English/Language Arts:

Writing job descriptions is a communication skill that will come in very handy later in life. Those that have some experience in writing job descriptions will impress their supervisors and therefore move up the ladder to supervision themselves. This career move brings more autonomy, responsibility, and higher pay. Ask all students to rewrite their job description from their notes.

Remind them that spelling, grammar, punctuation, and neatness are important.

After reading and discussing "I Hear America Singing," the students, in groups of 3 to 4, rewrote the poem using occupations of today. They also made a collage to accompany their vision of the poem.

– Pam Wieters
English Teacher
Stratford High School
Goose Creek, South Carolina

Optional

I Hear America Singing
by Walt Whitman
Read after completing page 165 in *Career Choices*

Pages 124-126

Job Description for:

Name _____

Predominant work behavioral style is: (circle one)   D   I   S   C

Company/Industry/Organization: _____

Job title: _____

Experience, skills, and training required: _____

_____

_____

Job duties:

1. _____

_____

2. _____

_____

3. _____

_____

4. _____

_____

5. _____

_____

6. _____

_____

7. _____

_____

8. _____

_____

Hours and working conditions: _____

Annual salary: _____

Instructor's Notes:

Chapter 7

Decision Making

The final step in choosing what you want is making a decision. As Anne Morrow Lindbergh said, "One cannot collect all the beautiful shells on the beach." Making a decision is difficult because choosing one thing inevitably means saying "no" to something else. For teens, this can be especially painful. It is essential, therefore, that they understand two points: that not making a decision is making a choice, and that most decisions can be changed.

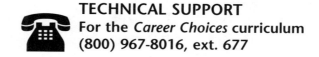

TECHNICAL SUPPORT
For the *Career Choices* curriculum
(800) 967-8016, ext. 677

Identifying Choices

Page 170   Page 80

Learning objective:

To help students discern the difference between long- and short-term goals and learn to take their hopes for the future into account when making daily decisions.

Presentation suggestions:

Ask a student to read Joyce's story aloud. Then have the class identify her two goals:

Becoming a doctor someday

Buying a car

What is Joyce's long-term goal? *Becoming a doctor.*

Right now, she is faced with deciding among three alternatives: getting a job so she can buy a car, becoming a candy striper to get medical experience, or spending more time on her studies.

Activities:

List on the board and discuss the choices students face every day to help them realize that they are already quite adept at making short-term decisions. Students usually have no trouble identifying at least ten decisions they make every day: what time to get up, what clothes to put on, what to eat, whether or not to go to school, what friends to call, what music to listen to, what subject to study first, what TV show to watch, whether or not to exercise, what time to go to bed.

Now ask them to list some longer term decisions they face in the next twelve months: what classes to take next year, whether to go out for a sport or school activity, when, and if, to date.

Now brainstorm some really long-term (five years to life) decisions they need to start making.

Do I want to take classes to qualify me for college or trade school?

Am I going to be sexually active (risk parenthood)?

Am I going to stay in school?

Am I going to work or give priority to my studies?

Ask students to discuss what kinds of choices are easiest to make and which are hardest. Why?

After reading and discussing pages 168-169, students need to see how decision making and problem solving are important in the business world as well as in their personal world. I split the class into small groups and assign them a section of the teachers' parking lot to examine. They are to identify the number of cars and their make so we can eventually determine how many are American-made, German-made, British-made, etc. Then the small groups share their numbers with the whole group until we know how many cars total were in the parking lot and how many are from other countries. We do a math lesson so students can create percentages! (Not a small feat in a Communications class!)

Next, we talk about the problems associated with so many cars being non-American. Then, students write a paragraph about their findings, including the importance of solving this problem in the marketplace. As students word process their paragraphs, they are also being taught how to convert their information into a spread sheet (we use the integrated package Microsoft Works), which will turn their percentages into a pie chart or bar graph. When students finish, they have a paragraph complete with pie chart showing the importance of companies solving problems in the workplace.

— Sharon Hurwitz
English Teacher and Technology Facilitator
Bethel High School
Hampton, Virginia

Gathering Information

Page 171

Page 80

Learning objective:

To help students understand that before they can evaluate their choices, they need to discover the facts and determine the effect of these realities on the outcome for any of the options being considered.

Presentation suggestions:

Review the material in the text and discuss in class. Other information that might be helpful to Joyce could include: whether the hospital would be willing to write a letter of recommendation to the college of Joyce's choice; whether her parents would let her use the family car several times a week in return for doing extra chores around the house; whether her hours on the job or at the hospital would be flexible enough to let her study when she needs to; and how much time she needs to study each week in order to keep up her grades.

Emphasize the importance of being resourceful when making decisions. Thinking beyond the obvious choices often results in win/win solutions. If Joyce could negotiate the use of the family car, for example, she could satisfy her short-term goal without putting her long-term hopes at risk.

Evaluating Choices

Page 172-174   Page 81-82

Learning objective:

To help students evaluate the *pros* and *cons* and the likelihood of success of different choices.

Presentation suggestions:

Continuing Joyce's story, have the class list the *pros* and *cons* and probability of success if she doesn't work at all. (*Pros:* more time for study, more flexibility. *Cons:* no money, no car, no experience. Probability of success: moot point.)

After the class has worked through Joyce's example, break into groups of two or three to consider Jessica's and John's stories.

Jessica

Choice 1: To take Algebra I. *Pros:* keeps options for college and future career open. *Cons:* more work, less time for other things. Probability of success: reasonably high, since she has done well at math in the past.

Choice 2: To take basic math. *Pros:* easier, less work. *Cons:* fewer future options. Probability of success: very high, since she has done well at math in the past.

Choice 3: Not to take math. *Pros:* easy way out. *Cons:* future options severely limited. Probability of success: moot point.

John

Choice 1: Quit school and go to work. *Pros:* no more school, earn money. *Cons:* little chance for advancement, fewer options for future. Probability of success: could probably get the job.

Choice 2: Graduate and go to vocational school. *Pros:* good chance for rewarding work and good pay. *Cons:* more school. Probability of success: good, since he already knows a lot about graphic design.

Choice 3: Graduate and join the army. *Pros:* training with pay. *Cons:* must commit several years to military service. Probability of success: good, if he can receive written assurance from the recruiter that he will get the training he wants.

Choice 4: Graduate and go to college. *Pros:* better prospects for high future earnings. *Cons:* must work very hard to bring up high school grades, must commit time and money to future education. Probability of success: depends on how hard he's willing to work.

Bring the class back together, and as a group brainstorm Jessica's and John's decisions. You might make a chart for each story on the board, listing all the alternatives thought of by students. Ask the students what they think are the best decisions for Jessica and John.

Activities:

Ask students to write a one-page essay entitled "My Current Dilemma" that outlines the choices they currently face. Ask two or three student volunteers to read their essays and let the group practice the decision making process with these problems. Emphasize that the final decision is up to the student involved, but that it's good to get the opinions of others when you are gathering information and evaluating choices.

We showed the video **Forrest Gump** *to help students explore how choices depend on personal values. We asked students to recall three values that were held by characters in the film. One student focused on Forrest's love of life, and commented, "If you put love of life above all the bad things that can happen in life, you'll probably never commit suicide." He was thinking about a rock star (who recently committed suicide) and concluded that if the rock star had had Forrest's perspective, he would probably be alive today.*

– Doug Campbell
Communication Department
San Gabriel High School
San Gabriel, California

Optional

The Monkey's Paw
A play based on the story by W.W. Jacobs
Read after completing pages 168-174 in *Career Choices*

Pages 127-138

Gloria's Chart/Your Chart

Page 176-177   Page 82-83

Learning objective:

To show students how their own resources, wants, and needs should enter into the process of making major life decisions.

Presentation suggestions:

As a class, discuss Gloria's chart. Note that a new element has been added to the process: considering Gloria's resources, wants, and needs. This is a step to take when making major decisions, such as what career to pursue, whom to marry, where to live, and so on. Can the class think of anything to add to Gloria's chart? What do they think Gloria should do?

Once they have completed the process for Gloria, ask students to review their own resources (strengths, skills, and passions), values, wants, and needs. Have them enter these on the chart on page 177, where their goal is to identify and evaluate four possible career choices. Ask them to complete the chart as best they can. Then break the class into small groups where students can help each other evaluate their choices and think of other options based on the person's resources and desires. Students should then make a choice (individually, not based on the group's decision).

Activities:

Using the format of the chart on page 177 of *Career Choices* ask students to complete this same process, this time making a decision about training for their future career. For example, someone who wants to be a hotel manager might decide whether he or she wants to go to trade school, go to college, or get a job in the field and work his or her way up.

> *When using "The Road Not Taken" we had students writing stories looking ahead into their own futures with two different scenarios.*
>
> – Suzanne M. Reese
> Teacher/Gifted Liaison
> R.L. Turner High School
> Carrollton, Texas

Optional

Pages 139-141

The Road Not Taken
by Robert Frost
Read after completing page 177 in *Career Choices*

239

Make a Decision

Page 178   Page 84

Learning objective:
To help students evaluate their decision-making strategies, their strengths, and their weaknesses.

Presentation suggestions:
Review the text on page 178, and ask students to check the box on the scale where they think their decision-making behavior is. There are no right or wrong tendencies. The purpose is to help students recognize the range of decision-making characteristics and learn to recognize how and when they use them.

English/Language Arts:
Ask student to write a fictional short story about three siblings (*à la* "The Three Pigs") who must make an important decision. Their choices could be autobiographical, about facing an important decision. Each sibling has a different decision-making style. One tends to avoid decisions, another tends to make decisions too quickly, and the third has a more rational or moderate approach. Suggest that students review the words on page 178 and perhaps use them in their story. They might also review page 20 of *Career Choices*.

To reinforce the decision-making process, the following value exercise was used: The students were asked to choose between two groups. In one they would get $5 a day just to show up to class. In the other, the first person who showed up would get $50, the second got $45, and so on down to zero for the 10th person and all those who followed.

Fifteen students chose the $5 group because they didn't want to compete. When asked what time the second group would arrive to class, one student said, "I'll show up an hour before to make sure I get in." The next said, "I'll show up two hours before." And a third said, "I'll sleep in the hallway!" They learned that if you pick a competitive field, someone will always "sleep in the hallway."

– Doug Campbell
Communication Department
San Gabriel High School
San Gabriel, California

Career Fair

At this point you might like to facilitate a student-directed career fair to be held later in the school year to which the whole school should be invited. This can be a one-class or multiple-class project.

Have students divide into committees by interest areas. Each committee will be responsible for:

1. Inviting one or more appropriate representatives in the career area

2. Gathering additional information about the career area with pamphlets from professional organizations, books, and so on

3. Designing and writing a fact sheet about the career that can be passed out at the fair

4. Display setup and cleanup

An organizational committee of five or six students should include a chair or co-chair(s), school publicity chair, and a facility chair.

After reading Julius Caesar by William Shakespeare, I ask, "Does Brutus make the right decision?" This is used as the culminating literary piece after studying the complete process of making decisions. Students then have to decide how they would have made a different decision than he did.

– Sharon Hurwitz
English Teacher and Technology Facilitator
Bethel High School
Hampton, Virginia

Optional

Pages 142-163

To Build a Fire
by Jack London
Read after reading page 179 in *Career Choices*

Instructor's Notes:

Chapter 8

Setting Goals and Solving Problems

Chapter 8 is the first of the "How to Get It" chapters that make up the remainder of the book. As they move through this final section, students will be making the plans, learning the skills, and acquiring the tools they will need to realize their dreams.

Solving problems and setting goals are two of the most important skills a person can learn. Fortunately, because new problems keep coming along and because there are always new goals to be set and achieved, everyone has ample opportunity to practice these skills!

Optional

Possibilities

Uphill
by Christina Rosseti
Read before beginning Chapter 8

Pages 164-165

Tools for Solving Problems

Page 183-185   Page 86

Learning objective:

To help students identify and apply the problem-solving techniques as presented in the text.

Presentation suggestions:

Discuss the way Hubert's problem relates to the four problem-solving tools: delaying gratification, accepting responsibility, dedication to truth or reality, and balancing. Then ask students to complete the exercise on page 185 individually or in small groups. Follow up with a class discussion.

Activities:

For further small group discussion, ask students to consider the following situations.

Jon has offered to lend his car to Pat for a weekend if Pat will let Jon copy his homework. Pat knows it's wrong to cheat and that he could be suspended from school if he's caught. But, he rationalizes, Jon isn't as good a student as he is, and the teacher really didn't explain the assignment well enough for him to understand.

What sacrifices or risks is Pat taking if he gives Jon his homework?

What sacrifices or risks is he taking if he refuses?

Who is responsible for solving Pat's problem? Jon's?

What are the facts in the situation?

What wishful thinking might enter into Pat's decision-making process?

What do you think Pat should do?

Lucy has been asked to go out drinking with a new group of friends on Friday night after work. Her friend Debbie plans to drive. Lucy knows it's not a good idea to drink and drive, but Debbie assures her that she knows when she's had enough. Lucy doesn't want to be left out.

What sacrifices or risks is Lucy taking if she goes with her friends?

What sacrifices or risks is she taking if she stays home?

Who is responsible for Lucy's safety?

What are the facts of the situation?

What kind of wishful thinking could enter into Lucy's decision-making process?

What do you think Lucy should do?

Assign the movie *Apollo13* for your Video Book Club (see page 96). It includes excellent examples of problem solving and has the added advantage of demonstrating that jobs in math, science and technology can be exciting, dramatic and even heroic.

Resources:

M. Scott Peck, *The Road Less Traveled.* A Touchstone Book, Simon and Schuster, Inc.

Reading assignment:

Romeo and Juliet by William Shakespeare

Romeo and Juliet exemplifies the theme of fate versus free will. Did the lovers bring about their fate through their actions or was it just meant to be?

Once students have completed their reading ask them to rewrite the ending to Romeo and Juliet using Peck's four problem-solving components.

Optional

The Myth of Sisyphus
by Albert Camus
Read after completing pages 182-185 in *Career Choices*

Pages 166-171

Setting Goals and Objectives

Page 186-190

Page 86

Learning objective:

To introduce students to a process for writing quantitative goals and objectives.

Presentation suggestions:

Setting goals and objectives is an extremely important skill, especially for teens who tend to think in vague generalities. Make a presentation from the text, carefully working through the examples. It is essential that students become familiar with the three questions every goal statement must answer:

What will be different?

By how much or how many?

By when?

Ask students to complete the exercises on pages 188 and 189 alone or in small groups. Ask a few volunteers to write and diagram on the board their goals and objectives from page 189.

You may want to provide additional practice by listing incomplete goal statements and having students indicate what component is missing. Examples:

Get a good job this summer.	*What will be different?*
Learn to speak Italian.	*When?*
Get some new school clothes.	*How much or how many? When?*
Learn to use a new word processing program.	*When?*
Make some new friends.	*How many? When?*

Activity:

Have students choose their most important goal for the next two weeks. Then ask them to write objectives for it. Ask them to keep this assignment at the front of their binder so they can glance at it over the next two weeks.

At the end of two weeks, have students share their goals and objectives in class discussion and report on how successful they were at meeting them.

When students have finished reporting, take a poll to see how many believe writing their goals and objectives down was helpful.

246

Note: If students are having trouble writing objectives for their goals, have them first identify the steps for reaching their goals. Then translate each step into quantitative objectives, with the three different components. It is helpful to list them in chronological order based on the date of completion.

Follow-up:

Encourage students to practice this skill by setting daily, weekly, and monthly goals and objectives. Suggest that they reward themselves for achieving their goals with small indulgences such as a new music CD or tickets for a special event.

Setting Goals and Objectives works very well with our business men and women who come into our classes and work with our students. The students, at first, struggle with the concept of goal setting....As the year progresses, they are asked to make weekly, monthly and long-term goals. Most of my students stated that this has helped them to improve their goals and also strengthen their organization skills.

– Dee Hennmann
English Teacher
Sandra High School
Albuquerque, New Mexico

Optional

Pages 102-110

Optional

Pages 178-211

Excerpt from *The Prince of Tides*
by Pat Conroy
Read after completing pages 182-191 in *Career Choices*

Instructor's Notes:

Chapter 9

Avoiding Detours and Roadblocks

The fact that everyone has some degree of difficulty in his or her life comes as a surprise to most people. We tend to think that things should run smoothly—and that they do for everyone else. It's easy, therefore, to give up when problems present themselves, or to turn to drugs or alcohol for relief from these difficulties. In this chapter, students should learn that problems are facts of life that must be faced head-on if they are to be overcome. Since they are responsible for their own lives, it is up to them to overcome any limitations they perceive.

In dealing with the issues of teen parenting, dropping out of school, and using drugs, we ask students to imagine how short-range "solutions" can affect their lives in the long run. A number of exercises in this chapter, in fact, give students a chance to think about long-range planning.

Students may also feel pressured to give up their dreams. This pressure can be external (from parents, society, and so on) or internal (based on irrational fears, anxiety, inability to take risks, and the like). Young women are especially prone to feelings of this sort. Review this material carefully, bringing in a school counselor or outside speaker if necessary. Remind students to turn back to this section any time in the future when they are discouraged and think they want to give up on a dream.

Optional

Pages 214-215

Mother to Son
  by Langston hughes
Read after completing pages 196-197 in *Career Choices*

What's Your Excuse?

Page 197-199   Page 89

Learning objective:

Students examine some of the reasons people use for not doing what they want to do, or can do, evaluate those excuses and determine what might be done to avoid using them.

Presentation suggestions:

Review the material on pages 197-199. Then ask students to check any "I can't do it because" statements which apply to them. After they have completed their charts, turn to page 199 and ask students to take turns reading items from the "They did it in spite of" chart. Discuss any additions that might be made to the chart.

Activities:

Invite someone who has overcome a significant handicap to address the class. Ask your guest to speak about both the physical and emotional processes experienced: not just the physical obstacles encountered in not being able to walk, for example, but how the debilitation affected attitudes and self-esteem.

Assign library research on others who have overcome handicaps. Have students write a one-paragraph summary of the research to share with the class.

One excuse area not covered in the text is the "social excuse." Brainstorm with students different social excuses such as:

I don't have time.

None of my friends do it.

My parents would object.

Evaluate those excuses. How inflexible are they? Are there situations where these excuses should not stand in the way?

If you are dealing with a population with a temporary problem (curable physical or emotional problems, incarceration, chemical dependency, or the like), encourage students to carry or display photos of themselves before the problem developed. It is helpful for them to be able to see themselves as healthy, functioning, changing, free individuals.

Reading assignment:

Ask students to read a biography or an autobiography of an individual who overcame an adversity. Brainstorm other individuals in addition to those mentioned on pages 198-199. One obvious choice is the biography of Helen Keller.

To add an element of fun to the class and to control excuse-making, we made a list of excuses—some of them wild ("bad hair day")—posted them, and point to them when students haven't finished an assignment, are late, etc. This was a humorous extension of the activity on page 197.

– Lynn Porter
 Coordinator of High School Diploma Program
 Santa Monica-Malibu Unified School District
 Santa Monica, CA

Optional

Pages 172-177

Hope
by Emily Dickinson

Expect Nothing
by Alice Walker

Read together after completing pages 194-199 in *Career Choices*

Taking Responsibility

Page 200

Page 90

Learning objective:

To help students evaluate excuses and reframe them so that they are accepting the responsibility for their problems and also opening new avenues for solving them.

Presentation suggestions:

Ask students to write some excuses they've recently used to absolve themselves from responsibility for solving their problems. Then, individually, or in small groups, ask them to reframe the excuses, this time *accepting* the responsibility.

As practice, it may be helpful to reframe the following examples in a class brainstorming session:

I can't take a job because I don't have any way to get there.

I can't do my homework because it's too noisy at home.

I can't go to the party because my parents won't buy me a new outfit.

I didn't make the team because the coach is out to get me.

I failed the test because the teacher expects too much.

Reframed examples:

I can't take a job because I haven't taken the time to investigate bus schedules or car pooling opportunities.

I can't do my homework because I don't want to go to the library.

I can't go to the party because I'm not imaginative enough to come up with something appropriate to wear.

I didn't make the team because I didn't practice hard enough.

I failed the test because I didn't seek out the extra help I need.

Be sure to remind your students that although they are responsible for their own actions and decisions, many sources of help are available. Another step to solving problems should be to identify those sources of help and support and determine when to use them.

Startling Statement Quiz

Page 201-202   Page 91

Learning objective:

To expose students to some of the statistics regarding teen pregnancy, dropping out of school, and substance abuse.

Presentation suggestions:

Quizzes such as this seem to have a lasting impact on students. Statistics that might be easily dismissed or forgotten in a text or lecture loom much larger in this context. Have students answer the questions to the best of their ability, then turn the page and review the correct statistics. When students have answered correctly, their impressions are reinforced. If they were wrong, the correct answer often makes a deep impression. Follow with group discussion.

Activities:

Instead of having students take the quiz individually, divide the class into groups of three students and give them time to come to a consensus about which are the correct answers. The ensuing discussions can be valuable as students examine their own thoughts and where they came from, as well as those of their classmates. Follow with large group discussion.

For extra credit, have students research a topic of interest to the class and write their own startling statement quiz, using the statistics they uncover.

Energizer:

Offer a prize to the group that gets the most correct answers to the quiz. This further reinforces the learning process because the students try even harder to come up with the right answers.

Detours and Roadblocks

Page 203-206   Page 92-93

Learning objective:

To allow students to examine some common problems and then project into the future to consider the possible long-term consequences of present actions.

Presentation suggestions:

Ask the class to read the three stories aloud and follow with group discussion, or have students complete the exercise on their own and then discuss in class. Another alternative would be to break into groups of about three students each and assign one of the problems to each group. Bring the class together and have the groups present their conclusions. If you have more than one group considering a particular story, compare answers to see how they differ and how they are alike.

Activities:

If you know of someone who actually dealt with one of the problems presented here approximately fifteen years ago, you might ask him or her to talk with the class about it and explain what he or she would do differently if given the chance to go back in time.

The section on roadblocks and detours was very rewarding because the students realized they were using some of those excuses now.

> – Hattie Burns
>   Business Education Teacher
>   Chesterfield Middle School
>   Chesterfield, South Carolina

The Detours and Roadblocks unit really helped students to think about choices they make. The Economics of Bad Habits lesson really opened some eyes and several students committed to stop smoking.

> – Sara L. Carter
>   Business Education Teacher
>   Garden City High School
>   Garden City, Michigan

Is It Worth Staying in School?

Page 207

Page 94

Learning objective:

To help students personalize the effect of dropping out of school on their eventual job satisfaction.

Presentation suggestions:

If members of your class are at high risk of dropping out of school, you should spend considerable time on this activity. Complete the steps outlined in the text. Revisit the library or career center so students can complete the Career Interest Survey on page 150 for jobs not requiring a diploma. As a class, discuss the questions at the bottom of page 207.

Activity:

Invite a panel of adults who dropped out of high school to speak to the class. One member of the panel should be someone who then went back to school to realize his or her dream.

This exercise is important even if your students are all college-bound. Dropping out of college can have devastating effects on their career satisfaction.

Resource:

Occupational Outlook Quarterly. Outlook 2000. This interesting governmental publication gives figures for various levels of education in each major occupational grouping.

Students finally understood the cost of an upscale lifestyle and, most importantly, that education plays a major part in determining lifestyle.

— Dan Somrock
Social Studies Teacher
Cass Lake-Bena High School
Cass Lake, Minnesota

The Economics of Bad Habits

Page 208-209

Page 95

Learning objective:

To enable students to comprehend the financial costs of bad habits. The concrete evidence presented in this exercise may be more readily grasped than information about the physical or emotional costs, which can seem abstract.

Presentation suggestions:

Review the material and then have students complete the exercise at the bottom of page 208. (Mathematical answers are on page 209. What each student would do with the money, of course, will vary.) Bring the class together for a group discussion. This is a good time to talk about retirement accounts, guaranteed incomes, and the like. While it may be difficult for most students to imagine that they will ever be of retirement age, you might ask them to think about some older people they know, preferably someone who has enough money to live comfortably and someone who just gets by. How do the lifestyles of these individuals differ? Who has more options for enjoying life? Who has more worries?

Break the class into small groups to consider the daily, weekly, and lifetime costs of nonproductive or even destructive habits. Use the chart at the bottom of page 209. Discuss the proactive nature of turning a negative activity (bad habit) into a positive one (saving for the future). How would that make them feel?

Activities:

Invite a guest speaker to discuss pensions and retirement accounts. Ask her or him to share charts that show how much income will be generated with different savings plans.

Ask a panel of senior citizens to speak to the class about their retirement planning and their current lifestyles. If possible, invite persons whose experiences range from satisfactory to struggling.

Optional

Pages 221-224

Over the Hill to the Poor-House
by Will M. Carleton
Read before completing pages 208-209 in *Career Choices*

If You're A Woman

Career Choices
Page 211-213

Workbook and Portfolio
Page 96-98

Learning objective:

To help students understand how flexibility and higher salary relate to mixing career and family, and to have young women consider how nontraditional careers may be the best option.

Presentation suggestions:

Young women who hope to have families often think that the best career options for them are the so-called traditional women's jobs: nursing, teaching, clerical work, retail sales, waitressing, and the like. On the surface, these choices seem reasonable. Nurses and secretaries can usually drop in and out of the workforce if they want to spend a few years at home with their children, and they can find work almost anywhere to accommodate a husband who may be transferred from place to place. Teachers share the same vacations as their children. Waitresses and sales clerks needn't think too much about their jobs when they're off duty.

Upon closer examination, however, this reasoning falls apart. Today, most women work outside the home even when they have small children. In fact, more than half of all women with children under the age of one year are in the workforce while a staggering number of women are the sole support of their families. We have reached a point where it is less important to be able to move into and out of the workforce than it is to earn a sufficient salary and to have the day-to-day flexibility required for responsible parenting, such as being able to take a few hours off to attend a school play or parent-teacher session.

The jobs that offer these benefits are likely to be those traditionally held by men, whether blue collar or professional. This exercise should help young women see that preparing for this kind of career is as important for them as it is for the young men in the class.

Review the instructions carefully, then have students complete the exercise on their own.

The amount needed for a woman and three children to live in minimum comfort will vary greatly from community to community. It might be a good idea to bring the class together to try to determine an appropriate figure for your community.

Activities:

Ask a woman who is successfully mixing career and family to talk with the class about her job, training, reasons for choosing that field. Consider blue-collar workers as well as professionals.

On the board, list a number of jobs traditionally held by women (see above) and an equal number most often held by men in the past. Discuss. What are the advantages and disadvantages of each? Which usually pay more? Which usually require more training? Is there anything about the work itself that makes it unsuitable or impossible for someone of the other sex to perform?

For a couple in which either partner is capable of supporting the family, brainstorm possible benefits such as taking time off, going back to school, taking a lower-paying job that is more emotionally rewarding, feeling less pressure, and so on. Discuss ways in which employers might make life easier for all working parents through job sharing, flexible hours, parental leave, child care facilities, allowing people to work at home, and so on.

Resource:

For more information, exercises, and activities, see *More Choices: A Strategic Planning Guide for Mixing Career and Family,* by Bingham and Stryker, Advocacy Press. See page 350 for ordering information.

I think in the exploration of non-traditional careers, the female students have realized that there is a whole "new" world that is open to them!

– Catherine M. Fitzpatrick
Family and Consumer Science Teacher
Humbolt Secondary Complex
St. Paul, Minnesota

I have seen former students enroll at Tech College because of what they learned in class.

– Janet Richards
Equity Teacher
Johnson High School
St. Paul, Minnesota

Optional

Pages 100-101

Before You Give Up Your Dream

Career Choices

Page 215

Workbook and Portfolio

Page 99

Learning objective:

To help students learn an evaluation technique to be used before acting rashly in abandoning a dream or plan.

Presentation suggestions:

Ask for a volunteer to identify a dream he or she is considering giving up. Then in "fishbowl" fashion (see page 85 of this *Guide*), work through the questions with that student. Ask the rest of the class to share problem-solving ideas they have with the student.

Optional

Possibilities

Pages 212-220

A Dream Deferred
  by Langston Hughes
Read after completing pages 214-215 in *Career Choices*

A Noiseless Patient Spider
  by Walt Whitman

All I Really Need to Know I Learned in Kindergarten
  by Robert Fulghum
Read after completing pages 216-217 in *Career Choices*

Developing
Anxiety Tolerance

Page 216-217   Page 100

Learning objective:

To help students overcome fears by seeing themselves be successful at whatever makes them anxious.

Presentation suggestions:

Refer to pages 169 and 216-217 in this *Guide* to review the process of this activity.

Ask students to identify an activity that makes them feel anxious and then, like Carlotta, break that activity down to its elements. Write a guided visualization that will help them become comfortable with the feeling, thereby defusing it.

A note on guided visualization: This technique is being used more and more by the established medical profession to control pain and anxiety and to promote healing and behavioral change. Yet it should also be pointed out to students that this technique is powerful and in the wrong hands can be used for brainwashing and manipulation.

Reading assignment:

The Tell-Tale Heart, by Edgar Allen Poe

A wonderfully gruesome tale of fear controlling and destroying a man's sanity. This can lead to excellent discussion on fear and anxiety! Good reading with excellent film and tape available.

Optional

    Pages 6-9

One Step at a Time

Page 218-221　　Page 101

Learning objective:

To expose students to a hierarchical approach to conquering anxieties.

Presentation suggestions:

Read Sally's story aloud and discuss what she did and how she did it. How might her life have been different if she had not taken these steps? After brainstorming, ask the class to think of common fears and list them on the board.

Ask students individually to list some of their own fears, and then to rank them from the easiest to deal with to the hardest. Can they come up with a plan to overcome these fears? Some students may want to discuss this in small groups. Others may prefer to do this project privately. Respect those wishes. This might be a good time to bring in the school counselor for a class discussion.

Emphasize the importance of identifying the stress response and then learning to tolerate that feeling. It helps to start with stress responses of lesser degree and work up to stress responses of greater degree.

A word of caution: While some phobic (severe stress reaction) responses can be cured in this fashion, it should not be attempted without the help of a trained professional. If you identify this potential in a student, be empathetic and supportive and suggest that he or she seek help from the school counselor or community counseling service. Check with your administration on school policy.

Optional

Pages 225-227

George Gray

by Edgra Lee Masters

Read after completing pages 216-221 in *Career Choices*

Yorik's Story

Career Choices
Page 222-223

Workbook and Portfolio
Page 102

Learning objective:

To give students an opportunity, in a third-person situation, to make long-range plans for the success of someone who could reasonably be expected to fail. Since this is the classic American dream, we hope the exercise will allow students who see themselves as outside the mainstream of American society to view their own situation with more optimism and determination.

Presentation suggestions:

This exercise could take up to two class periods. Point out that this is in preparation for the final exam (Chapter 12). You may decide to complete the exercise in small groups or as a class.

If you choose to do the exercise in class, begin with a review of setting goals and objectives. Remind students, too, that Yorik has both a vision (his goals) and the energy to realize it (his objectives, or action plan). Vision plus energy equals success.

HINT: It's often helpful to start with year ten and work backward.

Taking Risks

Page 224-225   No Workbook Page

Learning objective:

To help students see that taking calculated risks is an important skill.

Presentation suggestions:

Although the text contains no exercise on this topic, it's important to discuss it thoroughly. As the text states, taking a risk is a sort of cross between overcoming fears and making decisions. Review these concepts as part of your presentation.

Ask the class for examples of things they believe many people are afraid to do that are not life-threatening, such as public speaking, applying for a job, asking for a date, introducing yourself to a stranger at a party, and so on. List these on the board. Discuss possible outcomes for someone taking these risks. What is the worst that could happen? The best thing? Could it be worthwhile to take this risk?

Activities:

Ask students how they would complete the sentence "If I could do anything I wanted, I would…" Is this action desirable? Is it risky? Have the class evaluate the risks involved.

Ask students to give examples of times they took a risk. Did it pay off?

Brainstorm ways in which students could motivate themselves to take a calculated risk. They might break the action down into more manageable parts, for example, or offer themselves a reward.

Invite someone who has taken a major risk to address the class.

Making a Move - Investigating Other Areas of the Country

Curriculum sequence:

You may want to conduct this research following Yorik's Story and the section on risk taking in *Career Choices* (pages 224-226). It is also a good follow-up to the Internet Activity described on pages 226 and 227 in this *Guide*. This exercise is also appropriate for students completing the Home Affordability Across the Country and Where Do I Want to Live? exercises on pages 27-30 in *Lifestyle Math*.

Learning objective:

Students will learn how to design and conduct custom searches using key words on a variety of Internet search engines. They will also experience the power of the Internet and how it can answer all their questions if they take the time to learn simple Internet skills, practice basic logic and spend some time at a keyboard.

Methodology:

The thought of moving to another part of the country is frightening for some people. But sometimes specific career or educational plans mandate a move, at least for a period of time. The inability to be mobile or flexible could stagnate both career and educational plans and lead to a life of frustration such as the one described in *A Dream Deferred* (*Possibilities*, page 212). Therefore it is important to help students investigate what it would be like to live in another area of the country so they can view this as a feasible alternative.

Once students have located an interesting job in another region (page 226 of this *Guide*) or have identified a community that sounds intriguing from an economic standpoint (*Lifestyle Math*, pages 27-30), have them ask themselves, "What would it be like to live there?" This question will direct their search.

Internet directions:

Review the search engines available and how each one is used. We suggest you begin with http://www.yahoo.com/ because it is easy to expand a search directly from this search engine to another.

As a class, brainstorm the key words that will help the students investigate a community. For instance, by using key words, *Tampa Real Estate*, students will have access to a variety of real estate web sites from the Tampa area. When they surf these sites, they'll gather data on the housing available and its costs. Most of these web pages have complete descriptions of the homes available, as well as photos.

By using the key words, *Tampa Chamber of Commerce*, they may find an informative web site on a variety of lifestyle topics. Besides offering data, many sites encourage questions and correspondence. E-mail forms are included so students can request brochures and informational fliers.

Encourage your students to create key words that expand their custom searches. Ask them to share their key words and Internet adventures with their classmates.

This activity offers an opportunity to teach the skills of conducting custom searches on the web. For complete instructional details, visit our *Making It Real* site on our web page.

Additional *Making It Real* activities are available through the Academic Innovations home page on the World Wide Web. For more information on how you can access these Internet enhancement activities, see pages 36 and 37 of this *Instructor's Guide*.

Getting Back on Track
If You've Been Derailed

Page 226

No Workbook Page

Presentation suggestions:

If you know of individuals in the class who are "derailed," it's important that they learn what resources are available to them. A good way to accomplish this goal without singling anyone out is to have a guest speaker or school counselor talk about the various sources of help available in your community. This is valuable information for the whole class. Everyone has problems from time to time.

Reading assignment:

I Am the Cheese, by Robert Cormier

This is a story of a boy seemingly lost in a circle of memories and forgetfulness resulting from a traumatic experience. As he continues his symbolic trip, he comes closer and closer to discovering the truth and thereby freeing himself from the prison of his own mind and his surroundings. To do this, he must face his fears. This book leads to important discussions on self-discovery, overcoming fears, perseverance, and the freedom of self-knowledge.

Instructor's Notes:

Chapter 10

Attitude is Everything

Attitudes can be empowering—or limiting. To paraphrase the old adage, "You are what you think you are." In this chapter, we try to instill the attitudes that lead to success, as defined by each individual.

We have identified four areas of attitude for discussion here: attitudes toward excellence, attitudes toward the work ethic, attitudes toward a changing world, and, most important, attitudes that make any chosen career a dignified and noble pursuit.

TECHNICAL SUPPORT
For the *Career Choices* curriculum
(800) 967-8016, ext. 677

Affirmation

Page 231   Page 104

Learning objective:

To help students understand the power of affirmations in changing self-limiting attitudes.

Presentation suggestions:

Affirmations have been shown to be a powerful tool in changing attitudes. Ask students to think of attitudes they have that may damage their potential for future success: I'm too shy, too dumb, too lazy, too poor, too uncoordinated, and so on. Then have them write affirmations to help change these attitudes: I _____ am a confident person, I _____ am a good student, I _____ am willing to work hard for what I want, and so on.

Activities:

Provide 3 × 5 cards on which students can write their affirmations. Instruct them to take these home and tape them to their bedroom or bathroom mirrors so they can be repeated every time they comb their hair or brush their teeth.

Follow-up:

Remind students often to keep repeating their affirmations. Several weeks after they've begun, ask if any have noticed a difference in their behavior or thought patterns about themselves.

The Six Es of Excellence

Page 232-235   No Workbook
Page

Learning objective:
To recognize and evaluate the characteristics and attitudes of excellence.

Presentation suggestions:
Discuss the concept of excellence with the class. This goes beyond the "vision plus energy equals success" equation. Excellence requires added effort. Ask students if they can recall an instance in which they truly excelled at something, or can think of some part of their lives for which they must meet particularly high standards (playing a musical instrument or sport, for example). Then discuss the six Es as presented in the text, asking students to consider what part each of these characteristics plays in their own interest area. Emphasize that although performance is often judged by others, only the individuals concerned know for sure whether they gave it their best shot.

Activities:
Ask students to write a paper about something they have done or would like to do, relating how each of the six Es plays a part in this activity.

Or, ask the class to write about different activities in which they display each of the six Es (expecting to be a good student, having enthusiasm for basketball, putting energy into making friends, and so on). Can they think of ways to bring these activities together?

Reading assignment:
To Kill a Mockingbird, by Harper Lee

This classic novel opens up many wonderful areas of discussion on overcoming adversity and striving for what is right. The book deals with prejudice in a small southern town and one man's courage to do the right thing. The excellent movie based on the novel can be shown.

The Necklace by Guy de Maupassant

A young woman dooms herself to years of hard labor and poverty because of her inability to admit to her friend that she lost a necklace she borrowed to attend a special ball one evening. Years later, she meets her friend and explains to her that she appears old and worn out "because of her." Ironically, the friend reveals that the necklace had been a fake. Excellent story, excellent departure point for a discussion on "facing up to the truth" and dealing honestly with problems.

Optional

The Necklace
by Guy De Maupassant
Read after completing pages 232-235 in *Career Choices*

Pages 228-239

Going for It. . .Work Is an Aggressive Act

Page 236-237   Page 104

Learning objective:

To help students realize that action is necessary to achieve any goal.

Presentation suggestions:

This is a good exercise to have students read aloud. The correct answers are obvious, and class reaction should help reinforce the lesson to be learned. Young women especially should be assured that aggressive acts are often required at work in order to achieve excellence.

Activities:

Ask students to suggest aggressive words and phrases often used in the context of work and list them on the board. Examples: organize, manipulate, control, wrestle, grapple, make a killing, break a leg, knock 'em dead, sock it to 'em, whip into shape, beat into the ground, take a beating, take a blood bath, make a pitch, score a point.

Repeat the same activity with words which connote excellence, noting how they also imply aggression. Examples: superiority, supremacy, advantage, the height of, unsurpassed, overriding, transcending, unequaled, paramount, preeminent, above the mark.

There is no *work* without *effort*—and *effort* requires aggressiveness.

I had one student who completed his resume, submitted it to a prospective employer, and was hired. He graduates this year and wants to become a manager in his company's business.

– Lela Fay Roy
English Teacher
Somerset High School
Somerset. Kentucky

You're the Boss

Page 238-241   Page 105-107

Learning objective:

To clarify the concept of the work ethic and help students see how it relates to their lives.

Presentation suggestions:

Read the introductory paragraph to the class. Help students identify with Chris so that as they evaluate the employees, they can understand the employer's point of view. This person has made a large personal and financial investment in the business. If students were the employer, how would they feel about the people described in this exercise? Discuss individual employees in small groups. Have students identify the problem exhibited by each employee and design an objective to help him or her overcome it. What about Tim? What characteristics does he exhibit? (Dependable, helpful, creative, easy to get along with, honest and thoughtful, hard working. These are productive work habits.)

Brainstorm other productive work habits:

1. Doing your best

2. Finishing a task that you've begun

3. Cooperating with fellow employees

4. Recognizing that most workers have a boss

5. Teamwork toward the common goal

We tried to make our work environment in class as much like a work situation as possible. We used teams, projects, due dates set in advance, bonuses, etc.

–Linda Neef
9th grade English teacher
Pardeeville High School
Pardeeville, Wisconsin

Activities:

Ask students who have jobs whether the people they work with exhibit any of these negative or positive traits (no names, please). Which type of co-worker is most enjoyable?

Discuss the phrase *Puritan work ethic*. The term *work ethic* refers to something you do because you feel obliged to do so. In contrast, *work values* implies something you *choose* to do.

Ask students to evaluate their own work habits. Those who don't have jobs should apply these concepts to school and other responsibilities.

When students look at situations involving others, it helps them to address those same problems with themselves.

– Karen Michael
English Teacher
Bronson Junior-Senior High School
Bronson, Michigan

Optional

To Be of Use
by Marge Piercy
Read after completing pages 238-241 in *Career Choices*

Pages 249-251

The Employee of the Twenty-first Century

Career Choices
Page 242-245

Workbook and Portfolio
Page 108-109

Learning objective:

To demonstrate the attitudes that will be most in demand for workers in the future.

Presentation suggestions:

After reading the introduction, ask students to take the self-evaluation quiz and score their answers. Follow with class discussion, brainstorming objectives that can be used to adjust attitudes.

Activities:

Discuss technological advances most responsible for bringing about the changes in the way people work (jet travel, computers, fax machines, and so on).

Have a banker, stockbroker, or communications specialist talk with the class about international perspective in the workplace.

Divide the class into groups of three to five. Ask each group to invent an item or service and present their design to the class, answering the following questions:

Why is this needed?

Will it create new career opportunities?

What type?

What impact will it have on the future?

Some examples include:

Interactive videos for "at home" education

Gasless automobiles

Cure for the common cold

Servant robots

At-home water desalination machines

Energizer:

Read to the class *Tonia the Tree*, by Sandy Stryker, the 1989 winner of the Merit Award of Friends of American Writers. This charming allegory about dealing with change, the story of a tree that must be uprooted and moved in order to grow, will launch great class discussion.

Possible reading assignments:

Future Shock, by Alvin Toffler

Martian Chronicles, by Ray Bradbury

Writing assignment:

A.   Divide the class into small groups to brainstorm possible story lines about the following concepts:

1. Embracing change

2. Valuing people different from you

3. Curiosity and valuing learning

B.   Write an allegory based on one of these concepts.

Optional

Possibilities

Pages 240-248

Tonia the Tree
  by Sandy Stryker
Read after completing pages 242-245 in *Career Choices*

Be the Best of Whatever You Are
  by Douglas Malloch
Read after reading page 246 in *Career Choices*

Chapter 11

Getting Experience

This chapter introduces students to some of the most basic job-hunting skills: writing résumés, locating jobs, research interviews, filling out applications, job interviews. Because so much information is already available on these topics, we have not covered them in depth. You may want to refer students to other publications or library research if the materials are not sufficient for the needs of your class.

Here are resources you may want to review:

Martin Kimeldorf, *First Step to Employability*. Educational Design, Inc.

Martin Kimeldorf, *Pathway to Work*. Meridian Publishing Company.

Debbie Bloch, *How to Get and Get Ahead on Your First Job*. VGM Career Horizons.

Debbie Bloch, *How to Have a Winning Job Interview*. VGM Career Horizons.

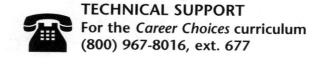

TECHNICAL SUPPORT
For the *Career Choices* curriculum
(800) 967-8016, ext. 677

Creative Idea: Students Create Multi-Media Presentations

Not every school is fortunate enough to have a sophisticated media lab, but California's San Gabriel High School has such a facility. Thanks to a state 1470 grant, English and Career Education teacher Elizabeth Farris makes good use of it.

When her ninth grade students had worked through a good portion of the *Career Choices* curriculum (in a year-long class), Farris assigned them to use HyperStudio, an authoring software program from Roger Wagner Co., to make a presentation on something they had learned. Some focused on a career of interest, others chose one of the topics from the text, such as Maslow's triangle, personal profiles, "why people work." To develop their projects, they used CD-ROMs, laser discs, clip art, drawings and scanned pictures, all put together in the media lab. One of the highlights came from several future firefighters who used segments of the movie *Backdraft*, complete with theme music and sound effects.

Later in the year, when the class was writing their resumes (Chapter Eleven of *Career Choices*), Farris reminded students, "You all have computer skills." "We do?" they replied. They'd been so involved, having so much fun, that they didn't realize they were also picking up some very high-tech skills along the way!

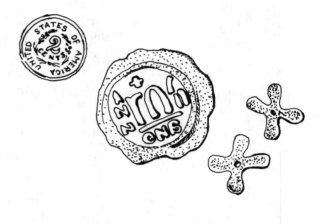

Reproduced from quarterly Focus on the Future *newsletter. To be added to our mailing list for this free publication, call (800) 967-8016.*

Your Resume

Page 250-253   Page 111

Learning objective:

To give students experience in writing a personal résumé.

Presentation suggestions:

Review the information and example in the text before students complete and turn in their own résumés. If the school has a computer lab, you may suggest that résumés produced by the laser printer will look the most professional.

Activities:

Using a job chosen from the local classified ads, students practice writing a cover letter for that position.

Cover letter checklist:

1. Title of position identified

2. How you found out about the vacancy

3. Brief highlights of your résumé related to the job requirements

4. How and when you can be contacted

5. Closure

If you know someone who works in a personnel office, see if you can get copies of about twenty résumés, ranging from very good to very bad. (Black out all personal information to assure privacy.) Divide the class into small "Personnel Department" groups to evaluate the résumés and decide on five to interview. Ask them to evaluate reasons for their choices.

When they are finished, ask these very important questions: "What impact did the neatness and correctness (spelling, grammar, punctuation, and so on) have on your impression of the applicant? Did you eliminate anyone from the interview process because their resume was not neat, complete, and readable?"

At this point, it should become clear to students how writing skills can have an impact on their lives.

Finding A Job…Conduct an Informational Interview

Page 254-255   No Workbook Page

Learning objective:

To give students experience in conducting informational interviews.

Presentation suggestions:

See page 218 in this *Guide*, the Shadow Program, for hints on finding people willing to be interviewed. Review the information in the text before students conduct their interviews. Be sure to review the etiquette involved.

Activities:

Ask students to write a paper about what they learned from their interviews.

Our 10th graders do a "Career Portfolio"—complete with actual résumé and model application form—to present to parents at our Spring Open House. Its purpose is for students to use when applying for summer jobs, as well as to demonstrate growth and achievement toward personal goals over the course of the year. It begins with a student letter to parents about "me in 1 to 5 years."

– Andrée Liscoscos
English Department Chair
Santa Maria High School
Santa Maria, California

Job Applications

Page 256-257   Page 112

Learning objective:

To give students experience in filling out job applications.

Presentation suggestions:

Review the material in *Career Choices*. Ask students to get any information they need and then to answer the questions on page 256. Remind them to bring this information along whenever they apply for a job.

Activities:

Go to a local bank or other large employer in the community and see if you can get copies of their application forms so students can have experience filling out an actual application. When they have completed the forms, break the class into small groups and ask students to evaluate each other's applications. Would they hire this person? Since most won't have much job experience to relate, the evaluations should center around neatness and completeness.

The Job Interview

Page 258-259   Page 113

Learning objective:
To provide information on, and experience in, being interviewed for a job.

Presentation suggestions:
Review the information and the questions in the text. To give students practice in being interviewed, use the application forms they filled out for the previous exercise. These should be for an entry-level job. Have students take turns conducting interviews for this job, or invite a real employer to interview individuals as the rest of the class observes.

Energizer:
If your school has video recording equipment, tape the interviews and play them back so individuals can judge their own performance. Perhaps a professional interviewer will be willing to watch with the students and offer hints for improvements. This is a frightening experience for most students, but it can be very valuable. You may want to get assistance from the vocational counselor or someone else in the school who has had experience with this type of activity.

The interviewing helps them to realize how important it is to present themselves appropriately for an interview.

–Ann Barber
Business Education Teacher
Lenox Memorial High School
Lenox, Massachusetts

Optional

Looking for Work
by Gary Soto
Read after completing pages 250-259 in *Career Choices*

Pages 254-261

Dealing With Rejection and Accepting a Job

Page 260-261   No Workbook
                          Page

Learning objective:
To help students gain information on how to deal with these two facets of a job search.

Presentation suggestions:
Review the materials in the text. Some students may wish to share experiences they've had in these areas.

This chapter is most effective when I take at least two weeks. My students are required to fill out job applications and compose a working résumé. After this is accomplished, we set appointments for a mock interview. The students are required to dress professionally and prepare for their interview. The interviews are videotaped. After completion, we view the results in class. Students can see their strengths as well as get tips on how to improve. Everyone learns something; it is a very positive experience.

– Stephanie Born-Mathieu
Business teacher
Edison High School
Minneapolis, Minnesota

Making Connections

Page 262-263   Page 114

Learning objective:

To help students gain an understanding of mentoring and encourage them to watch for opportunities to have or be a mentor.

Presentation suggestions:

Discuss the material in the book. Then review the questions on page 263, either individually, in small groups, or as a class. Ask students to relate their own experiences as mentors.

Activities:

When guest speakers come to class, ask them about their mentors.

You might have students write a paper about an experience they've had as a mentor. If they don't think they've ever been a mentor, try to jar their memories. Have they ever instructed a younger brother or sister? Helped a new student find his or her way around? Tutored a classmate?

Reading assignment:

Ask each student to read and report on a book whose major theme centers around one of their career interest areas. It could be fiction, biography, or autobiography. This is an ideal time to reinforce library research skills. Be sure to demonstrate the use of *Books in Print: Subject Directory*.

We had them write thank you notes to someone who
helped mentor them after reading "The Bridge Builder."

– Suzanne M. Reese
Teacher/Gifted Liaison
R.L. Turner High School
Carrollton, Texas

Optional

The Bridge Builder
by Will Allen Dromgoole
Thank You, M'am
by Langston Hughes
Read after completing pages 262-263 in *Career Choices*

Pages 262-269

Chapter 12

Where Do You Go from Here?

We've now reached the point in the course where students use the information they've gained and the skills they've developed to write their own plan of action. As they begin, remind them again that this is a tentative plan. It can and probably will be changed. The process, however, can be repeated as often as necessary.

This material can also be used by school counselors as they advise individual students. Recommend that students take their *Career Choices Workbook and Portfolio* to any counseling appointments.

This whole chapter could be assigned as a take-home final examination. Allow at least one week as several assignments require research and contemplation to be completed accurately and thoroughly.

My students worked in groups to produce bulletin boards throughout the school depicting themes learned in their class.

—Janet Richards
Teacher
Johnson High School
St. Paul, Minnesota

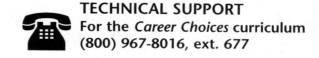

TECHNICAL SUPPORT
For the *Career Choices* curriculum
(800) 967-8016, ext. 677

Getting the Education or Training You Need

Page 267-269   No Workbook Page

Learning objective:

To help students understand the various training opportunities available to them.

Presentation suggestions:

Review and expand on available educational and training opportunities. This is also a good time to bring in various speakers: career counselors, vocational technical counselors, college placement officers, employment development workers, military recruiting officers, and the like.

Resources:

For private trade schools:

> National Association of Trade and Technical Schools
> 2251 Wisconsin Ave., N.W.
> Suite 200
> Washington, D.C. 20007

For private colleges:

> Association of Independent Colleges and Schools
> One Dupont Circle, N.W.
> Washington, D.C. 20036

Activity:

The Bureau of Labor Statistics projects that 16 percent of all workers will have less than a high school education by the year 2000. Brainstorm what kind of jobs those might be. What will be the characteristics of the jobs? Would class members be happy in those jobs?

One student, when asked why he was flunking math even when he said he needed it for his future job, paused then said, "Because I never thought of it like this before, that it would help me for my career."

> – Debra Kuperberg
> Special Education Teacher
> San Gabriel High School
> San Gabriel, California

On-line Research of College and Training Programs

Curriculum sequence: (optional)

This project could be assigned while students are working on pages 267-269 in *Career Choices*.

Internet directions:

Students will conduct key word searches using the Internet search engines along with searches of specific URLs gathered during their earlier research efforts.

Learning objective:

Students will learn how to conduct customized searches of colleges and employment training programs, as well as other institutions.

Methodology:

By this point in the course, students will have a good idea of the types of education and training required to meet their career goals. The Internet is an ideal vehicle for easily gathering comprehensive data on a variety of opportunities. By spending a few hours online, students can gather enough information to begin envisioning their life immediately following high school.

If you have completed a good number of the *Making It Real* activities prior to this, the students should have enough skills and confidence to take this project on with very little instruction from you. With some populations you may want to assign this project to pairs of students with common educational goals.

For the college bound: Students can go online and find detailed information on the majority of colleges throughout the United States and the world. Many universities even have their course catalog online.

For those bound for technical school: Many technical schools and trade associations have web sites where students can find information on their career field of choice.

For students entering the workforce following high school: Students can search trade association sites along with specific articles on their chosen fields to find out more about apprenticeships and internships.

For up-to-date URLs for colleges, technical schools and trade association home pages, visit our *Making It Real* web site.

Lesson extensions:

FINAL Internet project: This project will require that students use all the Internet research skills learned in earlier *Making It Real* lessons. It could be used as the final project and grading opportunity for this technological portion of the class.

Additional *Making It Real* activities are available through the Academic Innovations home page on the World Wide Web. For more information on how you can access these Internet enhancement activities, see pages 36 and 37 of this *Instructor's Guide*.

Where Is It You Want to Go?

Page 270-273

Page 116-118

Presentation suggestions:

Ask students to indicate their career choice in the space provided and then determine the kind of training they need and the duration of that training. Some students will have several options such as vocational school, apprenticeship, or the military. Urge them to consider the advantages and disadvantages of each course of action before making a decision.

The chart on page 271 should require additional research, but it is essential to allow time for this important activity.

Activity:

Knowing exactly what they need to do in order to accomplish their career goals will help students set priorities and make plans. They may be overwhelmed, however, by the thought of spending another ten to fifteen years preparing for and getting established in a job. To help them visualize this commitment as it relates to the normal lifespan of about eighty years, use the following exercise: Give students two pieces of 8½ × 11 graph paper (¼-inch blocks) each, and ask them to tape them together lengthwise. Assuming that each block represents one year, have them label each five-year segment, from age one to eighty. Now have them fill in the blocks representing the years they will need for their education or training. In this context, and considering the financial and emotional rewards involved, the investment of time should appear more justifiable.

You might consider recommending that students reproduce the charts on page 270 and 271 and complete them for at least one other job. This will enable them to compare the education and training requirements for each career.

Optional

Pages 270-272

If
by Rudyard Kipling
Read after completing pages 270-273 in *Career Choices*

286

Delaying Gratification

Page 274-275   Page 119-120

Learning objective:

To personalize the issue of delaying gratification by identifying the sacrifices and commitments required.

Presentation suggestions:

Break the class into small groups based generally on individual career plans, type and duration of training required, or general career field—whatever seems most appropriate. Since training for any career involves some type of delayed gratification, it should be fairly easy for groups to identify the types of sacrifices they will probably need to make. Having done this, they can help each other complete the questions on page 275.

Facing Fears and Anxieties

Page 276-277   Page 120-121

Learning objective:

To personalize the issue of facing fears and anxieties so students can take this into account when they write their own plan.

Presentation suggestions:

Ask students to review the material on overcoming anxieties in Chapter 9 and then to complete the exercises on pages 276 and 277. You might use yourself or a student volunteer as an example and run through the exercise as a class.

Your Plan

Page 279-280   Page 121-123

Presentation suggestions:

Depending upon the level of the class, this segment of the chapter might be used as the final exam. A more advanced or gifted class should be given the whole chapter as an exam. A class with lower abilities may need the assistance of class discussion in the previous exercises.

If you choose to use this as the final, we suggest making it a take-home exam, and allowing about a week for its completion. Statements should be written as measurable objectives with all three components: What will be different? By how much or how many? By when? Review this material in class, if necessary. You should also evaluate the plans according to how realistic they are, as well as the amount of time and thought students have given them.

Emphasize again the importance of being able to identify mentors.

Many of my students got really excited about creating their plan. I even received a few letters from parents.

– John Fishburne
Teacher
Cascade High School
Leavenworth, Washington

When we read "25th High School Reunion," it inspired the students to create a scrapbook that could be carried throughout their high school years so that they would have it for their 25th reunion. Also, they began work on a time capsule.

– Janet Sinclair
English I Teacher
Hancock High School
Kiln, Mississippi

Optional

Pages 273-283

Ex-Basketball Player
by John Updike
Read before beginning to work on "Your Plan" in *Career Choices*

25th High School Reunion
by Linda Pastan
Read after completing "Your Plan" in *Career Choices*

Mission in Life

Page 282

Page 124

Presentation suggestion:

Have students refer to their stated mission on page 61. Have they changed their minds? If not, ask them to copy the statement again at the end of the book. If they need to change their mission, now is the time to do so.

If students are willing to share their missions, you might post them around the room or provide the information to the yearbook editor. Be sure to respect any wishes for privacy, however.

As a Portfolio assignment at the end of the year, students read "We Are a Success" and wrote about how they have been successful over the year.

— Suzanne M. Reese
Teacher/Gifted Liaison
R.L. Turner High School
Carrollton, Texas

Back to the Future

Remembering Your Dreams and Goals

Students will have a clearer sense of themselves and their dreams for the future as they finish their *Career Choices* course. This vision should be captured for a future time when it might trigger renewed enthusiasm.

Have your students write two letters to themselves about their dreams and goals for their future. Tell them they will receive one letter in two years and the other in five years. Ask them to attach a copy of their 10-year plan along with a copy of the letter written from the activity on page 169 in this *Guide*.

Ask each student to bring two envelopes to school, each bearing double first class postage (to take into account any rate increases). The envelopes should be addressed to the students, in care of someone in their family who they feel is not likely to move. The return address should be that of a second relative who is likely to stay at the same address. This doubles their chances of receiving the letters.

After they have written and sealed their letters, box them up and store them for mailing. You'll want to label the boxes with the year they are to be sent. Then each year (perhaps with the new year) you'll deliver the appropriate envelopes to the post office.

Your students' letters just might arrive at a critical moment when they are considering giving up a cherished dream or goal. It could rekindle a passion or remind them of the benefits of staying on course and pursuing a goal.

Post Assessment:

At this time, the exercise "Envisioning Your Future" on page 14 of *Career Choices* should be administered again. Compare this version with the one completed at the beginning of the course. Do you see any growth in the students? Have their horizons been broadened? Perhaps their goals are more realistic for their capabilities. Have young women considered non-traditional careers? Do you sense better self-knowledge? Do their plans include post-secondary education?

If appropriate, share these two assessments with the school counselor. They could also be included in the students' files if appropriate and legal.

Turn back to the exercise "Defining Success" on page 140 of this *Guide*. You may be interested in doing the course wrap-up activity recommended there.

> During the last ten minutes on the final day of the course, we recommend reading aloud *Oh! The Places You'll Go!* by Dr. Seuss. This is a wonderful book for people of all ages, filled with many of the messages imparted in *Career Choices*. Published by Random House, New York, ISBN 0-6779-80523-3, it should be available in most bookstores. The summary provided by the Library of Congress is as follows: Advice in rhyme for proceeding in life; weathering fear, loneliness, and confusion; and being in charge of your actions.

SECTION FIVE

Restructuring Resources and Recommendations

In the past, education was structured using the following model:

THE TRADITIONAL ORGANIZATIONAL MODEL

Organization

Curriculum

Needs of students

The **ORGANIZATION** of education...
(so many "periods" that were so long, 8 am to 3 pm, five days per week, English, math, science, social studies departments, classrooms with desks in a row, lecture format leading to easily scored tests, etc.)

dictated the **CURRICULUM**
(50-minute lessons, broken into specific disciplines for students in a structured classroom studying for a test)

The **CURRICULUM** defined the "**NEEDS OF STUDENTS.**"

Industry and commerce were the first to recognize that the "needs of the customers" must dictate how businesses are run. This drove the restructuring process they have undergone in the last decade. Today education, too, is finding it must change its structure.

THE PROGRESSIVE STUDENT-CENTERED MODEL

Needs of students

Curriculum

Organization

Once the educational **NEEDS OF STUDENTS** are articulated, a **CURRICULUM** can be designed to meet them. When such a **CURRICULUM** is designed, then an **ORGANIZATIONAL STRUCTURE** to deliver the curriculum can be set in place. For an example, see pages 54-55 of this *Guide*.

Academic Innovations is committed to helping you provide your students with the best and most relevant education possible. The times ahead for education are likely to be both exciting and challenging and we know the more support and information you have, the better your chances of success. Therefore, we have included a variety of optional resources and suggestions that you may find helpful, not only as you introduce the *Career Choices* curriculum, but also as you and your fellow educators go about the important task of restructuring your school and district.

For that purpose we have established a telephone hotline to help you institutionalize the *Career Choices* curriculum in your school. Do not hesitate to call us on weekdays between 9 am and 3 pm PST. See Section Three, beginning on page 104.

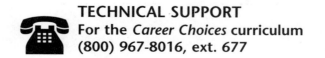

TECHNICAL SUPPORT
For the *Career Choices* curriculum
(800) 967-8016, ext. 677

Creating Buy-In for Your Course

Vision and teamwork are critical elements in any restructuring effort. However you plan to use the *Career Choices* curriculum, you will probably have to change some of the things you've done before, and change is a discomforting issue for everyone.

The first step to a positive and lasting change is creating buy-in from the individuals involved. If you plan a class where you are the only instructor, you will need to get buy-in from the administration and perhaps a school improvement committee (parents and community members). If you are planning an interdisciplinary curriculum, you will need to get active buy-in from the team of teachers who will work with you as well as the other instructors who will touch your students' lives at some level.

It is important to note that studies on the process of change suggest that the best way to get people to accept it is in one-to-one discussions. Therefore your first step is to "lobby" for your project. Meet with individuals over lunch or coffee and present your idea. Use this time to listen for any discomfort or concern and provide solutions right then or get back with more information. Once you feel you have addressed the concerns and have individuals at least comfortable with exploring the possibilities, it is time to call a meeting.

Our Web Site

Question	Go to URL:	You'll find:	Helpful hints & tips
I need to convince our administration that the Career Choices curriculum works. How can I print out stories and comments for other schools?	http://www. academicinnovations.com/ indepth.html	A listing of 20 programs using *Career Choices* in a variety of settings	*Scroll through and choose the stories that match your needs. Print them out to share with your administration.*
AND...	http://www. academicinnovations.com/ whatsay.html	A list of themes on which other educators have commented	*Hyperlink to* <u>Proven</u> *and print out the statements to incorporate into your report. Then surf any other relevant themes/issues to your proposed program.*
AND...	http://www. academicinnovations.com/ expert.html	A list of articles on a variety of topics about the special needs of adolescents.	*Read each hyperlink and then download the appropriate articles to include in your report. By downloading, you can later edit the text into your proposal.*

Creating a Shared Vision

We suggest opening your meeting immediately (after only a word or two of welcome) with the following group discussion:

If you could wave a magic wand and give your students any characteristics, attitudes or skills what would they be?

Have a large pad of paper and easel available to write on, so you can hang it on the wall for referral later. Following the rules of brainstorming (page 85 of this *Guide*), identify the needs of students. Once you have completed this exercise, and perhaps even prioritized and/or edited your list, present the concept of *The Progressive Model* on page 293.

This is a start to creating a shared vision. Now you can explain how the *Career Choices* curriculum meets the needs identified by the group (see pages 297-298 for examples).

Hint: Before you even begin lobbying, we recommend you call our office for technical support. Not only can we give you ideas and examples of how other schools with your demographic profile are using the curriculum, we can provide you with resources such as overheads and slides that might make your presentation planning easier.

Coming Summer 1997

http://www.academicinnovations.com/success.html

We're in the process of interviewing a variety of educators across the country who have successfully introduced *Career Choices* into their schools. You may want to visit to learn their techniques.

Notes from your meeting:

This list was created by 36 teachers and administrators during a brainstorming session at the beginning of one of our two-day workshops in Santa Barbara.

Would your list look similar?

Once you have read this list, fold back along the dotted line. →

What characteristics, attitudes and skills do we want for the teens we teach?

Critical thinking skills

Interpersonal skills

Pride in who they are

Adaptability to change

Value the educational system

Enthusiasm

Tolerance of people/cultures

Pride in workmanship

Ability to plan for the future

Setting goals/Planning

Stick-to-itiveness

Follow through

Risk taking

Good decision-making skills

Respect for others and self

Indulge creativity

Ability to handle stress

Initiative

Personal responsibility

Pursuit of excellence

Feeling entitled

Sense of humor

Good role models

Seek out mentors

Find out aptitudes/interests/strengths

Career exploration

Communication skills

Vocational skills

Empowerment

Introspection and self-evaluation

Being in charge of their destiny

Visionary

Access information

You'll want to evaluate all curriculum you choose for your invigorated school, based upon the list of "needs of students" you produce at your meeting.

☎ **TECHNICAL SUPPORT**
For the *Career Choices* curriculum
(800) 967-8016, ext. 677

Fold page 297 to here →

Sponsor a Parent-Student Workshop With the Adult Edition of *Career Choices*

Here's a great opportunity to facilitate parent-child communication. Why not sponsor a weekend workshop where the "teachers" are your students—who have completed their *Career Choices* class—and the "students" are their parents?

By popular demand, Mindy Bingham and Sandy Stryker have rewritten and re-edited *Career Choices* for the college and adult market. "Even though *Career Choices* was written for secondary schools," explains Mindy Bingham, "we have a number of colleges and adult programs using the materials. After all, the process of making wise life choices is the same no matter the age."

Therefore, this new edition, *Career Choices and Changes*, mirrors the original text, except that the examples and stories are geared for a more mature audience.

Take advantage of the fact that in most families midlife and adolescence happen at about the same time and organize your students to host a workshop for their parents. It could prove to be one of the most powerful experience of your teaching career.

To receive a 60-day examination copy of the adult edition, *Career Choices and Changes*, and a sample 10-hour parent-student agenda, fax your request on letterhead stationery to (805) 967-4357 or call (800) 967-8016.

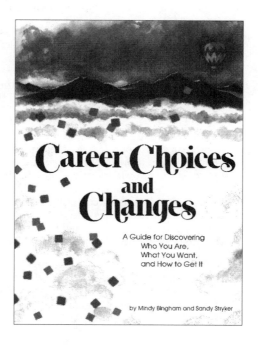

National Occupational Information Coordinating Committee

High School Student Competencies and Indicators

Self-Knowledge

COMPETENCY I: Understanding the influence of a positive self-concept.
Identify and appreciate personal interests, abilities and skills.
Demonstrate the ability to use peer feedback.
Demonstrate an understanding of how individual characteristics relate to achieving personal, social, educational, and career goals.
Demonstrate an understanding of environmental influences on one's behaviors.
Demonstrate an understanding of the relationship between personal behavior and self-concept.

COMPETENCY II: Skills to interact positively with others.
Demonstrate effective interpersonal skills.
Demonstrate interpersonal skills required for working with and for others.
Describe appropriate employer and employee interactions in various situations.
Demonstrate how to express feelings, reactions, and ideas in an appropriate manner.

COMPETENCY III: Understanding the impact of growth and development.
Describe how developmental changes affect physical and mental health.
Describe the effect of emotional and physical health on career decisions.
Describe healthy ways of dealing with stress.
Demonstrate behaviors that maintain physical and mental health.

Educational and Occupational Exploration

COMPETENCY IV: Understanding the relationship between educational achievement and career planning.
Demonstrate how to apply academic and vocational skills to achieve personal goals.
Describe the relationship of academic and vocational skills to personal interests.
Describe how education relates to the selection of college majors, further training, and/or entry into the job market.
Demonstrate transferable skills that can apply to a variety of occupations and changing occupational requirements.
Describe how learning skills are required in the workplace.

COMPETENCY V: Understanding the need for positive attitudes toward work and learning.
Identify the positive contributions workers make to society.
Demonstrate knowledge of the social significance of various occupations.
Demonstrate a positive attitude toward work.
Demonstrate learning habits and skills that can be used in various educational situations.
Demonstrate positive work attitudes and behaviors.

COMPETENCY VI: Skills to locate, evaluate and interpret career information.
Describe the educational requirements of various occupations.
Demonstrate use of a range of resources (e.g. handbooks, career materials, labor market information, and computerized career information delivery systems).
Demonstrate knowledge of various classification systems that categorize occupations and industries (e.g., Dictionary of Occupational Title).
Describe the concept of career ladders.
Describe the advantages and disadvantages of self employment as a career option.
Identify individuals in selected occupations as possible information resources, role models, or mentors.
Describe the impact of population, climate, and geographic location on occupational opportunities.

COMPETENCY VII: Skills to prepare to seek, obtain, maintain, and change jobs.
Demonstrate skills to locate, interpret, and use information about job openings and opportunities.
Demonstrate academic or vocational skills required for a full or part-time job.
Demonstrate skills and behaviors necessary for a successful job interview.
Demonstrate skills in preparing a resume and completing job applications.

Identify specific job openings.

Demonstrate employability skills necessary to obtain and maintain jobs.

Demonstrate skills to assess occupational opportunities (e.g., working conditions, benefits, and opportunities for change).

Describe placement services available to make the transition from high school to civilian employment, the armed service, or post-secondary education/training.

Demonstrate an understanding that job opportunities often require relocation.

Demonstrate skills necessary to function as a consumer and manager of financial resources.

COMPETENCY VIII: Understanding how societal needs and functions influence the nature and structure of work.

Describe the effect of work on lifestyles.

Describe how society's needs and functions affect the supply of goods and services.

Describe how occupational and industrial trends relate to training and employment

Demonstrate an understanding of the global economy and how it affects each individual.

areer Planning **COMPETENCY IX: Skills to make decisions.**

Demonstrate responsibility for making tentative educational and occupational choices.

Identify alternatives in given decision-making situations.

Describe personal strengths and weaknesses in relationship to post-secondary education/training requirements.

Identify appropriate choices during high school that will lead to marketable skills for entry-level employment or advanced training.

Identify and complete required steps toward transition from high school entry into post-secondary education/training programs or work.

Identify steps to apply for and secure financial assistance for post-secondary education and training.

COMPETENCY X: Understanding the interrelationship of life roles.

Demonstrate knowledge of life stages.

Describe factors that determine lifestyles (e.g. socioeconomic status, culture, values, occupational choices, work habits).

Describe ways in which occupational choices may affect lifestyle.

Describe the contribution of work to a balanced and productive life.

Describe ways in which work, family, and leisure roles are interrelated.

Describe different career patterns and their potential effect on family patterns and lifestyle.

Describe the importance of leisure activities.

Demonstrate ways that occupational skills and knowledge can be acquired through leisure.

COMPETENCY XI: Understanding the continuous changes in male/female roles.

Identify factors that have influenced the changing career patterns of women and men.

Identify evidence of gender stereotyping and bias in educational programs and occupational settings.

Demonstrate attitudes, behaviors, and skills that contribute to eliminating gender bias and stereotyping.

Identify courses appropriate to tentative occupational choices.

Describe the advantages and problems of non-traditional occupations.

COMPETENCY XII: Skills in career planning.

Describe career plans that reflect the importance of lifelong learning.

Demonstrate knowledge of post-secondary vocational and academic programs.

Demonstrate knowledge that changes may require retraining of employees' skills.

Describe school and community resources to explore educational and occupational choices.

Describe the costs and benefits of self-employment.

Demonstrate occupational skills developed through volunteer experiences, part-time employment, or cooperative education programs.

Demonstrate skills necessary to compare education and job opportunities.

Develop an individual career plan, updating information from earlier plans and including tentative decisions to be implemented after high school.

Where *Career Choices* Addresses Specific NOICC Competencies

Page	Activity / Assignment	I	II	III	IV	V	VI	VII	VIII	IX	X	XI	XII
10-14	Envisioning Your Future					•	•			•	•		•
15-17	Why People Work, Everybody Works			•		•			•		•		
18-19	Defining Success	•		•		•					•		
20-21	Making Career Choices									•			
24-27	Personal Profile — Identity	•	•	•							•		
28-29	Identifying Your Passions	•											
30-37	Work Value Survey	•				•						•	
38-45	Strength and Personality	•	•			•							
46-48	Skills & Aptitudes/Name That Skill	•			•	•							
49	Roles, Occupations & Vocations	•			•						•		
50-53	The Message Center	•	•									•	
56-59	Lifestyle/Maslow Triangle	•			•						•		
60-61	How Do You Want to Be Remembered?	•			•								
62-63	Components of Lifestyle	•		•			•	•	•		•		
64-71	Happiness is a Balanced Lifestyle, etc.	•	•	•		•			•		•	•	
74-76	What Cost This Lifestyle/Ivy Elm's Story			•					•			•	
77-92	The Budget Exercise				•			•				•	
93	What Salary Will Support this Lifestyle							•					
95-96	Over Your Head/Hard Times Budget							•					
97-101	Some Sample Budgets							•	•			•	
102-103	Poverty/Poverty Statistics	•									•	•	
104-105	Money Isn't Everything	•									•		
106-110	Rewards and Sacrifices Stories	•		•		•				•			
111-113	You Win Some… Lose Some/Avocation Choices	•		•		•				•			
114-115	Commitment				•	•							
116-119	An Investment in Education… Yields Dividends for a Lifetime				•	•				•			
120	Ask Someone Who's Been There	•	•			•	•	•	•	•	•	•	•
121	Easier Said Than Done	•			•	•			•	•			
124-125	Your Ideal Career	•					•	•		•	•		
126	Physical Settings	•					•	•		•	•		
127	Working Conditions	•					•	•		•	•		
128	Relationships at Work	•	•				•	•		•	•		
129	Psychological Rewards of Working	•		•		•	•	•		•	•		
130	Mixing Career and Family	•					•	•		•	•	•	
131	Financial Rewards	•					•	•		•	•		
132-134	Job Skills/Your Chart	•	•	•	•		•	•		•	•	•	
135-137	Consider Your Options	•		•			•	•	•	•	•		•
138-139	Employee or Employer	•					•	•			•	•	•
140-141	What About Status			•		•	•	•			•		
144-146	Career Research/Step One						•	•		•			•
147	Bring in Your Identity	•					•	•		•			•
148-155	Career Research/Survey	•		•	•		•	•		•	•	•	•
156-157	Visualize Your Career			•			•	•		•	•		•
158-159	The Shadow Program						•	•	•				•
160-161	Involvement: Volunteering/Entry Level				•	•	•	•			•		•
162-165	The Chemistry Test: Work Behavioral Styles	•	•			•							

Where *Career Choices* Addresses Specific NOICC Competencies

Page	Activity/Assignment	I	II	III	IV	V	VI	VII	VIII	IX	X	XI	XII
168-169	Decision Making				•		•			•			
170	Identifying Choices				•		•			•			
171	Gathering Information				•		•			•			
172-175	Evaluating Choices				•		•			•			
176-177	Your Choices - Evaluating				•		•	•	•	•			•
178	Making A Decision					•				•			
179	Keeping Your Options Open					•				•			
183-185	Tools for Solving Problems	•	•										
186-190	Setting Goals & Objectives		•		•			•		•			•
191	Change Process Style			•									
194-195	Avoiding Detours and Roadblocks	•		•									
196-197	I Can't Do It Because/What's Your Excuse?	•		•		•				•		•	
198-199	They Did It in Spite of...	•		•		•				•		•	
200	Taking Responsibility	•	•	•		•				•			
201-202	Startling Statements			•							•	•	
203-206	Detours & Roadblocks Lifestyle Choices			•	•	•					•	•	
207	Is It Worth Staying in School				•	•		•			•	•	•
208-209	The Economics of Bad Habits	•		•									
210	If You've Decided to Give Up Your Dream	•		•		•							
211-213	If You're a Woman	•		•	•	•		•	•		•	•	
214-215	Support for your Dream/If You Don't Think You Deserve It	•		•	•	•				•			
216-221	Anxiety Tolerance/Overcoming Fears	•	•	•	•	•							
222-223	10 Year Plan for Yorik (remedial plan)		•		•			•	•	•	•		•
224-225	Taking Risks	•		•		•							
226	Getting Back on Track if You've Derailed	•		•	•	•			•				•
230-231	Attitude is Everything	•	•	•		•							
232-235	The Six Es of Excellence	•	•	•	•	•		•					
236-237	Going for It ... Work Is an Aggressive Act	•	•		•	•		•				•	
238-241	You're the Boss/Work Ethic	•	•	•		•		•		•			
242-245	The Employee of the Twenty-first Century		•	•	•	•	•	•	•			•	•
246-247	A Final Note on Attitude	•	•	•		•							
250-253	Getting Experience/Your Resume							•					
254	Finding a Job							•					
255	Conduct an Informal Interview		•				•	•	•				
256-257	Job Applications							•					
258-259	The Job Interview		•					•					
260	Dealing With Rejection	•	•					•					
261	Accepting A Job		•					•					
262-263	Making Connections/Mentors		•				•						•
266	Where Do You Go From Here?				•	•				•			•
267-269	Getting the Education or Training You Need				•	•	•	•		•			•
270-273	Where Is It You Want to Go/Life Plan				•	•	•	•		•	•	•	•
274-275	Delaying Gratification		•	•		•				•	•	•	•
276-277	Facing Fears and Anxieties	•	•	•		•				•		•	•
278-283	Your Plan	•	•	•	•	•	•	•	•	•	•	•	•

Put SPIRIT into Your Classroom With SCANS

Quick, can you rattle off the SCANS Competencies and Foundation Skills? Perhaps you'll want to use the SPIRIT acronym as a mnemonic device to help you remember these very important components as you design your restructured curriculum.

The following chart outlines ways in which the *Career Choices* curriculum addresses the SCANS competencies and foundation skills.

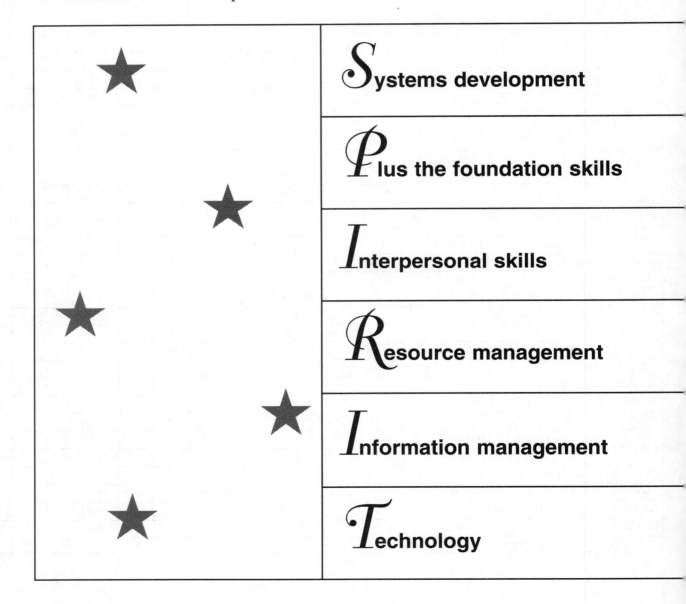

$\mathcal{S}$ystems development

$\mathcal{P}$lus the foundation skills

$\mathcal{I}$nterpersonal skills

$\mathcal{R}$esource management

$\mathcal{I}$nformation management

$\mathcal{T}$echnology

The *Career Choices* curriculum is filled with activities & exercises that help students understand how systems work & why students learn to master the processes that make individuals efficient & effective, beginning with simple tasks that become increasingly complex as they develop comprehensive plans for building a satisfying future.

A competency-based curriculum that offers relevant practice in reading, writing & mathematics, the *Career Choices* program gives concrete instruction in the areas of creative development, decision making & goal setting, problem solving & "seeing in the mind's eye." It promotes self-esteem, self-management, accountability & responsible citizenship.

Because *Career Choices* works best in a cooperative learning environment, students will have an opportunity to practice such interpersonal skills as working in teams, leading, negotiating & teaching others—all so important in the workplace. Specific activities & exercises help them perfect techniques that are valuable both in & out of the workplace.

Project-oriented activities throughout the *Career Choices* curriculum offer students the opportunity to practice resource management. As they complete their projects or case studies they learn to identify, organize, plan & allocate time, money, human resources & technology.

As they work through a life planning process, students gather, evaluate & organize data and produce a product or thesis based on that idea. A variety of information-gathering strategies are suggested throughout the course.

The value & use of technology is promoted throughout the curriculum. Optional activities offer opportunities for students to use electronic spreadsheets & graphs, desktop publishing & computer graphics, word processing programs & computerized information systems as they develop their projects.

Great Resources We'd Like to Recommend

Common Miracles

Correspondents Peter Jennings and Bill Blakemore reveal how we can help students realize their unique talents and learning abilities in the ABC News Special "Common Miracles: The New American Revolution in Learning." The documentary features penetrating interviews with instructors, principals, psychologists, parents and students and focuses on methods and schools which provide their students with freedom and options through education.

Illustrating several innovative and positive techniques which help young people grasp the "keys to a glorious future," Jennings and Blakemore go on location to schools across the nation. They find that traditional education—including tracking, factory model schools, and IQ-based assessment—is being replaced with cooperative learning, the use of computers, apprenticeships, parent and community involvement, and the philosophy that every child is gifted.

"Common Miracles" exposes the ultimate goal of educational revolution: to "liberate the human potential in all Americans." We recommend showing it at staff and parents' meetings.

To order a copy, available for $19.98 plus shipping, call MPI at (800) 323-0442.

The Lost Generation

If you want to convince parents or staff members of the need for career education, we suggest that you show them a video of the NBC News Special "The Lost Generation." Hosted by Tom Brokaw, it dramatically illustrates how the jobs now available to young people with just a high school education do not support the lifestyle their parents could afford with a similar education. It demonstrates, too, how this situation often leads not only to poverty, but to frustration, despair, crime, and alienation from society. The final segment of the exceptional video presents hope, as it shows how high schools can make their programs more relevant for those students who are not going on to a 4-year college. Copies are available for $36.45, plus shipping. Call (800) 777-TEXT. We recommend you show this at staff meetings and parent meetings during the coming year.

Our Web Site

Question	Go to URL:	You'll find:	Helpful hints & tips
Who are my state's Tech Prep coordinators and our School-to-Work contacts? How would I contact them?	http://www. academicinnovations.com/ tpfunds.html	Information on these federal programs along with directories of state contacts.	*Scroll down and find the names of your state contacts. Write them and ask to be put on their mailing list for future "Requests for Funding Proposals."*

Educated in Romance

Why are young women—even those who perform very well in school—less likely to be achievers in the world than their male counterparts? According to Dorothy C. Holland and Margaret A. Eisenhart, author of the fascinating book *Educated in Romance* (University of Chicago Press), the answer lies not so much in what or how much is learned, but in why they learn. In their longitudinal study, the authors found most females are more interested in pleasing others, attracting males, getting good grades or just getting by than they are in mastering knowledge or skills. Only those who saw a relationship between their education and future occupations went on to live up to their potential in the workplace.

The authors' findings provide strong support for comprehensive career education programs in secondary schools. By understanding the forces that can lead even gifted young women into dead-end futures, you can take steps to prevent this from happening to your students and your daughters. This book is available in paperback at bookstores, and we highly recommend it to you.

The Neglected Majority
by Dale Parnell

In his visionary book, *The Neglected Majority*, author Dale Parnell champions the cause of those high school students who are too often overlooked: the 75 percent who will not graduate from a 4-year college. For their sake, and for the country's, he argues, it is time for our high schools to develop and implement Tech Prep programs. If you haven't read this easy to understand blueprint for educational reform, you will find valuable strategies and solutions within its pages.

In the book's forward, Thomas A. Shannon, Executive Director of the National School Board Association, states, "Parnell makes a convincing case for the argument that the complex, technological world of the future is really already here. The emerging truth is that higher and more comprehensive skills must be developed, particularly by the middle two quarters of the workforce."

A copy can be obtained through your local book store or directly from the Community College Press at (800) 250-6557.

Road Map for Change

If you want to learn how high schools successfully improve, read *Making High Schools Work—Through Integration of Academics and Vocational Education*. Published by the Southern Regional Educational Board, this 200-page report speaks to reality, not theory, and is based on the experience of using SREB-recommended strategies. Loaded with specific experiences from consortium members in 19 states already restructuring and implementing Tech Prep programs, this book is highly recommended reading for administrators, teachers and counselors who want to avoid reinventing the wheel.

Available for $10.95 per copy from SREB, 592 10th Street-A, NW, Atlanta, GA 30318, (404) 875-9211. When you order five or more copies, pay only $5.00 each.

Network With Career Educators

As a valuable service for all career educators, Dr. Ken Hoyt, known as "the father of career education," has prepared *The National Career Education Leader Communication Network* (NCELCN) newsletter. Filled with ideas and activities developed by the 500 members from all parts of the country, it also provides names and phone numbers to facilitate networking.

While there is no financial commitment to belong to the network, you must be willing to share information about your activities. For a Network Enrollment Form, write Kenneth B. Hoyt, Ph.D., Kansas State University, College of Education, 362 Bluemont Hall, Manhattan, KS 66506.

Choosing a Career Exploration Computer Program

Looking for a way to make an informed choice about which computer software programs students will use in their career exploration and search? A "consumer guide" comparing computer information delivery systems (CIDS) is available to help you. The *Career Information Delivery Systems Inventory (1993)* highlights the similarities and differences among 25 computer-based career information delivery systems marketed in California. Not intended to be a definitive list, it includes VIEW/COIN, Career Visions, CAREERS 2001, CHOICES, EUREKA, to mention a few. Funded by the California Occupational Information Coordinating Committee (COICC) and produced by the Los Angeles County Office of Education, this free publication is available from COICC, (916) 323-6544. (There is a limit on copies per caller.)

Second to None: A Clear Vision

Educational reform and restructuring plans are taking shape across the country. Florida's *Blue Print* and Ohio's *Future at Work* are two excellent examples of action plans to modernize the educational process. California's vision of the future, *Second to None*, written by their High School Task Force, is another exemplary step toward 21st-Century schools.

Second to None begins with a vignette of a student's day at Bayshore High, a fictional school where students want to learn and teachers want to teach. The model program involves clusters, student-centered learning, and teachers who coach and support all students. As one reads this well-crafted description of the state's ambitious educational reform plan, it is not difficult to see how the wheels of educational change can spin more quickly. Seven of California's 30 Investment High Schools (educational reform demonstration sites) chose the *Career Choices* curriculum as an important component of their restructuring projects.

For a copy of Second to None, ($9.50 plus shipping and handling), write the California Department of Education, Publication Sales, Box 271-A, Sacramento, CA 95812, or call (916) 445-1260.

Tech Prep Student Guide Available

Are you in the process of developing articulation plans with your local community college? If so, you'll want to see Clackamas, Oregon's Tech Prep Guide.

An exemplary model, this catalog describes every Tech Prep program offered and was given to each high school student in the district. Clear, concise, and well designed, it could save your Tech Prep team hundreds of hours by providing a road map for your articulation efforts.

The guide was prepared by the Clackamas Educational Service District, Portland Community College, Mount Hood Community College, Clackamas Community College and the Oregon Career Information System. For a copy, send $7.00 to the attention of John Quiggle, Clackamas Educational Service District, P.O. Box 216, Marylhurst, OR 97036-0216. We hear that supplies are limited, so act quickly. If your goal is to encourage more students to obtain post-high school training using a Tech Prep model, you'll want to see this publication.

Reproduced from quarterly Focus on the Future *newsletter. To be added to our mailing list for this free publication, call (800) 967-8016.*

School-to-Work Web Site
http://www.stw.ed.gov/

If you are implementing School-to-Work programs, this is the place to find some of the best resources available. This site alone will make your effort well worthwhile if you don't already know how to use the Internet. (Request our free guide mentioned on this page to help.)

You'll find manuals, fact sheets, templates, presentations and documents you can download to your hard drive. Join in on conversations with others interested in School-to-Work or post your questions to their bulletin board for others to respond.

Here's where you'll find out the available federal/state funding and initiatives and who to contact for more information. By the time you're done surfing this site, you'll know just about everything there is to know about School-to-Work. Don't reinvent the wheel. Start here.

Why Do I Have to Learn This?
by Dale Parnell

One of the most frequently asked questions by students is "Why do I have to learn this?" Instead of responding with the typical answer, "You might need it someday," try using the approach which Dale Parnell provides in his first book dedicated primarily to teachers and students of K–Adult education.

In *Why Do I Have to Learn This?* ($16.00, CORD Communications, 1995), Parnell discusses the latest research in learning styles and outlines a common sense but ever-so-important strategy for improving teaching and learning. Previously available as *LogoLogic*, Parnell's book has been updated and re-titled. This book demonstrates the importance of providing a solid philosophical and academic base for the Tech Prep program.

A natural follow-up to *The Neglected Majority*, this insightful and thought-provoking book, by one of the leading educational reformers today, stresses the complexity and effectiveness of learning for meaning. Without meaning, students will continue to search for the answers to why education is relevant to their future.

To order, call CORD Communications at (800) 231-3015.

Classroom Connect

Classroom Connect is a practical guide for integrating the Internet into your classroom. Published nine times annually, this newsletter offers easy, cost effective solutions for upgrading technology in the classroom.

Classroom Connect contains unique ideas for using the Internet in a variety of core subject areas including math, science, and social studies. Included are favorite Internet sites and ways other schools and teachers are using this sophisticated resource. Each issue also defines computer terms to help you understand this quickly growing field. Additionally, *Classroom Connect* advertises "keypals" for instructors who are looking for e-mail partners, either domestic or international, for their students.

Classroom Connect offers a hands-on learning approach for students of all ages. We highly recommend taking a look at what they offer. For more information, write to *Classroom Connect* at P.O. Box 10488, Lancaster, PA 17605-0488 or call (717) 393-1000.

Interventions for Adolescent Identity Development

One of the challenges educators face today is how to best address the issues of adolescent development. *Interventions for Adolescent Identity Development* (edited by Sally L. Archer, SAGE publications, 1994) contains fifteen articles by education leaders addressing this and other important concerns.

The team of experts examines what is known about adolescent identity formation and how that information can be used to maintain effective communication with adolescents involving their life choices.

For example, Philip H. Dreyer contributes an article entitled "Designing Curricular Identity Interventions for Secondary Schools" that you'll want to take a look at particularly if you are restructuring your school (softcover, $24.95). To order, contact Sage Publications at (805) 499-0721.

Specialized Lesson Plans

The following pages (315-343) provide two complete versions of optional lesson plans for the *Career Choices* curriculum.

The Sample Nine-Week Interdisciplinary Lesson Plan (pages 314-323) can save your academic team hundreds of hours of planning time. This plan, which tracks not only vertically but horizontally as well, demonstrates how instructors can work together to present a relevant thematic, academically based curriculum.

The 180-Hour (one school year) Lesson Plan is designed to be used by one instructor who is presenting a comprehensive career guidance experience, grounded in the academic subjects. Even if you don't have two semesters for your course, you'll want to study this plan to see how the different textbooks fit together and also note the activities that are considered the most important by the authors and other instructors using the curriculum (starred in the last column).

We also have a number of other specialized sample lesson plans available for the *Career Choices* curriculum. Give our Technical Support Department a call to see if one fits your needs.

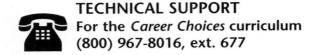

TECHNICAL SUPPORT
For the *Career Choices* curriculum
(800) 967-8016, ext. 677

You'll want to visit our web site and read the stories of 20 innovative educators who use the *Career Choices* curriculum. You may want to build some of their strategies into your lesson plan.

In-Depth Interviews with Innovative Educators

http://www.academicinnovations.com/indepth.html

At Bethel High School, and most of the high schools on the Virginia Peninsula, Career Choices is used in both the 9th grade and 10th grade Tech Prep Communications classes as a supplemental text. Since every city/division has its own adopted texts for literature, grammar, and writing, Career Choices became the one in-common text for everyone.

– Sharon Hurwitz
English Teacher and Technology Facilitator
Bethel High School
Hampton, Virginia

A Sample Nine-Week Interdisciplinary Lesson Plan

The following lesson plan is an example of what could be accomplished if an English/language arts, math, social studies and career, guidance, business or family and consumer science instructor form a cluster unit to teach a quarter class.

This nine-page example demonstrates the scope and sequence of the *Career Choices* curriculum in a multidimensional fashion. Not only does this plan work vertically which is the traditional way to create lesson plans, but it also relates horizontally. What the guidance component is discussing (column one) relates thematically to what the English, math and social studies teacher is presenting. Therefore what is being discussed in English will enrich the discussion in the math and guidance class. The problems worked on in math class will reinforce the dialogues in social studies, english and guidance component. It is our hope that this sample lesson plan will stimulate you to create similar interdisciplinary lesson plans for not only your *Career Choices* experience but other themes you present in your school.

It is important to note that this lesson plan is just one of many ways to organize the course. Teachers from various disciplines have taught from the different texts. For instance, column one, using primarily the *Career Choices* textbook, might be taught by a career or guidance professional, a business teacher, or family and consumer science instructor. Another possibility would be for the Social Studies instructor to teach this vertical lesson plan and therefore the teaching team would eliminate the last column in this lesson plan.

Or perhaps the English/language arts instructor wants to teach from both the *Career Choices* and *Possibilities* texts. Using this format, the first two columns would be combined and the course would be expanded to an 18-week semester unit. The "team" math teacher would then teach a thematic unit from *Lifestyle Math* at the appropriate times while working on other math lessons in between.

If you are working with an at-risk population or one that is performing below grade level, you will probably want to take more time on the individual lesson and therefore expand from a 9-week class to an eighteen week class.

As you have seen from the comments and quotes of educators using the curriculum, the possibilities of combinations are vast. The *Career Choices* curriculum provides the foundation and you provide the creativity and organization. Here is your chance to be innovative and meet the special needs of your population of students.

Note: You will want to have a copy of each of the textbooks available as you study this plan.

WEEK ONE

CAREER/GUIDANCE CURRICULUM

Text: Career Choices: A Guide for Teens and Young Adults and the Workbook and Portfolio

The following page examples correlate with those in the *Instructor's and Counselor's Guide or Career Choices*. Following each exercise is a definition as to what depth to explore the topic; what discussions, activities and ideas you will have time for.

Monday

Introduction, page 136
Presentation suggestions, Activities

Tuesday

Vision Plus Energy Equals Success, page 132
Presentation suggestions
Envisioning Your Future, page 134
Presentation suggestions

Wednesday

Defining Success, page 138
Presentation suggestions, Activities
Making Career Choices, page 141
Presentation suggestions

Thursday

Bulls Eye Chart, page 141
Identifying Your Passions, page 146
Presentation suggestions, Activities, English/Language Arts

Friday

Values Survey, page 148
Presentation suggestions
Homework: Follow-up, page 149

ENGLISH/LANGUAGE ARTS

Text: Possibilities: A Supplemental Anthology for Career Choices

Assign reading, journal entries and compositions as homework. Each day share themes of journal entries and proceed with discussions and activities in class.

Monday

Introduction
Explanation of journal writing

Tuesday

***The Secret Life of Walter Mitty* by** James Thurber
Discussion: Questions 1 - 5
Quick write: Question 6
Homework: Question 7, Envision Your Future

Wednesday

***A Psalm of Life* by** Henry Wadsworth Longfellow
Discussion: Questions 1, 4, 5, 6
Homework: Antonyms and Synonyms

Thursday

***Dreams* by** Langston Hughes
Discussion: The Formal Debate, pages 21 - 22

Friday

***I Have A Dream* ...** by Dr. Martin Luther King, Jr.
Discussion: Questions 1, 2, 3
Homework: Question 8

MATH

Text: Lifestyle Math: Your Financial Planning Portfolio: A Supplemental Mathematics Unit for Career Choices. Unless otherwise noted, all page numbers correlate with text Lifestyle Math.

Monday

Introduction and discussion, pages 3 - 4
What Is Your Attitude About Math, page 6
Math Anxiety, page 7

Tuesday

Your vision of being competent in math, *Career Choices*, pages 216 - 217
Writing Affirmation about Math
Career Choices, pages 230 - 231
Getting Help, page 8

Wednesday

What Cost this Lifestyle?
Debate from page 12
Read pages 76 - 77 in *Career Choices*
Complete page 12 in *Lifestyle Math*

Thursday

Housing Budget, pages 14 - 16

Friday

Renting or Owning, pages 18 - 20
Property Tax, Insurance, Association Fees, pages 21 - 22

SOCIAL STUDIES

Instructional materials: To be researched and developed. Use Career Choices textbook and Workbook and Portfolio weeks seven, eight and nine.

Instruction through use of lecture, video, readings, dialogue, activities.

Monday
Introduction

Tuesday
Visionaries in Our Culture, motivational videos

Wednesday
Characteristics of Visionaries
How each of us is a visionary

Thursday
The Societal Movements of the Last 30 Years

Friday
The Societal Movements of the Last 30 Years

WEEK TWO

CAREER/GUIDANCE CURRICULUM

Monday

Strengths and Personality, page 150
Presentation suggestions

Tuesday

Your Strengths, page 152
Presentation suggestions, Activities, Energizer

Wednesday

Name That Skill, page 155
Presentation suggestions
Skills Identifications, page 156
Presentation suggestions, Activities

Thursday

Roles, Occupations, and Vocations, page 158
Presentation suggestions, Activities, Follow-up

Friday

Message Center, page 160
Presentation suggestions, Activity, Debate

ENGLISH/LANGUAGE ARTS

Monday

Excerpt from *The Prophet* by Kahlil Gibran
Discussion: Questions 1, 2, 3, 4
Richard Cory by Edwin Arlington Robinson
Discussion: Question 5
Homework: Question 4

Tuesday

Sonnets From the Portuguese by Elizabeth Barrett Browning
Discussion: Question 2 and Figurative Language

Wednesday

Excerpt from *Alice in Wonderland* by Lewis Carroll
Discussion: Acrostic Poetry #3

Thursday

Excerpt from *I Know Why the Caged Bird Sings* by Maya Angelou
Discussion: Characterization and Autobiographical Incident
Homework: (extended) Writing Directions

Friday

Sympathy by Paul Dunbar
Discussion: Questions 2, 4
Personification
Life by Nan Terrell
Discussions: Questions 1, 2, 6

MATH

Monday

Utilities and telephone, pages 23 - 24
Make Your Choice, page 24
Rental Move-In Costs, page 25
Small group activity, page 26

Tuesday

Where Do You Want to Live?, pages 27 - 30
Home Ownership on One Income, page 31
Small group discussion: Last question

Wednesday

Transportation - Buying a Car, pages 32 - 33
Trade-In Time, page 34
Gasoline costs, pages 35 - 37

Thursday

Small group problem, page 38
Insurance and maintenance, page 41
Case Study, page 42

Friday

Yearly Clothing Budget, pages 43 - 44
Spouse and Children's budget, pages 45 - 47

SOCIAL STUDIES

Monday

Cultural Values
How they change
How they impact our lives

Tuesday

Individual Freedoms;
America's Foundation

Wednesday

Community and Shared
Responsibility

Thursday

Prejudice:
Ethnic, racial, gender, age, disability

Friday

Diversity:
What is it and why is it important?

WEEK THREE

CAREER/GUIDANCE CURRICULUM

Monday

Maslow's Triangle, page 166
Presentation suggestions, Activity
Read How Do You Want to Be
Remembered
Homework: Complete Mission Statement

Tuesday

How Do You Want to Be Remembered, page 167
Presentation suggestions; Panel of self-actualizers

Wednesday

Looking into the Future, page 169
Components of Lifestyle, page 170
Presentation suggestions

Thursday

Happiness is a Balanced Lifestyle, page 171
Presentation suggestions
The Modified Maslow Triangle, page 172
Presentation suggestions
Homework: Interview adult on his/her location on triangle

Friday

What About Your Life, page 173
Presentation suggestions, Activity (parent's triangle)

ENGLISH/LANGUAGE ARTS

Monday

Excerpt from *Self-Reliance* by Ralph Waldo Emerson
Discussion: Share and debate responses to Journal entry
Questions 2, 8, 9

Tuesday

***Growing Older* by R. G. Wells**
Discussion: Questions 1, 2 and journal entries

Wednesday

I Shall Not Pass This Way Again
Discussion: Questions 3, 6

Thursday

***Red Geraniums* by Martha Haskell Clark**
Discussion: Questions 1 - 4
The Writer's Notebook

Friday

The Mills of the Gods
Discussion: Journal entries, Questions 1, 4, 6
Discuss extra credit quote

MATH

Monday

Food Budget, pages 48 - 52
Planning Your Weekly Meals,, pages 53 - 55
Homework: Grocery shopping, pages 55 - 57

Tuesday

Monthly Entertainment Budget, page 64
Recreation is More than Just Fun, page 65

Wednesday

Saving Plan for Vacation, pages 68 - 69
Creative Planning, small group, page 70

Thursday

Child Care Budget, pages 71 - 73
Health Care Budget, pages 74 - 75

Friday

Furnishing Expenses, pages 76 - 77
Depreciation, Group Brainstorm, pages 78 - 79
Saving for Long-Term, page 80
Percentage you must save, page 81

SOCIAL STUDIES

Monday Appreciating Diversity

Tuesday Cultural Diversity
A historical perspective

Wednesday Cultural Diversity
Today's multicultural society

Thursday Gender Diversity

Friday Age Diversity
Diversity of Ability

WEEK FOUR

CAREER/GUIDANCE CURRICULUM

Monday

Budget Exercise, pages 176 - 188

Tuesday

Budget Exercise, pages 176 - 188

Wednesday

Hard Times Budget, page 189
Presentation suggestions

Thursday

Some Sample Budgets, page 190
Presentation suggestions

Friday

**A Few Words About Poverty,
pages 191-192**
Presentation suggestions

ENGLISH/LANGUAGE ARTS

Monday

The Savings Book by Gary Soto
Discussion: Questions 1, 2, 3

Tuesday

Activity from **The Savings Book**
Activity a: Group

Wednesday

Miss Rosie by Lucille Clifton
Discussion: Journal entry,
Questions 3, 4, 5

Thursday

Christmas Day in the Workhouse by
George Simms
Discussion: 2, 3
Group activity: 5

Friday

The Gift of the Magi by O. Henry
Discussion: Journal entries, Question 4

MATH

Monday

Miscellaneous Expenses, page 84
Group Think, **Saving Strategies,**
pages 82 - 83

Tuesday

Your Total Budget Profile, page 85
What Ends Up in Your Pocket,
page 86

Wednesday

Your Annual Salary Requirement,
page 87
Now Find a Job, page 88

Thursday

Group Project: **Hard Times Budget,**
pages 93 - 94

Friday

Charting Statistics, pages 95 - 97

SOCIAL STUDIES

Monday

Capitalism
How it works

Tuesday

Capitalism vs. Socialism

Wednesday

The Free Enterprise System: Small
business to Corporations

Thursday

Poverty in the U.S.

Friday

Poverty in the U.S.

WEEK FIVE

SOCIAL STUDIES

Monday The Changing Workforce/Workplace

Tuesday Changing Demographics

Wednesday Changes in Laws Affecting the Workplace

Thursday Changes in the Family Structure and the Workplace

Friday Technology and the Information Age

MATH

Monday Group presentations, pages 95 - 97

Tuesday Group presentations, pages 95 - 97

Wednesday **Comparing with National Average,** page 92

Thursday Group Project: **What Is Your Math Education Worth To You?,** pages 98 - 99

Friday Group Project: **What Is Your Math Education Worth To You?,** pages 98 - 99

ENGLISH/LANGUAGE ARTS

Monday **Creative Writing, page 101**

Tuesday *A Legacy For My Daughter* by James Webb
Discussion: 1 - 5, 7, 8

Wednesday *I Decline to Accept the End of Man* by William Faulkner
Discussion: 1, 5 - 10

Thursday *A Boy's Ambition* by Mark Twain
Discussion: 1 - 3, 8, 9

Friday *Lego*
Discussion: 1 - 6, 9 - 11

CAREER/GUIDANCE CURRICULUM

Monday **Money Isn't Everything, page 193**
Presentation suggestions
Psychological Cost: Sacrifices Versus Rewards, page 194
Presentation suggestions

Tuesday **You Win Some, You Lose Some, page 195**
Presentation suggestions
After-hours Rewards, pages 196-197
Presentation suggestions

Wednesday **An Investment In Education, page 198**
Presentation suggestions
Homework: **Ask Someone Who's Been There, page 200**

Thursday **Easier Said Than Done, page 201**
Presentation suggestions
Report out from homework assignment

Friday **Your Ideal Job, pages 204-205**
Presentation suggestions

WEEK SIX

CAREER/GUIDANCE CURRICULUM

Monday
Complete Your Ideal Job, from previous day
Consider Your Options, page 206
Presentation suggestions
Homework: **Employee or Employer, page 207**

Tuesday
Employee or Employer, page 207
Activities
What About Status, page 209
Presentation suggestions

Wednesday
Career Interest Areas, page 212
Presentation suggestions
Bring In Your Identity, page 213
Presentation suggestions

Thursday
Career Interest Survey, page 214
Presentation suggestions
Go to career library

Friday
Career Interest Survey, page 214
Presentation suggestions
Go to career library

ENGLISH/LANGUAGE ARTS

Monday
Essay on Fantasy Job, page 123

Tuesday
Presentation on Fantasy Job

Wednesday
To Build a Fire by Jack London
Discussion of Journal entry

Thursday
To Build a Fire by Jack London
Discussion: 1 - 8
Review Observational Writing

Friday
To Build a Fire by Jack London
Share observational writing assignment

MATH

Monday
Investment in Education, page 113,
Career Choices

Tuesday
Math Problem in *More Choices*, pages 144 - 147 *

Wednesday
Math Problem in *More Choices*, pages 144 - 147 *

Thursday
Job Research at career center on computers

Friday
Job Research at career center on computers

* From *More Choices: A Strategic Planning Guide for Mixing Career and Family* by Bingham and Stryker.

SOCIAL STUDIES

Monday
The history of vocations/work in the U.S. Colonial days to mid-1880's

Tuesday
The history of vocations/work in the U.S. The Industrial Revolution

Wednesday
The history of vocations/work in the U.S. Post-World War II to 1970

Thursday
The history of vocations/work in the U.S. The last 20 years

Friday
Predicting the future

WEEK SEVEN

CAREER/GUIDANCE CURRICULUM

Monday

**Seeing in the Mind's Eye,
pages 216-217**

Tuesday

**The Shadow Program,
pages 218-219**
Explain and write letters
Long-term homework: Arrange for
Shadow Experience

Wednesday

**Involve Me and I Understand,
page 225**
Presentation suggestions
The Chemistry Test, page 228
Presentation suggestions

Thursday

Identifying Choices, page 235
Presentation suggestions
Gathering Information, page 236
Presentation suggestions

Friday

Evaluating Choices, pages 237
Presentation suggestions
Gloria's Chart, page 239
Presentation suggestions
Make a Decision, page 240
Presentation suggestions

ENGLISH/LANGUAGE ARTS

Monday

I Hear America Singing by
Walt Whitman
Discussion: 1 - 4
Copy Change

Tuesday

The Monkey's Paw, a play adapted from
W.W. Jacobs' short story
Discussion: 4
Writing Dialogue

Wednesday

The Monkey's Paw, continued
Share dialogues and run survey of
class choices

Thursday

The Road Not Taken by Robert Frost
Discussion: 1 - 7

Friday

Hope by Emily Dickinson
Discussion: 3, 5, 6, 8
Expect Nothing by Alice Walker
Discussion: 1, 4, 5 - 7

MATH

Monday

Group Discussion: **Salary Estimation,**
pages 89 - 91

Tuesday

Group Energizer: **Planning a Party**
Spreadsheet lesson at the computer lab

Wednesday

Group Energizer: **Planning a Party**
Spreadsheet lesson at the computer lab

Thursday

Group Energizer: **Planning a Party**
Spreadsheet lesson at the computer lab

Friday

Party with **Math Baseball game,**
pages 66 - 67

SOCIAL STUDIES

Monday

The Six E's of Excellence
Career Choices, pages 232 - 235

Tuesday

Work is an Aggressive Act
Career Choices, pages 236 - 237

Wednesday

Work Ethic
You're the Boss exercise
Career Choices, pages 238 - 241

Thursday

Work Ethic
You're the Boss exercise
Career Choices, pages 238 - 241,
continued

Friday

The Employee of the Twenty-first
Century
Career Choices, pages 242 - 245

WEEK EIGHT

CAREER/GUIDANCE CURRICULUM

Monday

Tools for Solving Problems, page 244
Presentation suggestions
Setting Goals and Objectives, page 246
Presentation suggestions
Homework: Activities

Tuesday

Goals and Objectives, page 246
More practice
What's Your Excuse?, pages 250
Presentation suggestions
Taking Responsibility, page 252
Presentation suggestions

Wednesday

Startling Statement Quiz, page 253
Presentation suggestions, Activities
Detours and Roadblocks, page 254
Presentation suggestions
Homework: **Is It Worth Staying In School?, page 255**

Thursday

Is It Worth Staying In School?, page 255
Activities

Friday

Before You Give Up Your Dream, page 259
Presentation suggestions
Developing Anxiety Tolerance, page 260
Presentation suggestions

ENGLISH/LANGUAGE ARTS

Monday

Uphill by Christina Rossetti
Discussion: 1 - 9

Tuesday

The Prince of Tides by Pat Conroy
Discuss journal entry

Wednesday

The Prince of Tides by Pat Conroy
Vocabulary
Group Activity B

Thursday

The Prince of Tides by Pat Conroy
Character Development Activity

Friday

Dream Deferred by Langston Hughes
Discussion: 1, 6
Mother to Son by Langston Hughes
Discussion: 3, 5 - 10

MATH

Monday

Group Think: **Savings**, pages 82 - 83

Tuesday

Economics of Bad Habits
Career Choices, page 208

Wednesday

Saving for Retirement, page 100

Thursday

Economics of Women and Work
Career Choices, pages 211 - 213

Friday

Economics of Women and Work
Career Choices, pages 211 - 213

SOCIAL STUDIES

Monday

The Employee of the Twenty-first Century
Career Choices, pages 242 - 245, continued

Tuesday

Finding a Job in Today's World
Resume writing
Career Choices, pages 250 - 253

Wednesday

Conducting an Informal Interview
Career Choices, pages 254 - 255

Thursday

Job Applications
Career Choices, pages 256 - 257

Friday

The Job Interview
Career Choices, pages 258 - 259

WEEK NINE

SOCIAL STUDIES

Monday - Friday
Chapter 12, *Career Choices*
Complete pages 266 - 282 as in-class
and take-home final.

MATH

Monday
Developing an Action Plan,
pages 102 - 103

Tuesday
Developing an Action Plan,
pages 104 - 106

Wednesday
**Developing an Action Plan for Your
Dream,** pages 107 - 109

Thursday
**Developing an Action Plan for Your
Dream,** pages 107 - 109

Friday
**A new vision of yourself as math
competent**
Writing Affirmations, *Career
Choices*, page 231

ENGLISH/LANGUAGE ARTS

Monday
Excerpt from *All I Really Need to Know I
Learned In Kindergarten* by Robert Fulgram
Discussion: 3 - 5, 7, 8

Tuesday
Over the Hill to the Poor-house by
Will M. Carleton
Discussion: 3, 5 - 7
Writing assignment

Wednesday
George Gray by Edgra Lee Masters
Discussion: 1 - 4

Thursday
Ex-Basketball Player by John Updike
Discussion: 1 - 3
Writing assignment

Friday
25th High School Reunion by
Linda Pastan
Discussion: 1 - 5
Write your essay to be included in your
25th High School Reunion Booklet

CAREER/GUIDANCE CURRICULUM

Monday
One Step At a Time, page 261
Presentation suggestions

Tuesday
Yorik's Story, page 262
Presentation suggestions

Wednesday
Taking Risks, page 263
Presentation suggestions
**Getting Back on Track If You've
Been Derailed, page 265**
Presentation suggestions

Thursday
Homework: Write their own poem:
"WE ARE A SUCCESS." Use the
poem by Robert Louis Stevenson
on page 283 of *Career Choices*
as a model.

Friday
Defining Success, page 140
Follow-up at the end of the course
Energizer
During the last ten minutes of class,
read *Oh! The Places You'll Go!* by
Dr. Seuss

Career Choices Curriculum
180-Hour Lesson Plan

Designed for:

- one instructor
- using all four textbooks
- in daily 50-minute periods
- for one complete school year

Ideal for:

- Freshmen orientation programs
- A careers course
- Academic classes with a self-discovery theme
- Motivational courses for at-risk students

This specialized lesson plan augments the material of the *Career Choices* curriculum and assists you in your daily planning. In detailed format, it shows how the textbooks work together, some of the activities to use and the order of the activities. It is our hope that this lesson plan will save you hundreds of hours of planning time and present proven strategies for classroom success.

Career Choices: A Guide for Teens and Young Adults: Who Am I? What Do I Want? How Do I Get It?

Workbook and Portfolio for Career Choices

Possibilities: A Supplemental Anthology for Career Choices

Lifestyle Math: Your Financial Planning Portfolio

Computerized Correction Key and Portfolio for Lifestyle Math

The Goals of this Lesson Plan

This plan was written for instructors whose goals include facilitating the student guidance and planning process. Students will leave this class with an understanding of the importance of education and the role it plays in their future satisfaction. They will have a strong sense of direction for the balance of their educational experience and the skills to change plans if circumstances dictate.

This is a competency-based course. Students will soon understand the necessity of acquiring basic skills if they hope to have a satisfying adult life. Never again will they ask, "Why do we have to learn this?" Yet while the activities in this lesson plan will give students daily practice in reading, writing, speaking and mathematical computation, the self-exploration activities of the curriculum have been chosen rather than the academic drill and skill exercises. More of these exercises may be added at the instructor's discretion.

Because this curriculum teaches an important decision-making process that students will use throughout their lives, it has a strong scope and sequence (curriculum lingo for 'order'). Therefore, skipping around is not recommended. Particular activities may be deleted or substituted, but it is important to note that some exercises are critical to the success of the course. The awareness and skills learned earlier in the books are used as the students finalize their plans. Those lessons have been noted in the far right margin with a star ☆.

This lesson plan requires each student to have a copy of:

- *Career Choices: A Guide for Teens and Young Adults: Who Am I? What Do I Want? How Do I Get It?*
- *Workbook and Portfolio for Career Choices*
- *Possibilities: A Supplemental Anthology for Career Choices*
- *Lifestyle Math: Your Financial Planning Portfolio*
- *Computerized Correction Key and Portfolio for Lifestyle Math*

As the instructor, you will use the *Instructor's and Counselor's Guide for Career Choices* on a daily basis.

Getting Started

First you'll need a copy of each textbook and the *Instructor's Guide* handy so you can turn to the pages and exercises noted in the lesson plan.

It is a strong recommendation that as the instructor you actually work through your own copy of the main textbook, *Career Choices*, completing the activities and exercises for yourself. This will help you integrate the total process, understand the scope and sequence, and provide you with discussion material and examples for your class based on your own experience. Students love to hear teachers' responses! You might want to pretend you are searching for a second career when you retire from teaching. As an adult, this task should take 20 hours or less. Most educators find this an enjoyable and enlightening experience.

How to Use this Lesson Plan

- You'll note the lesson plan is set up in an hour-by-hour format. (Column one)

- The next column notes which textbook(s) the students will use for that lesson, along with the specific pages. This is the reading material for the day. In the case of *Career Choices*, you may want to assign all or a portion of the next day's reading as homework so the students come to class somewhat familiar with the topic and ready to discuss and complete the activities.

- The third column shows the title of the activity or exercise in the texts. If the title is in parenthesis, it is a description of the lesson.

- The next column directs the instructor to the pages in the *Instructor's and Counselor's Guide* for that particular lesson. It also notes what exercises are suggested for that page. For example, if it says "Presentation suggestions" you will read and execute the directions under that topic on that particular page. The same is true for other topics such as Activities, Energizers, Resources, etc. This does not mean you shouldn't use other topics on the page if you have the time or inkling.

- The last column presents Special Directions that completes this special lesson plan and are not included in the *Instructor's and Counselor's Guide*. You will want to combine the information in this column with the directions detailed in the fourth column.

- In the right margin, lessons are starred (☆) that we consider critical to the success of the program. We suggest you not delete these if you decide to do other activities not noted on this lesson plan. You may want to, or need to, spend more time on some of the required lessons.

Hour	Textbook	Lesson	Instructor's Guide	Special Directions (beyond those given in *Instructor's Guide*)	
20	*Career Choices*, p. 30 *Career Choices*, pp. 31-37 *Workbook*, pp. 13-16	(James and Letitia) Work Values Survey	p. 148, Presentation suggestions	Dramatic Reading Review the survey together, discuss any words or concepts they don't understand. It is important to be very non-judgmental about statements read. Note the suggestion of the "value totem" on page 149.	☆

Example

Career Choices Curriculum
180 hours of instruction

Hour	Textbook	Lesson	Instructor's Guide	Special Directions (beyond those given in *Instructor's Guide*)	
1	*Career Choices*, pp. 6-7	Introduction	p. 130, Presentation suggestions Activities	Give students a piece of 8½ × 11 white paper and ask them to "create" something that flies. Responses will vary greatly. Optional: Let students decorate the outside of their *Workbook and Portfolio*. Perhaps allow them to decoupage their books, using pictures they find meaningful or their names in decorative art forms.	☆
2	*Career Choices*, pp. 10-13 *Workbook*, p. 5	Vision + Energy = Success	p. 132, Presentation suggestions		☆
3	*Career Choices*, pp. 10-13 *Workbook*, p. 5	(Visualizer activity)	p. 135	Divide students into groups of three to develop, design and build their visualizer. Have groups "model" and explain their visualizers to the rest of the class. Leave visualizers hanging in the room with permission to use if needed at any time.	☆
4	*Career Choices*, pp. 14-17 *Workbook*, p. 6	Envisioning Your Future	p. 134, Presentation suggestions	Visual Assessment: Videotape students presenting their Envisioning Your Future essay during the first week of class. Then, during the last week of class, have students rewrite their essays and videotape the new responses. Compare the two videotapes. Share the final production not only with the students but with administrators and funders. This is powerful!	☆
5	*Career Choices*, pp. 15-16 *Career Choices*, p. 17 *Workbook*, p. 7	Why People Work Everybody Works	p. 136, Presentation suggestions p. 137, Presentation suggestions		☆
6	*Career Choices*, pp. 18-21 *Workbook*, pp. 8-9	Defining Success	p. 138, Presentation suggestions		☆
7	*Career Choices*, pp. 18-21 *Workbook*, pp. 8-9	Defining Success *(continued)*	p. 138, Activities	Have students write the first of their success statements: p. 21 of *Career Choices*.	☆
8	*Possibilities*, pp. 37-39	"Richard Cory" by Edwin Arlington Robinson		Have the Simon and Garfunkel song "Richard Cory" playing as the students enter the classroom. Read story aloud. Have students discuss journal entry and question 5.	
9	*Possibilities*, p. 38	"Richard Cory" *(continued)* Question 7 How to gather data and conduct an interview		Present the project: Choose an outcome. For example, present findings to the school newspaper or submit to a community paper's editorial page. Where to find people to interview. How to take notes. Homework: Conduct interviews.	
10	*Possibilities*, p. 38	"Richard Cory" *(continued)* Question 7 How to analyze data		Students report out on findings from their interviews. Group decides how to composite findings.	
11	*Possibilities*, p. 38	"Richard Cory" *(continued)* Question 7 How to summarize data		Summarize findings: Discuss and brainstorm ideas. Record findings. Invite school news reporter to sit in on discussion to write an article for the paper [or have a class member(s) write and submit the article].	

Special Directions (beyond those given in *Instructor's Guide*)

Hour	Textbook	Lesson	Instructor's Guide	Special Directions	
12	*Career Choices*, p. 20 *Workbook*, p. 9	Making Career Choices	p. 141, Presentation suggestions	After you've discussed as per *Instructor's Guide*, make a chart for classroom wall with the characters' names and a descriptive title. For example, Eric/wishful thinker, Louisa/escape artist, etc. Throughout the course, let students identify the decision making patterns of friends, characters in stories and even themselves. "Today I'm reacting like Harold (procrastinator) when I wait until the night before to start my social studies report."	☆
13	*Possibilities*, pp. 11-18	"Secret Life of Walter Mitty" by James Thurber		Read Thurber's story aloud. Use dramatic inflection of voice or invite a senior drama student to do the reading. As a class, discuss question 8 in *Possibilities*.	☆
14	*Possibilities*, p. 17	"Secret Life of Walter Mitty" (*continued*) Question 9		Break into groups of three to discuss and complete chart. Share charts as a class. As a class, discuss question 5.	☆
15		(Identity activity)	p. 144, Activity	Personal Collage: Who am I? What do I want? What are my dreams? On a very large sheet of paper, mark off a quarter section to be used for this assignment. Other parts of the collage can be added later, after they complete other activities that help them identify their dreams and goals.	
16		(Identity activity)	p. 144, Activity	Personal Collage: Time to complete. Ask each person to explain his or her collage.	
17	*Career Choices*, p. 24	(James and Letitia)		Choose three students who are able to confidently read aloud to be (1) a narrator; (2) James and (3) Letitia. Their story is told throughout chapter 2 of *Career Choices* (pp. 24-50). Each time the class arrives at a portion of their story, ask the "actors" to read their parts.	☆
	Career Choices, pp. 25-27 *Workbook*, p. 11	(Your Personal Profile) (Bull's Eye Chart)	p. 144, Presentation suggestions, Energizer	On their own, create the "first draft" of their charts.	
18	*Career Choices*, p. 28 *Career Choices*, pp. 28-29 *Workbook*, p. 12	(James and Letitia) Identifying Your Passions	p. 146, Presentation suggestions, Activities	Dramatic Reading Show the film clip of Dr. Martin Luther King presenting his *I Have a Dream* speech. Discuss King's passion and vision.	☆
19	*Career Choices*, pp. 28-29 *Workbook*, p. 12	Identifying Your Passions (*continued*)	p. 146, English/language arts lesson	Break into small groups and have each group member help the others describe their ideal day. Ask each person to report out. *Note: Follow-up statement on p. 147 of Instructor's Guide.*	☆
20	*Career Choices*, p. 30 *Career Choices*, pp. 31-37 *Workbook*, pp. 13-16	(James and Letitia) Work Values Survey	p. 148, Presentation suggestions	Dramatic Reading Review the survey together, discuss any words or concepts they don't understand. Be non-judgmental about statements read. Note the suggestion of the "value totem" on p. 149.	☆
21	*Career Choices*, pp. 31-37 *Workbook*, pp. 13-16	Work Values Survey (*continued*)		Students take the survey. They must take it alone, not in groups. *Note: Follow-up suggestion on p. 149 of Instructor's Guide.*	☆

Hour	Textbook	Lesson	Instructor's Guide	Special Directions (beyond those given in *Instructor's Guide*)	
22	*Career Choices*, pp. 31-37 Workbook, pp. 13-16	Work Values Survey *(continued)*		Students score the survey. Discussion of each category.	☆
23	*Career Choices*, pp. 31-37 Workbook, pp. 13-16	Work Values Survey *(continued)*		As a class, brainstorm careers for each student, given his or her top three work values. Ask each student to write his or her top three values on the board. Open the discussion up to the floor so classmates can make suggestions. This is an introductory activity and will need a lot of support from teachers and adults. You might even invite two or three other individuals (career counselor, guidance counselor, principal, etc.) to help brainstorm.	☆
24	*Career Choices*, pp. 31-37 Workbook, pp. 13-16	Work Values Survey *(continued)*	p. 148, Gender Equity Activity	Reading and discussion of the story *My Way Sally*. Invite a special guest to read (drama student or teacher, favorite adult or teacher, principal). Call (800) 967-8016 to order.	
25	*Career Choices*, p. 38 *Career Choices*, pp. 38-42 Workbook, pp. 17-19	(James and Letitia) Strengths and Personality	p. 150, Presentation suggestions	Dramatic reading Review the definitions on p. 39 of *Career Choices* before students complete the activity. Complete the activities individually.	☆
26	*Career Choices*, p. 43	(How personality impacts career choices)	p. 150, Presentation suggestions	Discussion of styles. Brainstorm the types of careers in which each style might be happiest.	☆
27	*Career Choices*, pp. 44-45 Workbook, p. 20	Your Strengths (Developing your strengths)	p. 152, Presentation suggestions, Activities		☆
28	*Instructor's Guide*, p. 114	(Contributing your strengths to the team)	pp. 153-154, Energizer		
29	*Possibilities*, pp. 43-46	Excerpt from *Alice in Wonderland* by Lewis Carroll Question 3		Have students form editorial teams to help each other write their poems. Two students can choose to work together. Each will complete a poem with the other's help and input. Discussion: Acrostic poetry, question 3.	☆
30	*Possibilities*, pp. 43-46	Excerpt from *Alice in Wonderland (continued)*		Have the students make their acrostic poem into a poster (art project) and hang them around the room.	☆
31	*Career Choices*, p. 46 *Career Choices*, pp. 46-48 Workbook, p. 21	(James and Letitia) Skills and Aptitudes, Name That Skill	p. 155, Presentation suggestions	Dramatic reading	☆
32	*Career Choices*, p. 48 Workbook, p. 22	Skills Identification	p. 156, Presentation suggestions		☆
33	*Career Choices*, p. 48 Workbook, p. 22	Skills Identification *(continued)*	p. 156, Activities	You may want to break into small groups to brainstorm and then ask each group to report out. Energizer: Name That Skill toss. Using a ball, have the students sit in a circle and, when tossed the ball, call out a skill they have as they throw to the next person.	☆
34		(Interest Inventory)	p. 157, Resources	Work with the Guidance Department and administer the interest inventory of choice.	

Hour	Textbook	Lesson	Instructor's Guide	Special Directions (beyond those given in *Instructor's Guide*)	
35		(Work behavioral style inventory)	p. 151	Optional: Administer the Carlson Personal Profile System Assessment. For ordering information, call (800) 967-8016.	
36	*Career Choices*, p. 49	Roles, Occupations, and Vocations	p. 158, Presentation suggestions, Activities	Energizer: Using a "family tree" format, ask students to research their family tree (through great grandparents), including the roles, occupations and vocations of these people. This may be a long-term project.	☆
37	*Career Choices*, p. 49	(Who Am I? - Becoming identity achieved)	p. 159, Chapter Follow-up	Chapter follow-up: Complete chart on p. 27 of *Career Choices* with information discovered from activities on pp. 28-49. Post charts around the room for all to see.	☆
38	*Career Choices*, p. 49	(Who do I want to become) (Character analysis)	p. 159, Chapter Follow-up p. 151	Compare bull's eye chart of hero/heroine with their own bull's eye chart. Activity and discussion. Complete a bull's eye chart for one of the following people in their future: Employer, best friend, business partner, spouse.	
39	*Career Choices*, p. 50 *Career Choices*, pp. 50-53 *Workbook*, pp. 23-24	(James and Letitia) The Message Center	p. 160, Presentation suggestions	Dramatic reading	☆
40	*Possibilities*, pp. 61-62 *Career Choices*, pp. 50-53	"Life" by Nan Terrell Reed Message Center Debate: Does society give girls and boys different messages.	p. 160, Activity p. 160, Debate	Discuss the messages which society gives individuals based on their gender, race, age, physical appearance, physical ability, social status, intellectual capacity, educational achievement, and so forth. See p. 22 of *Possibilities* for a description of a Formal Debate. Energizer: Break students into teams of four or five. Give each team a large piece of art paper. Have students draw a box with lines dividing it into quarters (two rows, two columns). Along the horizontal axis, write "Good Messages" above the left-hand quadrant and "Bad Messages" above the right-hand quadrant. Along the vertical axis, write "Female" next to the top quadrant and "Male" next to the bottom quadrant. Have each group brainstorm the good and bad messages given to them by family, peers and society. You can also have them use magazine pictures to illustrate the messages.	☆
41		(Projecting into the future)		Divide into triads and ask the student teams to project into the future and write the script for James and Letitia. Describe their lives at age 20, 25, 30, 40 and 50. Keep in mind their described passions, values, strengths, etc.	☆
42	*Possibilities*, p. 24	(Long-range planning) "Dreams" by Langston Hughes		Have each group report on how they saw the lives of James and Letitia unfolding. Read the poem "Dreams" and discuss the journal entry question.	☆
43	*Career Choices*, pp. 56-59 *Workbook*, p. 26 *Career Choices*, pp. 60-61 *Workbook*, p. 27	(Maslow's Triangle), Where Are You Now? How Do You Want to be Remembered?	p. 166, Presentation suggestions p. 167, Presentation suggestions	Ask students to complete Mission Statement over the next two or three days.	☆

Hour	Textbook	Lesson	Instructor's Guide	Special Directions (beyond those given in *Instructor's Guide*)	
44	*Career Choices*, pp. 60-61 / Workbook, p. 21	How Do You Want to be Remembered? *(continued)*	p. 167, Activity	You'll want to look for this panel a few weeks ahead and loan them a copy of *Career Choices* so they can read chapter 3.	
45	*Possibilities*, pp. 69-71	"Growing Older" by R.G. Wells Discussion Questions 1, 2 and Journal Entry	p. 169, Looking into the Future	After reading the poem aloud and discussing questions, follow directions on p. 169 of the *Instructor's Guide* for a guided writing assignment. Make copies of the letters to be used with lesson "Remembering Your Dreams and Plans" (Hour 177).	☆
46	*Possibilities*, pp. 72-73	"I Shall Not Pass This Way Again" Discussion: Questions 3 and 6		Use as art project (optional).	
47	*Career Choices*, pp. 62-63 / Workbook, p. 28	Your Lifestyle, Components of Lifestyle	p. 170, Presentation suggestions		☆
48	*Career Choices*, pp. 64-69	Happiness is a Balanced Lifestyle, The Modified Maslow Triangle	p. 171, Presentation suggestions		☆
49	*Career Choices*, pp. 70-71 / Workbook, p. 30	What About Your Life	p. 172, Presentation suggestions		☆
50	*Possibilities*, pp. 76-79	"The Mills of the Gods" Discussion: Journal entries, Questions 1, 4, 6 Quote	p. 173, Presentation suggestions, Activity (parents' triangle)		
51	*Career Choices*, pp. 74-77 / *Lifestyle Math*, p. 12	(Ivy Elm's story, Family Profile)	pp. 176-178	Read and discuss Ivy's story. Have students complete their own family profile. Then have them share their plans with the class.	☆
52	*Career Choices*, p. 78 / *Lifestyle Math*, pp. 14-16	Housing Budget (Do you want to own or rent?) Presentation suggestions - Real estate professional	p. 179 / p. 179, Activity	Hand out copies of classified ads and real estate booklets. Be sure to have scissors and glue. Ask a professional if he or she can arrange a shadowing opportunity for class members. Saturday or Sunday is best.	☆
53	*Lifestyle Math*, pp. 18-19	Renting or Owning		As a class, figure at least one fictional example of a mortgage using steps on pp. 18-19 of *Lifestyle Math*. Use calculators if necessary.	☆
54	*Lifestyle Math*, p. 20	Your Mortgage Payment		Have students figure their own mortgage payment for house and condo chosen. Check on computer.	
	Lifestyle Math, pp. 21-22	Property Taxes Insurance Home Owner's Association Fees		Find out ahead if your state has a special formula for property taxes. Explain each of these "hidden costs" of owning a home. Check figures on computer. Homework: Bring in copies of utility bills from home.	☆
55	*Lifestyle Math*, pp. 23-24	Utilities Telephone		Ask students to total and share their families' utility costs for a month. Brainstorm ways to save on utilities. Complete calculations and check on computer.	☆

Hour	Textbook	Lesson	Instructor's Guide	Special Directions (beyond those given in *Instructor's Guide*)	
56	*Lifestyle Math*, p. 25	If Renting is Your Choice… How Much will it Cost to Move In?		Brainstorm pros and cons of renting. Explain move-in deposits and terms. Have each student complete p. 25 of *Lifestyle Math* and check on computer.	☆
57	*Lifestyle Math*, p. 26	How Numbers Can Help You Make the Best Choices		As a class, complete questions 1-3. Divide into three to four groups (no more than five per group) and answer question 4. Make sure there is at least one capable math student in each group. Ask each group to share final choice and tell why.	☆
58	*Lifestyle Math*, pp. 27-30	Home Affordability Across the Country Where Do You Want to Live?		Discuss topic. Practice formula on board using fictional example. Ask students to complete the first two problems on p. 30 of *Lifestyle Math*. Check on computer.	
59	*Lifestyle Math*, pp. 31	Affording Home Ownership on One Income		Discuss relocation. Ask students to share experiences. Brainstorm pros and cons. Complete An Affordable Location (bottom of page 30 and the exercise on page 31) of *Lifestyle Math*.	
60	*Lifestyle Math*, p. 31	(Reasons to move to a more affordable location)		Brainstorm this list (last question at bottom of page) in small groups. Report out. Optional: Conduct Internet searches of four or five cities students identified. Go to search engine such as Yahoo. Search (name of city) + "real estate" (*see Making It Real*).	☆
61	*Lifestyle Math*, p. 31	(Reasons to move to a more affordable location - *continued*)			
62	*Lifestyle Math*, pp. 32-34	Transportation - Buying a Car Trade-In Time	p. 180	*See Instructor's Guide.* Check on computer.	☆
63	*Lifestyle Math*, pp. 35-36	Planning Monthly Gasoline Costs		Ask students to break into pairs and make a weekly and monthly log detailing the mileage they think they'll travel on average under these headings: Weekly Trips - type of trip, how many times per week, how many miles per trip; Monthly Trips - type of trip, how many times per month, how many miles per trip. After they multiply their weekly trips by 4 and add their monthly trips, they'll have the miles per month they plan to travel. Complete p. 36 in *Lifestyle Math*. Check on computer.	☆
64	*Lifestyle Math*, pp. 39-40	Transportation, Insurance and Maintenance		Invite an insurance agent to speak to the class or ask an agent to give you charts to help students estimate costs. Review the insurance laws in your state. Ask students to interview parents to find monthly maintenance budget of their cars. Good chance for discussion of savings by doing your own tune-ups.	☆
65	*Lifestyle Math*, pp. 41-42	Public Transportation Case Study		Ask students to research bus fares. Divide into groups of three to five classmates and complete Case Study and presentations.	☆
66	*Career Choices*, p. 82 *Lifestyle Math*, pp. 43-47	Yearly Clothing Budget	p. 182	Students may have to complete as homework if they projected several children. Divide into groups of two or three students to brainstorm column C of each worksheet if you sense some students don't know average costs. Check on computer.	☆

Hour	Textbook	Lesson	Instructor's Guide	Special Directions (beyond those given in *Instructor's Guide*)	
67	*Lifestyle Math*, pp. 43-47	Yearly Clothing Budget (*continued*)			☆
68	*Lifestyle Math*, pp. 43-47	Yearly Clothing Budget (*continued*)			
69	*Career Choices*, pp. 84-85 *Lifestyle Math*, pp. 48-52	Preparing a Food Budget	p. 183	Prepare students to complete weekly meal cost by reading and discussing the noted pages in *Career Choices* and *Lifestyle Math*.	☆
70	*Lifestyle Math*, pp. 53-54	Planning Your Weekly Meals (Consumer of the Week award) (optional)		Advise students that an award will be given to the student whose weekly plan is judged most nutritious *and* economical (recruit home ec teacher to judge). Prize: lunch or dinner with you, the instructor. Collect weekly grocery ads for numerous weeks to be used for reference. Allow students to work in teams if you like.	☆
71	*Lifestyle Math*, p. 55	Sample Grocery List		Once they decide on the meal plan, they can make a grocery list.	☆
72	*Lifestyle Math*, pp. 56-57	Find Your Weekly Grocery Costs		Either assign a trip to the grocery store for homework (to investigate the costs of their list) or have resources in the classroom such as food advertisements from grocery stores or inventory price printouts from the stores. Check on the computer.	☆
73	*Lifestyle Math*, p. 64	Monthly Entertainment Budget	p. 184	Be sure to advise students they don't need a figure in each line item. Newspaper entertainment sections, catalogs, and brochures for health clubs and the YMCA would be good to have as resources. You may want to brainstorm column B as a class. Check on the computer.	☆
74	*Lifestyle Math*, p. 65	Recreation is More Than Just Fun		Review topic with students. Ask students to choose a hobby they'd like at age 29. Divide class into groups of individuals who have similar ideas so they can brainstorm their budget/start up cost together. Share your hobby with them. Include your start up costs and strategies.	
75	*Career Choices*, p. 87 *Lifestyle Math*, pp. 68-70	Saving and Planning for a Vacation / Creative Planning	p. 184	Have teams of students first complete p. 70 of *Lifestyle Math*, Creative Planning, and make a presentation to the class. Begin research for pp. 68-69 of *Lifestyle Math*. Use Sunday travel section from the newspaper.	☆
76	*Lifestyle Math*, pp. 68-70	Saving and Planning for a Vacation (*continued*)		If students have similar plans, suggest they form research teams to figure costs. Check on the computer.	☆
77	*Career Choices*, p. 88 *Lifestyle Math*, pp. 71-73	Child Care Budget	p. 185	Divide into groups of three to complete p. 71 of *Lifestyle Math* and brainstorm other child care options.	☆
78	*Lifestyle Math*, pp. 71-73	(Raising a child on your own)	pp. 90-94	Invite a panel of single mothers (from teen to adult) to present the challenges of single motherhood. One (widowed or divorced) should be successful due to education and career planning.	
79	*Lifestyle Math*, pp. 71-73	Child Care Budget (*continued*)		Either individually or in groups, complete questions and chart. Check on the computer.	☆

Hour	Textbook	Lesson	Instructor's Guide	Special Directions (beyond those given in *Instructor's Guide*)	
80	*Career Choices*, p. 89 *Lifestyle Math*, pp. 74-75	Health Care Budget Savings for Medical Deductibles	p. 185	Using classified ads and medical bills, work through pp. 74-75 of *Lifestyle Math* as a class. Most students will have little knowledge of health care costs. If one student has had extensive medical experience within their family, ask if he or she would like to share the story. Discuss generic medications vs. regular, HMOs, and other health insurance options. This can be overwhelming so present gingerly. Check on computer.	☆
81	*Career Choices*, p. 89 *Lifestyle Math*, pp. 76-77	Furnishing Expenses	p. 186	Have merchandise catalogs available for research. Divide into groups to complete chart on p. 77 of *Lifestyle Math*. Check on computer.	☆
82	*Career Choices*, p. 89 *Lifestyle Math*, p. 80	Saving for the Long Term	p. 186	Review each line item and, as a class, brainstorm Savings Plan on p. 80 of *Lifestyle Math*. Check on computer.	☆
83	*Lifestyle Math*, p. 100	Saving for Retirement		Ask a retirement specialist to come in and present growth potential on annual deposits in IRA if begun early. Ask students to complete graph on p. 100 of *Lifestyle Math*.	☆
84	*Lifestyle Math*, p. 81	What Percentage of Your Salary Must You Save per Month?		This is an important concept to understand. You may want to use the figures of a couple of students and work through this formula. Discuss the question at the bottom of the page as a class. If you are willing, share your savings philosophy and compare it to your parents' philosophy.	☆
85	*Lifestyle Math*, p. 84	Miscellaneous Expenses	p. 186	First complete a fictional example on the board. Then ask students to complete their own annual and monthly costs. Check on computer.	☆
86	*Lifestyle Math*, pp. 85-87	Your Total Budget Profile What Ends Up in Your Pocket Your Annual Salary Requirement	pp. 187-188	You'll want to briefly talk about payroll deductions and gross pay versus net pay. It is important that your students understand that their salary requirement will be higher (by at least 20%) than what they expect to spend each month. You may want to share copies of payroll stubs (from your older students) so they can see what is taken out of a paycheck. Check on the computer.	☆
87	*Lifestyle Math*, p. 88	Find a Job That Will Support Your Lifestyle		Resources: *The American Almanac of Jobs and Salaries* can be ordered from a full service bookstore.	☆
88	*Lifestyle Math*, p. 88	Find a Job That Will Support Your Lifestyle *(continued)*		Ask students to share what they found and which occupations they starred. As a class, brainstorm the last question: If you have trouble finding appropriate careers that would support your desired lifestyle, what other options do you have?	☆
89	*Possibilities*, pp. 80-86	"The Savings Book" by Gary Soto Discussion: Questions 1, 2, 3		After you read Gary Soto's story (autobiographical) as a class, brainstorm answers to questions 1, 2 and 3 on p. 84 of *Possibilities*.	
90	*Possibilities*, pp. 80-86	"The Savings Book" *(continued)* Activity A: Group		Break students into groups of three and ask them to write a 30-second spot as described in the Activity. At the end of class, ask each group to "present" their spot.	

Hour	Textbook	Lesson	Instructor's Guide	Special Directions (beyond those given in *Instructor's Guide*)	
91	*Career Choices*, pp. 95-96 *Workbook*, p. 43	In Over Your Head?; Hard Times Budget	p. 189, Presentation suggestions	You'll need to research ahead of time the amount for AFDC and unemployment in your state. Complete this activity either in small groups or as a class.	☆
92	*Possibilities*, pp. 87-89	"Miss Rosie" by Lucille Clifton Discussion: Journal entry, Questions 3, 4, 5		Before reading the poem, discuss the journal entry on p. 87. Break into small groups and ask each group to describe Miss Rosie's life at age 15 (question 4) and then report out their ideas. As a class, discuss question 5. For homework, ask students to write a first person narrative of a day in a homeless person's life.	☆
93	*Possibilities*, pp. 90-94	"Christmas Day in the Workhouse" by George R. Sims Discussion: Journal question, Questions 2, 3, 4, Group activity 5		Before reading the poem, discuss the scenario in the journal entry. Let students break into teams and choose to complete one of the following questions: 3, 4 or 5.	
94	*Career Choices*, pp. 97-101 *Workbook*, pp. 44-45	Some Sample Budgets	p. 190, Presentation suggestions	Break the class into four groups and assign each group a different budget on pp. 98-101 of *Career Choices*. Once the groups debate and decide on their budget, ask each one to report out on their budget and justify their choices.	☆
95	*Career Choices*, p. 102 *Workbook*, p. 46 *Career Choices*, p. 103	A Few Words About Poverty Could You Become a Poverty Statistic?	pp. 191-192, Presentation suggestions	After discussing the points on p. 102 of *Career Choices*, ask students to individually complete the questions at the bottom of p. 103. Inviting a panel of single parents is also an option here.	☆
96	*Lifestyle Math*, pp. 95-97	Statistics - Developing Charts and Graphs		As a class or in small groups, complete the activities on these pages. Spend time discussing what the students found shocking about their graphs.	
97	*Career Choices*, pp. 104-110 *Workbook*, pp. 46-48	Money Isn't Everything (Psychological costs – sacrifices vs. rewards)	p. 193, Presentation suggestions p. 194, Presentation suggestions	After discussing these two topics, choose one of the activities listed in the *Instructor's Guide*.	☆
98	*Career Choices*, pp. 106-110	(Individual's stories)		Break into groups of three or four and assign each group a story. Ask each group to first read the story, discuss the questions following each story and then report their conclusions. Do class members have anything to add?	☆
99	*Career Choices*, pp. 111-113 *Workbook*, pp. 49-50	You Win Some, You Lose Some (After-hours rewards)	p. 195, Presentation suggestions, Activities pp. 196-197, Presentation suggestions	As a class, brainstorm the possibilities on p. 111 of *Career Choices*. Break into groups of three and have each group help its members list the rewards and sacrifices of one or two careers each student is considering. As a class, discuss and brainstorm points on pp. 112 and 113.	☆

Hour	Textbook	Lesson	Instructor's Guide	Special Directions (beyond those given in *Instructor's Guide*)	
100	*Possibilities*, pp. 95-102	"The Gift of the Magi" by O. Henry / Discussion: Journal entry Creative Writing		Before reading the story, discuss the journal entry questions. Ask individuals to give examples. If you can, arrange for a dramatic reading of this story. Break into groups of four or five and ask each group to brainstorm the creative writing assignment. Give extra credit to any group that wants to complete the Creative Writing assignment over the next week.	
101	*Career Choices*, pp. 116-117 / Workbook, pp. 51-53	An Investment in Education ...Yields Dividends for a Lifetime	p. 198, Presentation suggestions	Ask students to study the chart on p. 116 of *Career Choices* and interpret what it demonstrates. Then ask them to individually complete computations on p. 117.	☆
102	*Career Choices*, pp. 118-119 / Workbook, pp. 51-53 / *Career Choices*, p. 120 / Workbook, p. 54	An Investment in Education ...Yields Dividends for a Lifetime (*continued*) / Ask Someone Who's Been There	p. 199 / p. 200	Help students as they individually complete their bar graph on p. 118 and worksheet on p. 119 of *Career Choices*. Ask students to share their findings. Assign homework: *Career Choices*, p. 120.	☆
103	*Career Choices*, p. 121 / Workbook, p. 55	Easier Said Than Done	p. 201, Presentation suggestions,	Report out from homework and follow directions on p. 201 of the *Instructor's Guide*.	☆
104	*Career Choices*, pp. 124-134 / Workbook, pp. 57-62	(Your ideal career)	pp. 204-205, Presentation suggestions	Ask students to complete pp. 124-134 in *Career Choices*. They will need to work individually on this assignment. You'll want to follow procedure outlined in the *Instructor's Guide*.	☆
105	*Career Choices*, pp. 124-134 / Workbook, pp. 57-62	(Your ideal career) (*continued*)	pp. 204-205	After students have completed their charts, begin brainstorming possible careers that meet their essential career characteristics (see *Instructor's Guide*, p. 204.) If you have a career technician or counselor, you might ask her to attend this class to assist.	☆
106	*Career Choices*, pp. 135-137 / Workbook, p. 63	Consider Your Options	p. 206, Presentation suggestions		☆
107	*Career Choices*, pp. 138-139 / Workbook, pp. 64-65	Employee or Employer?	pp. 207-208, Presentation suggestions	After completing the activity as outlined in *Instructor's Guide*, you may want to debate the question "Which worker would have the most options for parenting, someone in a structured job or someone who is self-employed?"	☆
108	*Possibilities*, pp. 118-123	"Lego" Discussion: Journal entry, Questions 1-6, 9-11		Discuss the Mark Twain quote before reading the story. After reading this true story, discuss questions 1-6 and 9-11. Spend the most time on question 11. This is an important concept for students to understand. Then present the project described in the Writing Assignment so students can ponder it that evening.	☆
109	*Possibilities*, p. 123	"Lego" (*continued*) Essay on fantasy job		Have students spend the class time designing their fantasy job and writing a description of it. Encourage their imaginations to run wild.	☆
110	*Possibilities*, p. 123	Presentation on fantasy job		Ask students to give a short presentation on their fantasy job.	☆
111	*Career Choices*, pp. 144-147 / Workbook, p. 67	(Career interest areas) Bring In Your Identity	p. 212, Presentation suggestions / p. 213, Presentation suggestions	After completing these activities, ask students to write down three careers that they may want to pursue.	☆
112	*Career Choices*, pp. 148-149	Career Research		Review text. Take a tour of the career center/library.	☆

Hour	Textbook	Lesson	Instructor's Guide	Special Directions (beyond those given in *Instructor's Guide*)	
113	*Career Choices*, pp. 150-155 *Workbook*, pp. 68-73	Career Interest Survey	p. 214, Presentation suggestions	You'll want to recruit the assistance of your career librarian or career technician and spend the next three days in the library or career center.	☆
114	*Career Choices*, pp. 150-155 *Workbook*, pp. 68-73	Career Interest Survey (*continued*)	p. 214, Presentation suggestions		☆
115	*Career Choices*, pp. 150-155 *Workbook*, pp. 68-73	Career Interest Survey (*continued*)	p. 214, Presentation suggestions		☆
116	*Career Choices*, pp. 156-157 *Workbook*, pp. 73-74	Seeing in the Mind's Eye	pp. 216-217, Presentation suggestions		☆
117	*Career Choices*, pp. 158-159 *Workbook*, p. 75	The Shadow Program	pp. 218-219, Presentation suggestions	Explain and write letters. Long-term homework: Arrange for Shadow Experience. Optional: This project will be completed over a period of time and require outside work on your part (either finding job shadowing placements or better yet, a Director of Mentors), but the added effort is well worth it. This is an impressive activity for a high school student! See pp. 220-224 in the *Instructor's Guide*.	
118	*Career Choices*, pp. 160-161 *Workbook*, p. 76	Involve Me and I Understand	p. 225, Presentation suggestions	Optional Energizer: "What's My Line" guest panel. Invite in three individuals from the community who have unique jobs. Divide the class into two teams and have each team take turns asking questions and guessing their profession.	☆
119	*Career Choices*, pp. 162-165 *Workbook*, pp. 77-78	The Chemistry Test	pp. 228-231, Presentation suggestions	Read the story on p. 162 aloud. After discussing the topic as a class, work through the questions on pp. 163 - 164. Ask students to individually answer the questions on p. 165 of *Career Choices*.	☆
120	*Career Choices*, pp. 168-170 *Workbook*, p. 80	Identifying Choices	p. 234, Presentation suggestions, Activities		☆
121	*Career Choices*, p. 171 *Workbook*, p. 80	Gathering Information	p. 236, Presentation suggestions		☆
	Career Choices, pp. 172-174 *Workbook*, pp. 81-82	Evaluating Choices	pp. 237-238, Presentation suggestions	After the class has worked through Joyce's example, break into groups of three to consider Jessica and John's stories and complete their charts on pp. 173-174 of *Career Choices*.	
122	*Career Choices*, pp. 176-177 *Workbook*, pp. 82-83	Gloria's Chart	p. 239, Presentation suggestions	As a class, discuss and vote on Gloria's choice. Then have each student complete the chart on p. 177 of *Career Choices*, using the three careers researched earlier as their choices.	☆
123	*Possibilities*, pp. 127-135	*The Monkey's Paw* by W. W. Jacobs		A theatrical reading. Assign parts to students.	
124	*Possibilities*, pp. 127-135	*The Monkey's Paw* (*continued*) Question 4 Writing Dialogue		Discuss question 4 as a class. Break into groups of three and ask each group to write the dialogue for Morris (described in Writing Dialogue). Then have each group share their scenes.	

Hour	Textbook	Lesson	Instructor's Guide	Special Directions (beyond those given in *Instructor's Guide*)	
125	*Career Choices*, p. 178 *Workbook*, p. 84	Make a Decision	p. 240, Presentation suggestions	Brainstorm a list of important choices you might make as a working parent. Using the Edward De Bono exercise—Plus, Minus, Interesting—ask the students to brainstorm what is positive about each choice, negative about each choice and interesting about each choice. After discussion of decision making styles and a review of the terms on p. 178 of *Career Choices*, ask each student to complete the chart at the bottom of p. 178. Discuss the topic on p. 179.	☆
	Possibilities, pp. 139-141	"The Road Not Taken" by Robert Frost Homework: Question 7		End the class with the Robert Frost poem, "The Road Not Taken" in *Possibilities* and assign question 7 for homework.	
126	*Career Choices*, pp. 182-185 *Workbook*, p. 86	Tools for Solving Problems	pp. 244-245, Presentation suggestions, Activities		☆
127	*Career Choices*, pp. 186-190 *Workbook*, p. 86	Setting Goals and Objectives	pp. 246-247, Presentation suggestions	Energizer: Hand out a paper clip and a one-foot piece of thin string to each student. Folding the string in half, slip a paper clip through until the half way point and then, holding the two ends of the string, dangle the paper clip. Ask students not to move their hand but to think about the paper clip swinging. It will. The point: What we focus on will eventually happen.	☆
128	*Career Choices*, p. 190 *Workbook*, p. 86	Setting Goals and Objectives *(continued)*	pp. 246-247, Activities	If you have time, you'll want to have your students complete pages 102-106 of *Lifestyle Math*. This exercise demonstrates how to use goals and objectives to develop a timely, quantitative plan.	☆
129	*Career Choices*, pp. 197-199 *Workbook*, p. 89	What's Your Excuse?	pp. 250-251, Presentation suggestions, Activities		☆
130	*Career Choices*, p. 200 *Workbook*, p. 90	Taking Responsibility	p. 252, Presentation suggestions	Break into small groups of three students. Write the excuses found in the *Instructor's Guide* on the board and ask the groups to reframe them. Bring the class together and have groups present their conclusions.	☆
131	*Possibilities*, pp. 178-206	*Prince of Tides* by Pat Conroy		Because Pat Conoy's stories are so beautifully written, read this story to the class or ask a drama student to read it.	
132	*Possibilities*, pp. 178-206	*Prince of Tides (continued)* Group Activity B		Break into small groups or use the Fish Bowl technique described on p. 85 of the *Instructor's Guide*.	
133	*Career Choices*, pp. 201-202 *Workbook*, p. 91	Startling Statement Quiz	p. 253, Presentation suggestions, Activities, Energizer		☆
134	*Career Choices*, pp. 203-206 *Workbook*, pp. 92-93	Detours and Roadblocks	p. 254, Presentation suggestions, Activities		☆
135	*Career Choices*, p. 207 *Workbook*, p. 94	Is It Worth Staying In School?	p. 255, Presentation suggestions, Activities		☆
136	*Career Choices*, p. 207 *Workbook*, p. 94	Is It Worth Staying In School? *(continued)*	p. 255, Presentation suggestions, Activities	Energizer: Break class into teams to build a tower. Each team gets two sheets of card stock, 10 paper clips and one pair of scissors. The point: the need for a good foundation.	☆

Hour	Textbook	Lesson	Instructor's Guide	Special Directions (beyond those given in *Instructor's Guide*)	
137	*Career Choices*, pp. 208–209 Workbook, p. 95	Economics of Bad Habits	p. 256, Presentation suggestions		☆
138	*Career Choices*, pp. 208–209 Workbook, p. 95	Economics of Bad Habits (*continued*)	p. 256, Presentation suggestions, Activities	Panel: Senior citizens	
139	*Career Choices*, pp. 211–213 Workbook, pp. 96–98	If You're a Woman	pp. 257–258, Presentation suggestions		☆
140	*Career Choices*, pp. 211–213 Workbook, pp. 96–98	If You're a Woman (*continued*)	pp. 257–258, Activities	Guest speaker: Mixing career and family	
141	*Career Choices*, p. 215 Workbook, p. 99	(Before you give up your dream)	p. 259, Presentation suggestions		☆
142	*Possibilities*, pp. 212–215	"Dream Deferred" by Langston Hughes Discussion: Question 6 "Mother to Son" by Langston Hughes Discussion: Questions 3, 8–10		At the beginning of class, have a dramatic reading of "Dream Deferred." Discuss the journal entry question as a class. Ask students to individually complete the activity described in question 6 on p. 213 of *Possibilities*. Then have a dramatic reading of "Mother to Son" followed by a class discussion of questions noted.	
143	*Career Choices*, pp. 216–217 Workbook, p. 100 *Lifestyle Math*, pp. 6–7	(Developing anxiety tolerance)	p. 260, Presentation suggestions	Have students complete the inventory on p. 6 of *Lifestyle Math* and review the text on p. 7. Then read pp. 216–217 of *Career Choices* and help students write a guided visualization to overcome math anxiety.	☆
144	*Career Choices*, pp. 218–221 Workbook, p. 101	One Step at a Time	p. 261, Presentation suggestions		☆
145	*Career Choices*, pp. 222–223 Workbook, p. 102	Yorik's Story	p. 262, Presentation suggestions		☆
146	*Career Choices*, pp. 222–223 Workbook, p. 102	Yorik's Story (*continued*)	p. 262, Presentation suggestions	Extra Credit: Create a rap song around the theme of "I Hear America Singing," pp. 124–125 in *Possibilities*.	☆
147	*Career Choices*, pp. 224–225	Taking Risks	p. 263, Presentation suggestions, Activities		
148	*Career Choices*, p. 226	Getting Back on Track If You've Derailed	p. 265, Presentation suggestions	Invite a guest speaker who can review the resources and services available in the community to help an individual get back on track. An optional homework assignment would be to have each student volunteer three to four hours at a social service agency (such as serving at a soup kitchen, assisting at a day care center for children of the homeless, helping at a church/synagogue fund raiser to assist the less fortunate, or planning a class fund raiser to help with a particular family or agency).	☆
149	*Lifestyle Math*, pp. 93–94	Hard Times Budget		Brainstorm reasons as a class. Divide into groups of three students each and have groups complete pp. 93 and 94 of *Career Choices*.	☆

Hour	Textbook	Lesson	Instructor's Guide	Special Directions (beyond those given in *Instructor's Guide*)	
150	*Lifestyle Math*, pp. 93-94	Hard Times Budget (*continued*)		Finish work and ask each group to report out their plans and strategies.	☆
151	*Career Choices*, pp. 230-231 *Workbook*, p. 104	(Affirmations)	P. 268, Presentation suggestions, Activities		☆
152	*Career Choices*, pp. 232-235	The Six E's of Excellence	p. 269, Presentation suggestions, Activities	Energizer: The Seventh E - Entrepreneurship. Have students play the game An Income of Her Own. To order a copy, call National Resources for Girls and Young Women at (800)360-1761.	☆
153	*Career Choices*, pp. 236-237 *Workbook*, p. 104	Going For It... Work Is an Aggressive Act	p. 270, Presentation suggestions, Activities		☆
154	*Career Choices*, pp. 238-241 *Workbook*, pp. 105-107	You're the Boss	pp. 271-272, Presentation suggestions, Activities	As a class, read and discuss this section. Then break into small groups and assign each group one of the employees to evaluate, and then diagram their objectives.	☆
155	*Career Choices*, pp. 242-245 *Workbook*, pp. 108-109	The Employee of the Twenty-first Century	p. 273, Presentation suggestions, Activities	You will probably want to give each group inventing a new item or service a couple of days to think about their invention. Once presentations are made, you may want to ask the class to vote for the best idea.	☆
156	*Possibilities*, pp. 240-247	*Tonia the Tree* by Sandy Stryker Questions 4-8		The full color picturebook of *Tonia the Tree*, winner of the Friends of American Writers Merit award is available from Academic Innovations at (800) 967-8016. Adults as well as children delight in this book.	☆
157	*Career Choices*, pp. 2250-253 *Workbook*, p. 111	Your Resume	p. 277, Presentation suggestions		☆
158	*Career Choices*, p. 256 *Workbook*, p. 112	Job Applications	p. 279, Presentation suggestions, Activities	As outlined in the activity section, you'll need to arrange to get copies of actual résumé/application forms prior to this class.	☆
159	*Career Choices*, pp. 258-259 *Workbook*, p. 113	The Job Interview	p. 280, Presentation suggestions, Energizer	If you want to expand this into a community project, see pp. 123-126 of the *Instructor's Guide*. The Job Interview Night described on p. 126 is an excellent year-end project.	☆
160	*Career Choices*, pp. 262-263 *Workbook*, p. 114 *Possibilities*, p. 262	Making Connections	p. 282, Presentation suggestions, Activities	At the beginning of class, read the poem "The Bridge Builder." After discussing text on p. 262 of *Career Choices*, ask students to break into pairs and answer questions on p. 263 of *Career Choices*.	☆
161	*Possibilities*, pp. 264-268	"Thank You, M'am" by Langston Hughes Questions 1, 2, 3 and 5		After reading the story (either aloud or individually), discuss questions as a class. Break into groups of three and brainstorm question 5. Report out.	☆
162	*Lifestyle Math*, pp. 89-91	Computing Salaries In Your Head – Quickly! Numbers to Memorize		Break into groups of four or five students and ask them to discuss these problems and formulate group answers. Then have each group report their findings problem by problem. Review formula. Have students team up and practice computing annual salaries quickly.	

Hour	Textbook	Lesson	Instructor's Guide	Special Directions (beyond those given in *Instructor's Guide*)	
163	*Lifestyle Math*, pp. 66-67	Energizer - Math Baseball		Using the Math Baseball format on pp. 66-67 of *Lifestyle Math*, create flash cards for hourly wages for careers and use for game. Objective: Students compute annual salaries from hourly wages. Ask each correct respondent to write the title and salary on the chalkboard so the class can review the annual salaries. Use the *American Almanac of Jobs and Salaries* (see p. 88 of *Lifestyle Math*) for research.	
164	*Career Choices*, pp. 260-261	Dealing with Rejection, Accepting a Job	p. 281, Presentation suggestions	Review with class the text on pp. 260 and 261 of *Career Choices*. Here is a chance to invite in a personnel manager of a large business to discuss employment issues.	☆
165	*Career Choices*, pp. 266-269	Getting the Education or Training You Need	p. 284, Presentation suggestions, Activity	During the last two weeks of school, arrange for students to spend time with their counselor or advisor to map out the classes that meet their career and educational goals for the balance of their high school years. Students will want to incorporate those classes into their 10-year plan.	☆
166	*Lifestyle Math*, pp. 98-99	What is Your Math Education Worth to You? Working As a Team	SCANS	Following the directions and format on p. 99 of *Lifestyle Math*, ask each team to develop their project. As a class, discuss possible strategies, resources and production aids.	
167	*Lifestyle Math*, pp. 98-99	Working As a Team (*continued*)		Goal for today: Complete first, second and third steps.	
168	*Lifestyle Math*, pp. 98-99	Working As a Team (*continued*)		Goal for today: Work on fourth step - data collection.	
169	*Lifestyle Math*, pp. 98-99	Working As a Team (*continued*)		Goal for today: Analyze data and produce graph.	
170	*Lifestyle Math*, pp. 98-99	Working As a Team (*continued*)		Report out: Groups report not only on their findings but their process. Ask math department chair, principal and economics instructor to attend presentations. Showcase graphs in your school display area, school newspaper or community newspaper.	
171	*Career Choices*, pp. 270-273 Workbook, pp. 116-118	Where is it You Want to Go?	p. 286, Presentation suggestions, Activity	Hang their charts around the room once completed.	☆
172	*Possibilities*, pp. 270-271	"If" by Rudyard Kipling Journal question Delaying Gratification		Open the class with a discussion of the journal question. Then read "If" aloud, giving each student two lines from text. Line up in order for the reading.	☆
	Career Choices, pp. 274-275 Workbook, pp. 119-120		p. 287, Presentation suggestions		
173	*Possibilities*, pp. 252-253	"Be the Best of Whatever You Are" by Douglas Malloch Facing Fears and Anxieties	p. 287, Presentation suggestions	At beginning of class, read poem on p. 252 of *Possibilities* aloud to class. Ask students to individually complete pp. 276 and 277 in *Career Choices*. If students have built up their level of trust, ask some to share their concerns and their goals.	☆
	Career Choices, pp. 276-277 Workbook, pp. 120-121				

Hour	Textbook	Lesson	Instructor's Guide	Special Directions (beyond those given in *Instructor's Guide*)	
174	*Career Choices*, pp. 278-281 *Workbook*, pp. 121-123	Your Plan	p. 288, Presentation suggestions	Everything they have been doing in this class leads to this 10-year plan. Include a copy in their school folder. Also provide a copy for the student's next year's academic teachers. A parent-student meeting to present their plans would also be advantageous. It is important that students' plans and dreams are reinforced by everyone with whom they work and play.	☆
175	*Career Choices*, pp. 278-281 *Workbook*, pp. 121-123	Your Plan *(continued)*	p. 288, Presentation suggestions		☆
176	*Possibilities*, pp. 277-283	25th High School Reunion		After reading the poem aloud, ask students to write their "contribution" to their booklet for their 25th high school reunion. Make into a booklet for high school archives or bury as a time capsule to be unearthed by the group the day before their 25th reunion.	☆
177		(Remembering your dreams and plans)	p. 290	Project: Ask students to write two letters to themselves detailing their dreams and plans. One will be mailed to them in two years and the other in five years. Attach a copy of their 10-year plan along with a copy of the letter (written in Hour 45). Then ask each student to address two envelopes to themselves using the address and return address of two different relatives who are likely to be at the same address over the next five years. You will keep these letters together, labeled, to be mailed after the first of the year of each appropriate year.	☆
178	*Career Choices*, p. 282 *Workbook*, p. 124 *Possibilities*, p. 283	(A mission in life) "We Are A Success…" by Robert Louis Stevenson Course wrap-up	p. 289, Presentation suggestions p. 140, Energizer	You may want to share the art pieces at the next school staff meeting or even the next school board meeting.	☆
179	*Instructor's Guide*, p. 100	Course Wrap-Up		Energizer	
180	Graduation party	*Oh! The Places You'll Go* by Dr. Seuss		Have a spaghetti dinner potluck using recipes from *Lifestyle Math*, p. 60. Read Dr. Seuss book aloud.	☆

Course Follow-Up

Guidance Portfolio

Upon completion of this course, you will want to collect the students' *Workbook and Portfolio* and photocopy the following **completed** pages to form the students' guidance portfolios. This list is found on page 6 of the *Workbook and Portfolio* and permission is granted to photocopy the students' pages for inclusion in their school files.

Pages 6, 11, 28, 42, 83, 87, 112, 113, 121, 122, 123, 124

We also recommend that you give a copy of this guidance portfolio to *each* of their academic teachers for next year. You will probably want to write a brief cover letter to introduce the long-range educational and career plans of the student. This document will provide the data to each instructor so there can be continuity of support for that student's plans and dreams. This is very important!

Lifestyle Math Computerized Portfolio

Once students completes *the Computerized Correction Key for Lifestyle Math*, you can reformat their computer disk to become *a Financial Planning Portfolio* (see the manual). This way, throughout the time they are attending your school, they can revisit the computer loaded with the master program and run new budget projections. In this format, the answers are provided so it is a quick process. With their Financial Planning Portfolio disk, they can make projections of their financial needs and then they are better equipped to readjust educational plans to match their career and lifestyle plans. Also, they will learn and practice the very important life habit of periodical budget review.

Bibliography

Bingham, Mindy, Judy Edmondson, and Sandy Stryker. *Challenges: A Young Man's Journal for Self-awareness and Personal Planning*. Santa Barbara, CA: Advocacy Press, 1984.

Bingham, Mindy, Judy Edmondson, and Sandy Stryker. *Changes: A Woman's Journal for Self-awareness and Personal Planning*. Santa Barbara, CA: Advocacy Press, 1987.

Bingham, Mindy, Judy Edmondson, and Sandy Stryker. *Choices: A Teen Woman's Journal for Self-awareness and Personal Planning*. Santa Barbara, CA: Advocacy Press, 1983.

Bingham, Mindy, Lari Quinn, and William P. Sheehan. *Mother Daughter Choices: A Handbook for the Coordinator*. Santa Barbara, CA: Advocacy Press, 1988.

Bingham, Mindy, and Sandy Stryker. *Women Helping Girls with Choices. A Handbook for Community Service Organizations*. Santa Barbara, CA: Advocacy Press, 1989.

Bingham, Mindy, and Sandy Stryker. *More Choices: A Strategic Planning Guide for Mixing Career and Family*. Santa Barbara, CA: Advocacy Press, 1987.

Bolles, Richard Nelson. *What Color Is Your Parachute?* Berkeley, CA: Ten Speed Press, 1972.

Chess, Stella, M.D., and Alexander Thomas, M.D. *Know Your Child. An Authoritative Guide for Today's Parents*. New York: Basic Books, 1987.

Comiskey, James. *How to Start, Expand and Sell a Business: A Complete Guidebook for Entrepreneurs*. San Jose, CA: Venture Perspectives Press, 1985.

Crystal, John C., and Richard Bolles. *Where Do I Go from Here with My Life?* Berkeley, CA: 1974.

de Bono, Edward. *Lateral Thinking: Creativity Step by Step*. New York: Harper & Row, 1970.

Dyer, Dr. Wayne W. *What Do You Really Want for Your Children?* New York: William Morrow and Company, 1985.

Erikson, Erik. *Childhood and Society*. New York: W. W. Norton, 1963.

Fritz, Robert. *The Path of Least Resistance: Principles for Creating What Your Want To Create*. New Hampshire: Stillpointe, 1986.

Gelatt, H. B., Barbara Varenhorst, and Richard Carey. *Deciding: A Leader's Guide*. New York: College Entrance Examination Board, 1972.

Goldberg, Herb. *The Hazards of Being Male*. New York: New American Library, 1976.

Goldberg, Herb. *The New Male*. New York: New American Library, 1979.

Goldberg, Joan Rachel. *High-tech Career Strategies for Women*. New York: Collier Books, 1984.

Hewlett, Sylvia Ann. *A Lesser Life: The Myth of Women's Liberation in America*. New York: William Morrow and Company, 1986.

Hopke, William, *Encyclopedia of Career & Vocational Guidance*. J.G. Ferguson Publishing Co., 1987.

Horton, Thomas R. *What Works for Me?* New York: Amacom, 1989.

Hoyt, Kenneth B. *The Concept of Work: Bedrock for Career Development*.

James, Jennifer, Ph.D. *Women and the Blues. Passions That Hurt, Passions That Heal*. San Francisco: Harper & Row, 1988.

Jongeward, Dorothy, and Dru Scott. *Women as Winners*. Reading, MA: Addison-Wesley Publishing Company, 1976.

Kanter, Rosabeth Moss. *When Giants Learn to Dance*. New York: Simon and Schuster, 1989.

Knowles, M. and H. *Introduction to Group Dynamics*. Chicago: Association Press, Follett Publishing, 1972.

Lenz, Elinor, and Barbara Myerhoss. *The Feminization of America*. Los Angeles, CA: Jeremy P. Tarcher, 1985.

Marston, William Moulton. *Emotions of Normal People*. Minnesota: Persona Press, 1979.

Maslow, Abraham H. *Toward a Psychology of Being*. New York: D. Van Nostrand Company, 1968.

Mitchell, Arnold. *The Nine American Lifestyles: Who We Are and Where We're Going*. New York: Warner Books, 1983.

Morrison, Ann M., Randall P. White, Ellen Van Velsor, and The Center for Creative Leadership. *Breaking the Glass Ceiling: Can Women Reach the Top of America's Largest Corporations?* Massachusetts, 1987.

Naisbitt, John. *Megatrends*. New York: Warner Books, 1982.

Naisbitt, John, and Patricia Aburdene. *Re-inventing the Corporation*. New York: Warner Books, 1985.

Occupational Outlook Handbook. U.S. Department of Labor—Bureau of Labor Statistics. 1988—89 Edition.

O'Neill, Nena, and George O'Neill. *Shifting Gears*. New York: Avon Books, 1974.

Peters, Tom. *Thriving on Chaos: Handbook for a Management Revolution*. New York: Alfred A. Knopf, 1988.

Poynter, Dan, and Mindy Bingham. *Is There a Book Inside You? How to Successfully Author a Book Alone or through Collaboration*. Santa Barbara, CA: Para Publishing, 1985.

Ricci, Larry J. *High Paying Blue-Collar Jobs for Women*. New York: Ballantine Books, 1981.

Rohrlich, Jay B., M.D. *Work and Love: The Crucial Balance*. New York: Summit Books, 1980.

Sanderson, Jim. *How to Raise Your Kids to Stand on Their Own Two Feet*. New York: Congdon & Weed, 1983.

"Saving Our Schools." *Fortune* Magazine. 121, No. 12, Spring 1990.

Schaevitz, Marjorie Hansen. *The Superwomen Syndrome*. New York: Warner Books, 1984.

Scholz, Nelle Tumlin, Judith Sosebee Prince, and Gordon Porter Miller. *How to Decide: A Workbook for Women*. New York: Avon Books, 1978.

Simon, Sidney B., Leland W. Howe, and Howard Kirschenbaum. *Values Clarification: A Handbook for Teachers and Students*. New York: A and W Publishers, 1972.

"The New Teens: What Makes Them Different. Who Are Their Heroes?" *Newsweek*. Summer/Fall 1990.

Viscott, David., M.D. *Risking*. New York: Pocket Books, 1979.

Biographical Sketch

Mindy Bingham

Innovative educational approaches have always been a mission for Mindy Bingham. As a part-time college professor, seminar leader for educators, author, and community activist, Mindy has dedicated herself to improving schools. She has traveled around the country conducting workshops for teachers and curriculum specialists. In 1985, she was named one of the outstanding women in education by the Santa Barbara County Commission for Women.

To date, titles authored or coauthored by Mindy Bingham have sold nearly three-quarters of a million copies. They include the best-selling *Choices: A Teen Woman's Journal for Self-awareness and Personal Planning* and *Challenges*, the young man's version. Her children's picture books include the Ingram number one best-seller *Minou* and *My Way Sally*; the 1989 Ben Franklin Award winner. Mindy is the founder of Advocacy Press in Santa Barbara and was executive director of the Girls Club of Santa Barbara for fifteen years. She received a bachelor of science degree with honors in animal science from California State Polytechnic University at Pomona.

Sandy Stryker

Sandy Stryker is coauthor of the best-selling *Choices: A Young Woman's Journal for Self-Awareness and Personal Planning, Challenges* the young man's version, *More Choices: A Strategic Planning Guide for Mixing Career and Family* and *Changes: A Woman's Guide for Self awareness and Personal Planning*. Her first children's book, *Tonia the Tree*, was the 1988 recipient of the Merit Award from the Friends of American Writers. She is coauthor of The World of Work Job Application File and has edited numerous other publications. She holds a degree in journalism from the University of Minnesota.

Rochelle S. Friedman

Rochelle S. Friedman received her doctorate in education from the State University of New York at Buffalo. She has been an administrator and teacher in both the public and private sector. Dr. Friedman has served as a consultant to schools in Louisiana and Florida and has served as an adjunct faculty member at both Nova University and Louisiana State University. She has been honored as Outstanding Educator of the Year both for program development and for classroom teaching. Dr. Friedman is currently the Principal of Murray High School in Albemarle County, Virginia. Murray is a nontraditional high school whose primary mission is to meet the needs of students at risk who drop out or graduate below potential.

Laura Castle Light

Laura Light is a mother of two daughters and a foster daughter, a professional musician, an artist, and a teacher of literature, French, and art at Murray High School, an alternative school in Ivy, Virginia. A graduate of Stanford University in creative writing and literature, Laura worked and traveled as a musician for ten years, including two years in France. She completed her M.Ed. at Ohio University in 1984. Currently living in Charlottesville, Virginia, Laura continues to develop as an artist and teacher, putting her talents to good use in the innovative environment of Murray. Her current projects include developing the curriculum for the "Hire Education" program at Murray and developing ways to incorporate art into the English/Humanities curriculum.

Acknowledgments:

The authors would like to thank the following individuals for their assistance in the production of the manuscript: Shirley Cornelius, Robin Sager, Chas Thompson, Nancy Marriott, copy editing; Michele Julien, layout; Betty Stambolian, Pat Lewis, Linda Wagner, editing; Jim Johnson; Christine Nolt, design and layout; Itoko Maeno, Janice Blair, and Diana Lackner, art; Delta Lithograph, printing.

We would also like to thank the following individuals for contributions to this guide: Kathy Araujo, Kyle Brace, Mikell Becker, Deb Carstens, James Comiskey, Sara Lykken, M.Ed., Shirley Myers, M.Ed., Edward Myers, Susan Neufeldt, Ph.D., Penelope Paine, Robert Shafer, Betty Shepperd, Linda Wagner, and the hundreds of educators who have used the *Choices* series over the last several years and have shared their ideas.

And finally a very special thanks to Kenneth B. Hoyt, Ph.D., for the hours he spent reviewing the manuscript, giving constructive criticism, and challenging our assumptions. His advice, guidance, and contributions to this *Instructor's and Counselor's Guide* were invaluable. So, to this steadfast pioneer, we dedicate our effort to infuse career education into the core curriculum.

About the *Choices* Series

In 1983 the first of the *Choices* series, *Choices: A Teen Woman's Journal for Self-awareness and Personal Planning* by Bingham, Stryker, and Edmondson, was first introduced to the educational community by Advocacy Press. In 1984 the first companion edition, the male version, *Challenges* followed. Since 1984 over 1,000 high schools across the country have used this innovative curriculum. Based on the premise that young women and young men have received different messages as to the options open to them, this pre-career awareness curriculum prepares all students for career education and ultimately taking advantage of educational opportunities. We recommend that this curriculum be used in either the seventh or eight grade. If you are currently using *Career Choices*, you might consider mentioning this curriculum to your middle school curriculum committee.

One of the major conflicts young people face today when choosing a career is how to mix career and family. Many times career choices are based on yesterday's realities and role models. Young women lower their career aspirations and young men abdicate their parenting role. In 1987 a third book, *More Choices: A Strategic Planning Guide for Mixing Career and Family* (Advocacy Press) was introduced into the *Choices* series. This coed curriculum focuses on career choices based upon parenting requirements. Never before have career education and family life issues been combined in the same course. While separate approaches to these issues may have been appropriate when those duties were performed by separate individuals in the family, in the 1990s, career and family issues must be combined to meet the needs of our changing society. *More Choices* assists the learner in sorting out the conflicting messages in a period of radical change and promotes the theme that the higher your aspirations on the career scale, the more freedom you will have to be a parent. We recommend this 9- to 18-week curriculum for Home Economics or Family Life classes as a great follow-up for high school students who have completed *Career Choices*.

An instructor's guide and consumable workbooks are available for these *Choices* editions.

In addition, there is an adult woman's version. *Changes: A Woman's Journal for Self-awareness and Personal Planning*, it was developed so mothers and daughters could work side-by-side toward self-discovery. A national program, Mother-Daughter Choices, was developed with funds from the Lilly Endowment of Indianapolis, Indiana. A handbook and video are available for schools and individuals who want to start small groups of middle school girls and their mothers.

For ordering information on the above titles, please see page 350.

Ordering Information

Throughout this *Instructor's and Counselor's Guide*, we have noted resources and materials you can order directly through Academic Innovations. Satisfaction is guaranteed. If the resource is not what you need, return the merchandise within 30 days of the invoice in resaleable condition for a refund.

SCHOOL ORDERS

We can fill your order faster and more accurately when you include school purchase order number, quantity, full title, name of school, district, school and name of person placing order, date the books are needed, shipping, and billing addresses.

SHIPPING

Be sure to allow at least four weeks delivery time unless you want special shipping. Prices quoted are FOB Santa Barbara, and shipping and handling costs will be added to your invoice.

Career Choices: A Guide for Teens and Young Adults, by Mindy Bingham and Sandy Stryker. Softcover, 288 pages. ISBN 0-878787-02-0. $22.95.

Instructor's and Counselor's Guide for Career Choices, by Mindy Bingham and Sandy Stryker. Softcover, 352 pages. ISBN 0-878787-04-7. $21.95.

Workbook and Portfolio for Career Choices, by Mindy Bingham and Sandy Stryker. Softcover, 128 pages. ISBN 0-878787-03-9. $6.95.

Possibilities: A Supplemental Anthology for Career Choices, by Janet Goode and Mindy Bingham. Softcover, 288 pages. ISBN 1-878787-05-5. $9.95.

Lifestyle Math: Your Financial Planning Portfolio, A Supplemental Mathematics Unit For Career Choices, by Mindy Bingham, Jo Willhite and Shirley Myers. Softcover, 112 pages. ISBN 1-878787-07-1. $6.95.

or

Lifestyle Math workbook <u>and</u> the *Computerized Correction Key and Portfolio.* Call for pricing.

Career Choices and Changes: A Guide for Discovering Who You Are, What You Want, and How to Get It, by Mindy Bingham and Sandy Stryker. Softcover, 304 pages. ISBN 1-878787-15-2. $24.95.

EXAMINATION COPIES

Due to rapidly increasing publication costs, examination copies are available only on a 60-day approval basis. Once you have examined the copy, and you find it is not what you need, return it in saleable condition before 60 days. If you decide to keep the book, you will be invoiced after 60 days.

Publications Available from Academic Innovations

Career Choices: A Guide for Teens and Young Adults: Who Am I? What Do I Want? How Do I Get It?, by Mindy Bingham and Sandy Stryker. Softcover, 288 pages. ISBN 1-878787-02-0. $22.95.

Workbook and Portfolio for the text Career Choices, by Mindy Bingham and Sandy Stryker. Softcover, 128 pages. ISBN 1-878787-03-9. $6.95.

Instructor's and Counselor's Guide for Career Choices, by Mindy Bingham and Sandy Stryker. Softcover, 352 pages. ISBN 1-878787-04-7. $21.95.

Possibilities: A Supplemental Anthology for Career Choices, edited by Janet Goode and Mindy Bingham. Softcover, 288 pages. ISBN 1-878787-05-5. $9.95.

Lifestyle Math: Your Financial Planning Portfolio, by Mindy Bingham, Jo Willhite, and Shirley Myers. Softcover, 112 pages. ISBN 1-878787-07-1. $6.95.

Computerized Correction Key and Portfolio for *Lifestyle Math* and *Lifestyle Math* workbook. Call for pricing.

Career Choices and Changes: A Guide for Discovering Who You Are, What You Want, and How to Get It, by Mindy Bingham and Sandy Stryker. Softcover, 304 pages. ISBN 1-878787-15-2. $24.95.

Choices: A Teen Woman's Journal for Self-awareness and Personal Planning, by Mindy Bingham, Judy Edmondson, and Sandy Stryker. Softcover, 240 pages, ISBN 0-911655-22-0. $19.95.

Challenges: A Young Man's Journal for Self-awareness and Personal Planning, by Mindy Bingham, Judy Edmondson, and Sandy Stryker. Softcover, 240 pages. ISBN 0-911655-24-7. $19.95.

Workbook for Choices and Challenges. Softcover, 103 pages. ISBN 0-911655-25-5. $6.95.

Changes: A Woman's Journal for Self-awareness and Personal Planning, by Mindy Bingham, Sandy Stryker, and Judy Edmondson. Softcover, 240 pages. ISBN 0-911655-40-9. $19.95.

Workbook for Changes. Softcover, 104 pages. ISBN 0-911655-1-7. $6.95.

More Choices: A Strategic Planning Guide for Mixing Career and Family, by Mindy Bingham and Sandy Stryker. Softcover, 240 pages. ISBN 0-911655-28-X. $19.95.

Workbook for More Choices. Softcover, 104 pages. ISBN 0-911655-29-8. $6.95.

Instructor's Guide for Choices, Challenges, Changes and More Choices. Softcover, 272 pages. ISBN 0-911655-04-2. $19.95.

Mother-Daughter Choices: A Handbook for the Coordinator, by Mindy Bingham, Lari Quinn, and William Sheehan. Softcover, 144 pages. ISBN 0-911655-44-1. $14.95.

Women Helping Girls with Choices, by Mindy Bingham and Sandy Stryker. Softcover, 192 pages. ISBN 0-911655-00-X. $14.95.

Minou, written by Mindy Bingham, illustrated by Itoko Maeno. Hardcover with dust jacket, 32 pages with full-color illustrations throughout. ISBN 0-911655-36-0. $14.95.

My Way Sally, written by Mindy Bingham and Penelope Paine, illustrated by Itoko Maeno. Hardcover with dust jacket, 48 pages with full-color illustrations throughout. ISBN 0-911655-27-1. $14.95.

Tonia the Tree, written by Sandy Stryker, illustrated by Itoko Maeno. Hardcover with dust jacket, 32 pages with full-color illustrations throughout. ISBN 0-911655-16-6. $14.95.

Berta Benz and the Motorwagen, written by Mindy Bingham, illustrated by Itoko Maeno. Hardcover with dust jacket, 48 pages with full-color illustrations throughout. ISBN 0-911655-38-7. $14.95.

Is There A Book Inside You? A Step-by-Step Plan for Writing Your Book, by Dan Poynter and Mindy Bingham. Softcover, 236 pages. ISBN 0-915516-68-3. $14.95

Personal Profile System Assessment Instrument, Adult Version. Call or write for ordering information.

Joyce Lain Kennedy's Career Book by Joyce Lain Kennedy and D. Laranore.

Things Will Be Different for My Daughter: A Practical Guide to Building Her Self-esteem and Self-reliance, by Mindy Bingham and Sandy Stryker. Softcover, 1995. Penguin. $14.95.

It's too bad more students don't have an opportunity to have this class and use these materials.

—Ann Dabb
Teacher
Wahlquist Junior High School
Ogden, Utah

COMPLETELY REVISED

"User-friendly" for student and instructor alike, *Career Choices* helps teens and young adults learn more about the most important and interesting subject in their world: Themselves!

This edition of the *Instructor's and Counselor's Guide* offers comprehensive guidance, a 180-hour interdisciplinary lesson plan and links to technology so that all students can be computer-literate by the time they complete the course. You'll find exercise-by-exercise organization plans, discussion outlines, resource materials, classroom extension ideas, vocabulary lists, recommended reading lists and much more.

Use *Career Choices* in:
► English/language arts and/or math
► Tech Prep or School-to-Work programs
► Career education classes
► Life planning and family life courses
► Private counseling
► Drop-out prevention programs

This lively curriculum:

☑ is competency based with special application for English/Language Arts core curriculum.

☑ is highly suitable for use in both the classroom and the counseling office.

☑ complements traditional career planning topics with practical advice on overcoming obstacles and fears, solving problems dealing with rejection and anxiety, developing good attitudes and work habits, recognizing and using mentors, and much more.

☑ projects students into the 21st century to identify and develop the skills and attitudes that will be required for career and life satisfaction.

☑ demonstrates the consequences of quitting school, using drugs, becoming a teen parent, and other self-destructive behavior, and helps get students back on track.

☑ helps students identify the passions, values and personality styles that will greatly affect career satisfaction. Leads them to greater self-knowledge, enabling them to make their own best decisions about their futures.

☑ empowers students to write their own plans for a rewarding future based on their newly acquired self-knowledge, confidence and motivation.

ISBN 1-878787-04-7